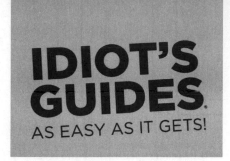

IDIOT'S
GUIDES.
AS EASY AS IT GETS!

D0337945

U.S. Government and Politics

Second Edition

by Franco Scardino

WITHDRAWN

ALPHA

A member of Penguin Random House LLC

Publisher: Mike Sanders
Associate Publisher: Billy Fields
Acquisitions Editor: Jan Lynn
Development Editor: Phil Kitchel
Cover Designer: Lindsay Dobbs
Book Designer: William Thomas
Compositor: Ayanna Lacey
Proofreader: Laura Caddell
Indexer: Brad Herriman

Dedicated to all my students and colleagues—past and present—who have made the teaching of government and politics one of the most rewarding experiences of my life.

Second American Edition, 2016
Published in the United States by DK Publishing
6081 E. 82nd Street, Indianapolis, Indiana 46250

Copyright © 2016 Dorling Kindersley Limited
A Penguin Random House Company
16 17 18 19   10 9 8 7 6 5 4 3 2 1
002-295786-SEPTEMBER2016

Published in the United States by Dorling Kindersley Limited.

IDIOT'S GUIDES and Design are trademarks of Penguin Random House LLC

ISBN: 9781465454355
Library of Congress Catalog Card Number: 2016930607

Note: This publication contains the opinions and ideas of its author(s). It is intended to provide helpful and informative material on the subject matter covered. It is sold with the understanding that the author(s) and publisher are not engaged in rendering professional services in the book. If the reader requires personal assistance or advice, a competent professional should be consulted. The author(s) and publisher specifically disclaim any responsibility for any liability, loss, or risk, personal or otherwise, which is incurred as a consequence, directly or indirectly, of the use and application of any of the contents of this book.

Trademarks: All terms mentioned in this book that are known to be or are suspected of being trademarks or service marks have been appropriately capitalized. Alpha Books, DK, and Penguin Random House LLC cannot attest to the accuracy of this information. Use of a term in this book should not be regarded as affecting the validity of any trademark or service mark.

DK books are available at special discounts when purchased in bulk for sales promotions, premiums, fund-raising, or educational use. For details, contact: DK Publishing Special Markets, 345 Hudson Street, New York, New York 10014 or SpecialSales@dk.com.

Printed and bound in the United States of America

idiotsguides.com

Contents

Introduction

If you have an interest in how political decisions are reached and who has the power to influence them, you will enjoy this book. We are living at a time when the knowledge of government and politics has never been more important. The nation is facing some of the most difficult economic challenges in 70 years, and it is starting a new chapter in American politics. Most people think the study of government and politics is simply about elections and politicians. However, the study of American government and politics is much more complex because it is the product of all of us: U.S. citizens participating in the political process on many different levels.

The American experiment with a new form of democratic governance has been a work in progress for over 200 years. This book will by no means be the definitive source on the topic, but it will be a valuable resource that will help you understand the fundamental principles of government and the complex relationships that exist in U.S. politics. Thomas Jefferson once said, "I know of no safe depository of the ultimate powers of the society but the people themselves; and if we think them not enlightened enough to exercise their control with a wholesome discretion, the remedy is not to take it from them, but to inform their discretion by education."

This book will provide you with an important foundation about what you need to know about the U.S. government and American politics, including the following:

- The Constitution, separation of powers, and federalism

- How Americans develop their political beliefs and how they behave politically

- The history of and role political parties, interest groups, and the media play in politics

- The structure of the U.S. government: Congress, the presidency, the bureaucracy, and the courts

- How public policy is formulated

- Civil rights and civil liberties

This book seeks to illustrate why studying government and politics and the Constitution is so critical to your future, and why we cannot have a civilized democratic society unless citizens of the United States and the world understand fundamental facts rather than ill-founded beliefs. We are looking for truth. Once we know the truth, we can decide what, if anything, to do about it.

There are essentially three kinds of people in the world: those who make something happen, those who wish something would happen, and those who wander in a daze wondering, "What happened?"

What kind of person are you? Aim low and you will achieve it and be one of those wandering in a daze. Aim high and you have a chance to make something happen. I hope this book will be a small step on your path to forge positive change. Step forward rather than marking time or stepping back. By the time you are done with this book, I hope you will have the knowledge and the tools needed for active citizenship. What does that mean? Register to vote, become informed on issues and candidates, and vote! Make phone calls, send emails, and write letters to elected leaders to let them know how you feel about the issues. Participate in politics. Volunteer for campaigns. Network! Run for office! Only through the active participation of citizens can the republic thrive.

How This Book Is Organized

This book is divided into six parts:

Part 1, The American System, starts with the fundamental principles of government and how a political system is constructed. You will then read about the documents and traditions that influenced the creation of the Constitution, and the key principles of federalism and separation of powers.

Part 2, The Political Process, is primarily about how people form their basic political values and how Americans share and disagree about certain aspects of politics and governance. In this part, you will read about the history of political parties, how congressional and presidential candidates are selected, and how campaigns are run for election to office.

Part 3, The Legislative Branch, is where you will read about the powers given to Congress by the Constitution and the important functions it plays in our government. You will also read about the unique roles both the House of Representatives and the Senate play and navigate through the steps involved with passing a law.

Part 4, The Executive Branch, describes the powers bestowed on the president by the Constitution. You will also read about the office of vice president, presidential succession, and how the U.S. government is organized by departments and agencies within the executive branch.

Part 5, The Judicial Branch, will inform you on how the judicial branch operates a co-equal branch of government. You will learn the role the courts play in our constitutional form of government and the freedoms that protect individuals from the government and the struggle for equality before the law.

Part 6, The Politics of Public Policy, will expound upon the constitutional protection that has allowed special interest groups to exist and flourish in our democracy and the critical role the media plays in our democracy. You will also learn about the process of transforming issues and interests into public policy.

In the back of the book, a glossary explains important terms.

Extras

This book also contains sidebars with additional information and asides:

 DEFINITION

This sidebar will offer explanations and definitions that will make you politically savvy.

 MISINFORMATION

This sidebar will clarify concepts or events that are often misinterpreted or misused.

 ON THE RECORD

This sidebar will give you important quotations in American political history.

REAL-LIFE FACTS

This sidebar will provide facts and important points that will make you a political trivia pro.

Online Extras

As a bonus to this book, we've included additional information online—a copy of the U.S. Constitution, a listing of major governmental departments and agencies, and the civics questions from the U.S. citizenship test. Point your browser to idiotsguides.com/usgovernment.

Acknowledgments

I would like to extend my sincere thanks to my family, colleagues, and former students, who are too many to name, for believing in me and encouraging me every day.

The American System

The United States is the world's oldest constitutional democracy. Yet after more than 200 years, the experiment with American democracy is still a work in progress. To understand how our government works, we must first examine the two main questions about politics: Who governs in a society? What are their goals?

Ever since the adoption of the Constitution, the question of what the relationship between the federal government and the states should be has been a major political question and source of conflict. The Constitution structured our federal system of government in a way to deal with political, economic, and social developments. The political history of federalism in the United States is filled with various shifts of power between the federal government and the states.

Principles of Government

The United States is the world's oldest constitutional democracy. Yet after more than 200 years, the American experiment in democracy is still a work in progress.

In this chapter, we will discuss some of the questions and principles that are fundamental to the construction of any political system. Furthermore, we will explore the two main questions about politics: Who governs in a society? What are the goals of those who govern?

Government is a conduit of power and action. Looking at these two questions together helps us understand how the actions of those who rule affect us.

In This Chapter

- Politics and political power
- Principles of government
- Variations of democracy
- Principles of American government
- Power and governance in the United States

What Is Government?

People often disagree on the size and scope of government. They also disagree on what exactly the government should do and how it should carry out its functions. Let's take a moment and discuss how to define a government. A government is a system of authority that exercises sovereign power to enact laws, execute justice, and enforce public policy. American government has three main goals: to enforce laws in order to maintain order, to provide citizens with goods and services to benefit and enable their well-being, and to ensure equality and justice among all members of society.

The U.S. government acts to achieve these goals through the work of Congress, the president, and the judiciary. Many appointed officials and bureaucrats work in the institutions that make up the various government branches at all levels to carry out these responsibilities. Altogether, these players fulfill their responsibilities through their authority to carry out the functions of government.

What Is Politics?

Politics is the science of *government*, the art concerned with the control of government and public policy. Aristotle, in his book *Politics*, states that humans are, by nature, political animals. Politics can best be understood as the process by which organizations of people in a society resolve conflicts and decide who gets what, when, and how.

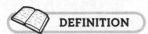 **DEFINITION**

> A **government** is a political institution that has the power to enforce rules and impose order and stability on a society.

In early human society, politics was fairly informal. Decisions were usually made by tribal elders or chiefs. As society became more complex and humans became settlers rather than hunters, resolving problems became more important, particularly with the development of property rights and inheritance. Politics developed into the process by which these questions, and others, were answered.

Society is made up of individuals and groups with unique needs, perspectives, and values. It is inevitable that conflicts will arise, so a political process is required to help resolve them. Some of these conflicts include the following:

- Personal, religious, and cultural beliefs
- The goals of the society

- Protection of personal and property rights

- How to spend the resources of the society

What Is Political Power?

Power is generally defined as the ability of a person to get another person or group to act according to his or her intentions or wishes. Sometimes power is exhibited in obvious ways. More often than not, however, power is exercised in more subtle ways. For example, a president may order a military assault—an obvious show of his power. However, if his advisers persuade him to lift sanctions on a country, the advisers are exhibiting subtle power, because they have gotten the president to act according to their wishes.

People who exercise political power may or may not have the authority to do so. Formal authority is the rightful use of power that compels obedience. Decisions made by people of authority are accepted and carried out. The president, members of Congress, and judges have formal authority.

When authority is appropriate and rightful, it is considered legitimate. In the United States, the Constitution is considered the source of legitimate authority of the government. Laws have been made and officials have been elected and selected according to a political process that represents the citizens of the country.

 MISINFORMATION

The difference between a republic and a democracy lies in the majority of whose votes determine the outcome. A democracy is simply one person, one vote. A republic is a government made up of democratically elected representatives. It is a democratic form of government.

Origins of the Nation-State

The nation-state is a political organization or unit of people within a defined territory who share a common culture, language, values, and history. The nation-state is best thought of as geopolitical rather than ethnically defined. For example, in the classical period of early civilization, the nation-state of China was made up of various kingdoms unified under one ruler. The United States today is also a political unit of various regions and ethnicities but who share a common national identity.

What factors bring about the birth of a nation-state? Many historians, philosophers, and political scientists have attempted to answer this question, but there are no definitive answers, only several important theories.

Many experts believe that the nation-state was born of force. People who share a geographic area, whether a common ethnic group or not, are forced to submit to the will of a person or group who physically controls the area.

The evolutionary theory maintains that the nation-state naturally evolved from the family. Because primitive families had a head of household, the theory maintains that was an early form of government. Over the years, this network of related families grew into clans. In time, clans became tribes. Once tribes settled and developed agriculture, the nation-state was established.

The divine-right theory maintains that God created the nation-state and specifically gave those of "royal" birth the right to govern. This theory was widely accepted by many ancient civilizations and in the Western world from the fourteenth through the eighteenth centuries. Many of these rulers were considered to be gods themselves.

The social-contract theory, developed during the seventeenth and eighteenth centuries by several philosophers, including John Locke, Thomas Hobbes, and Jean Jacques Rousseau, maintains that humans are born free in a state of nature and that they come together to form an agreement by which they give up powers to the state to create an environment of well-being for everyone. The social-contract theory argues that the state is born out of voluntary actions of free people and, therefore, exists only to serve the people. In this theory, as opposed to the divine-right theory, the people are the source of power.

Forms of Government

Governments can be structured in many different ways. The structure of government may depend on the needs of the citizens and/or the historical experience of the society.

Unitary government is a centralized government that possesses all political power. The central government might create agencies to help it govern, but power remains with the central government. Most governments in the world are unitary. The extent of the central government's political power depends on the authority it has been given. The British Parliament is an example of this.

In a federal government, power is divided between a central government and *sovereign local governments*. Both levels of government act according to the authority that they have been assigned. The United States is an example of this.

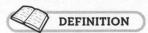 **DEFINITION**

A **sovereign local government** is fully independent and determines its own affairs.

A confederate government is an alliance of sovereign and independent states under a central government that only has the power assigned to it by the member states. U.S. history had two examples of this type of government: under the Articles of Confederation immediately after the Revolutionary War, and the Confederate States of America during the Civil War.

A presidential form of government features at least two branches of government: an executive and legislative branch. Sometimes it may include a third branch, the judiciary. The branches are independent of each other and considered co-equal—a separation of powers that creates a system of checks and balances on power.

In a parliamentary government, the executive or prime minister is selected by a majority of the legislative branch—the parliament. The prime minister and his or her cabinet stay in power as long as they have the support of a majority of the parliament, or general elections are held that create a different majority in parliament.

Dictatorship is among the oldest forms of government in history. All dictatorships are authoritarian—they are systems of government that hold absolute and unchallengeable power. A dictatorship exists when the person or group that rules is not held responsible to the will of the citizens it rules over. Despotism is government rule by a single leader, with all citizen/ subjects considered slaves. Monarchy is rule by an individual who has inherited the role and expects to bequeath it to their heir. This type of government was historically based on the Divine Right theory.

Oligarchy is government by a small group of people who share similar interests or family relations. Plutocracy is government composed of the wealthy class. (Several political observers have noted that the rising cost of campaigns is driving some democracies to resemble plutocracies.) Theocracy is government rule by a religious elite or a religious priest class. The Islamic Republic of Iran is an example of a modern-day theocracy.

What Is Democracy?

Political decisions are made many different ways. When a small group controls all the political power, it is called an oligarchy, meaning rule by a few members of an elite group. Another form of government by a group is known as an aristocracy, usually an upper socioeconomic class. Rule by the people is known as democracy. Historically, this has been limited by citizenship, age, gender, and sometimes property-ownership requirements. The people, however, hold the sovereign power, and the decisions of the government are conducted with the consent of the people. The distinguishing characteristic of democracy is that the government derives its authority and legitimacy from the people.

In a direct democracy, the citizens debate and vote directly on all the laws and policies of the government. This form of government results in a high level of participation from every citizen, but can also lead to instability if the voting majority frequently changes positions on laws and policies. In the United States, New England town meetings of the colonial era are an example of direct democracy. Today, direct democracy is at work in the United States when citizens vote on a *referendum*.

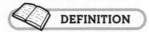 **DEFINITION**

A **referendum** is a process by which a law is referred to voters for final approval or rejection.

Representative democracy, to use Plato's term, is a republic. In a republic, citizens elect government officials to represent them and to make laws and policies. In a representative democracy, government officials are held accountable through regular elections and constitutional limits. This book uses democracy and republic interchangeably.

Constitutionalism embodies the principle that the people are sovereign. The government is given certain powers by the people and then it is held legally and politically accountable for how it exercises these powers. Government officials must listen to, sometimes negotiate with, and explain themselves to the people before they act on laws and policies.

Foundations of American Democracy

Democracy in America exists because the American people share a common set of beliefs:

- Citizens are entitled to personal liberty, a wide degree of individual freedom.
- Equality of opportunity for all persons.
- Respect for the individual.
- Popular consent or majority rule.
- The necessity of compromise.

 ON THE RECORD

"Democracy is worth dying for, because it's the most deeply honorable form of government ever devised by man."

—President Ronald Reagan

The Distribution of Power in a Democracy

Democracy in the United States is based on free and fair elections held at regular intervals. Political competition and choice are critical for the success and existence of democracy. In the United States, citizens have a choice to vote for candidates from different political parties, organizations made up of individuals who share a common philosophy or set of beliefs about public policy.

Majoritarian politics is when elected representatives closely follow the preferences of the majority of the citizens. They act in a manner that reflects the will of the people if the law or policy were put to a popular vote. However, the low level of voter turnout in presidential elections (and even less in congressional elections) means that democracy in the United States is far from true majoritarian democracy. If the citizens are not all involved in the election process, political power is distributed only to a majority of the participants, commonly referred to as political elites, a group that possess a disproportionate share of power.

If ordinary cititizens are not really making policy decisions, who is? These are two common views on who really governs in the United States: the elite theory and the pluralist view.

The American sociologist C. Wright Mills in his work *The Power Elite* (Oxford Press, 1956), posits that a loose coalition of three groups—corporate leaders, top military officials, and a handful of political leaders—makes important policy decisions in this country. Some say that the leaders of labor and the media should be added to this group. Whatever the composition, the main point is that government policies are made by an elite few to serve their own social, economic, or political interests.

 ON THE RECORD

"All tyranny needs to gain a foothold is for people of good conscience to remain silent."

—Thomas Jefferson

The pluralist view maintains that competition among interest groups or associations that represent the vast interests of the American people results in compromise and accommodation so that each group is satisfied to some extent.

Neither of these theories can be proven, yet it is important to note that unless large sums of money can be raised for campaigns from wealthy supporters or interest groups, candidates have little chance of success. This could result in political power being dominated by a financial elite, or democracy for a few. Additionally, some groups have become so large and powerful that public policy is designed only for their respective interests.

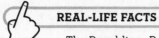

REAL-LIFE FACTS

The Republican Party was formed in 1854 by Free Soil Party, Whig, and northern Democrat members who opposed the spread of slavery in new states. The party of Abraham Lincoln was committed to preserving the Republic during the Civil War.

The Role of Government in American History

Since the Colonial Period, government has always been important to Americans. Government has affected economic and social life in America since the first arrival of the colonial European powers. From the time of the first settlements, citizens have expected their government to provide basic law, order, and protection from foreign invasions. However, government has always played a much larger role than that.

From the earliest days of British colonial rule, government has played a large role in developing and regulating the economy. During colonial times, the government helped finance new ventures, developed trading ports, and constructed roads and waterways. After the United States gained independence, new laws were enacted that established rules for organizing government and selling land in the large territory between the Ohio and Mississippi Rivers and the Great Lakes. This set of laws is commonly known as the Northwest Ordinance. Another example of the government's prominent role in the economy is the 1803 purchase of the Louisiana Territory from France.

The role of the U.S. government continued to expand in the nineteenth and twentieth centuries. The Great Depression—an economic crash that left millions of Americans jobless and homeless—greatly expanded the role of government as it attempted to solve the economic and social problems that had never been experienced at such a scale before. The federal government was managing the economy in ways it never had before by creating jobs for unemployed Americans, placing price controls to hold down prices, and regulating how businesses should conduct their affairs.

This explosion of new government activity was designed to promote economic and social stability. Soon a bureaucracy was born, the size of which has grown beyond most people's imagination at the time. Today, most Americans are affected directly or indirectly by such programs as Social Security, student loans, housing mortgages, Federal Emergency Management Agency (FEMA), Medicare, Medicaid, school lunches, unemployment benefits, and tax incentives.

In addition to economic and social interests, the government has taken on an expanded role in environmental policy and management ranging from emissions regulations, global climate initiatives, and developing new energy sources. To achieve some of these goals, the government has mandated lower speed limits on major roads, advocated for the development of nonfossil fuel energy sources, and signed international agreements to lower emission levels. The agreement signed by the United States at the 2015 United Nations Climate Change Conference in Paris commits our government to aiding the goal of reducing emission levels to preindustrial levels to prevent harmful levels of global climate warming.

Since the 1990s, a large number of Americans have come to the conclusion that the government has grown too big. Some efforts to reduce the scope of government, including Bill Clinton saying, "The era of big government is over," have reduced the scope and size of government. But the events of September 11, 2001, in addition to hurricanes Katrina and Sandy, have slowed the efforts to reduce government action, and in some ways have produced calls for more government action and programs. Instead of shrinking the size of government, the conversation seems to have turned to refocusing and reorganizing government so that it functions more efficiently and focuses on the threats and needs to which we are most vulnerable. This is one of many paradoxes in American politics: the yearning for small government (and low taxes) and the seemingly infinite number (and cost) of services we expect the government to provide.

Who Governs?

In theory, one should be able to clearly answer who governs and how political power is distributed in a society. However, the answers are not simple or obvious.

Political power does rest in the hands of elected officials, but it can also be found in many nongovernment institutions. Unions, lobbyists, consumer groups, the media, and other special-interest groups wield an enormous amount of political power in the United States. These nongovernment entities influence policies, laws, and elections, so it's important to understand the role they play in governance.

This book will give you an understanding of the underlying principles of American government and also give you the tools to analyze the two fundamental questions of politics: who governs in a society and what are their goals?

The Least You Need to Know

- Politics is the science of government and how people make decisions and solve societal problems.
- Government is the institution through which a society makes and enforces laws and policies.
- Political power is used to affect who governs and for what purpose.
- There are many forms of government, and several important theories that explain the birth of the nation-state.
- Democracy in the United States is based on several important principles, including the recognition of equality of each person, faith in majority rule, and an insistence on individual freedom.

The Constitution

The motto of the United States, *E Pluribus Unum,* is from the Latin meaning "from the many, one." This motto describes the system of government established by the framers of the Constitution meeting in Philadelphia in 1787.

The original, unamended Constitution contains just 4,543 words, yet it is the oldest written constitution, and it established an experiment in free government that is still working today, adapting to the needs of the people. It offers both hope and optimism as a framework of governance, and it serves as a protection against government tyranny and oppression. The Constitution is the supreme and binding law of the land.

In This Chapter

- Origins of the American constitutional system
- The development of the government from the colonial period to the Revolution
- Successes and failures under the Articles of Confederation
- Formation of the Constitution
- Changing the Constitution

English Roots of American Constitutionalism

American democratic and constitutional roots can be traced to several important documents in English history and from colonial America. Together with the *Enlightenment*, these roots formed a political culture and tradition that influenced the delegates at the Constitutional Convention in 1787. The founders had developed a philosophy about how people should be governed.

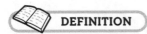 **DEFINITION**

> The **Enlightenment** was a European intellectual movement of the late seventeenth/ early eighteenth centuries emphasizing reason and individualism rather than tradition. The main philosophers who contributed to this movement were Rene Descartes, John Locke, and Sir Isaac Newton.

The Magna Carta: The Great Charter

The Magna Carta is the seminal document that establishes rights and protections in English history. Signed in 1215 by King John, it established limits on the king's absolute authority over the nobility. Over time, these rights and protections were extended to all English citizens. Among the fundamental rights established by the Magna Carta were trial by jury and due process of law—the protection against the taking of life, liberty, or property at the monarch's discretion.

The Petition of Right

Many English monarchs ignored the spirit of the Magna Carta. In 1626, King Charles I called a session of Parliament in an effort to obtain desperately needed funds to continue his unsuccessful war with Spain. In response to this request and a number of perceived violations of the law by Charles I in the first years of his reign, Parliament proposed the Petition of Right. By 1628, the English Parliament—a representative body that made laws—had grown in power and influence. It forced the monarch to sign the Petition of Right before it would allocate any more money to war efforts.

The Petition of Right limited the king's ability to imprison critics without a trial and his ability to force subjects to shelter troops without their consent. Finally, it declared that taxes could not be imposed without the consent of Parliament. All together, these components of the Petition of Right challenged the idea of the divine right of kings—the notion the monarch derives his or her authority to rule from God, and therefore cannot be questioned.

The English Bill of Rights

In 1688, after many years of civil war and turmoil, the English Parliament offered the crown to William and Mary of Orange. To prevent abuse of power by future monarchs, the Parliament first had William and Mary agree to a Bill of Rights establishing the supremacy of Parliament over the monarch. All elections to Parliament had to be free, and all laws had to be written and executed with the consent of Parliament. Additionally, only Parliament could levy taxes. This event in English history is also known as the Glorious Revolution.

Natural Rights

The assumption that people have natural rights is an Enlightenment notion advanced by the English philosopher John Locke. In his 1690 work, *Two Treatises on Government*, Locke maintained that people possess certain natural rights given to them by God, including the right to life, liberty, and property. He also argued that the main purpose of government is to protect these rights. This is the foundation of the social contract—the agreement between people to form a government to rule over them and to abide by its rules. If the government does not protect the natural rights of the people, the people can overthrow or change the government.

Colonial America

The first state governments of the United States differed in many ways, but they all shared common democratic features:

- Government by the consent of the governed, also known as popular sovereignty.

- Powers delegated to the government was limited.

- Citizens had certain rights that the government must respect, or a Bill of Rights.

- A division of power between an executive, legislative, and judicial branch of government, which created a system of checks and balances.

The English first established outposts in America in the late sixteenth century. In 1607, the English government established Jamestown, in what is now Virginia. This settlement became the basis for the first colony in America. The English government gave the authorities in Jamestown the authority to establish laws for the settlement. The colonists in Jamestown established the colonies' first representative assembly. Several other important documents contributed to this democratic tradition in colonial America.

The Mayflower Compact

Massachusetts was the first colony to be established in New England. In 1620, a group of individuals who sought to break with the Church of England landed at Plymouth. Before going onshore, the Englishmen drew up and signed the Mayflower Compact, named after the ship on which they had sailed. The document was an agreement by the settlers to submit to the authority of a government that would be established by the consent of the people.

Fundamental Orders of Connecticut

The Fundamental Orders of Connecticut appears to be the first written constitution in the Western tradition to have created a government. It is considered to be the prototype of the U.S. Constitution adopted 150 years later.

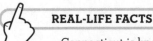

REAL-LIFE FACTS

Connecticut is known as the "Constitution state." The origin of this title is uncertain, but the nickname is assumed to reference the Fundamental Orders of 1638-1639.

Massachusetts Body of Liberties

In 1641 Massachusetts published the Body of Liberties. This document contained 100 liberties that were to guide the governing authorities at the time. It incorporates rights that were later judged to be ahead of their time, some of which eventually appeared in the Bill of Rights. For example, the Body of Liberties incorporated the notions of equal justice and the right of appeal, and banned cruel punishment.

The Flushing Remonstrance

The Flushing Remonstrance was a 1657 Colonial American petition to Peter Stuyvesant, the governor of the Dutch colony of New Amsterdam, in which several citizens (none of them Quakers themselves) requested an exemption to his ban on Quaker worship. It is considered a precursor to the U.S. Constitution's provision on freedom of religion in the Bill of Rights.

Pennsylvania Frame of Government

In 1682, King Charles II of England granted William Penn the colony of Pennsylvania. Penn in turn drafted the Pennsylvania Frame of Government as a constitution for the new colony of Pennsylvania.

The Frame of Government significantly influenced the development of American democracy. It protected many rights and liberties, including trial by jury, freedom of the press, and religious toleration. Use of the death penalty was much more limited than it was in other societies at the time. The Frame was also the first constitution to allow for an amendment process.

In 1701, Governor William Penn signed the Pennsylvania Charter of Privileges, formally establishing a stable frame of government that was remarkably liberal. This document granted a set of individual rights to protect freedom of religion among all *monotheists.*

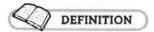 **DEFINITION**

Monotheism is the belief that there is only one God.

The Continental Congresses and Independence

In response to several harsh tax and trade policies of the British government, including the Stamp Act, the American colonies organized and formed the First Continental Congress in Philadelphia in 1774. The British Parliament imposed a series of taxes in order to assert their authority over the American colonies. The colonies, however, lacked elected representation in the governing British Parliament; many colonists considered the laws to be illegitimate and a violation of their rights as Englishmen. The meeting in Philadelphia resulted in a list of grievances to the king and a request that the British government repeal all taxes and trade regulations on the colonies. Furthermore, it required the colonies to raise their own troops.

 REAL-LIFE FACTS

The phrase "No taxation without representation!" was coined by Reverend Jonathan Mayhew in a sermon in Boston in 1750.

In 1775, the Second Continental Congress met with the main objective of establishing an army. Virginian George Washington was selected as the commander in chief. By 1776, many military encounters with British forces had occurred, and on July 2, 1776, the Second Continental Congress adopted a Resolution for Independence. On July 4, 1776, the Second Continental Congress passed Thomas Jefferson's Declaration of Independence, one of the world's most famous decrees in the development of free democracy:

> "We hold these truths to be self-evident, that all men are created equal, that they are endowed by their creator with certain unalienable rights, that among these are life, liberty, and the pursuit of happiness …."

With these words, the United States of America was formed.

The Articles of Confederation

The Second Continental Congress established the first American government with the passage of the Articles of Confederation in 1777. However, not until 1781 did all of the 13 original states join the confederation. The limited central government that was established was a voluntary association of independent, sovereign states. The central government was composed of a unicameral—one-house—assembly called the Congress, with each state represented by one vote. Only Congress could declare war and make peace.

The Articles of Confederation did not provide for an executive, but it did allow the assembly to elect a presiding officer for a one-year term. The government also lacked any independent sources of revenue.

The government could settle disputes between the states. Claims by certain states to western territories were settled and the Northwest Ordinance of 1787 was passed. This act established a pattern of government for new territories not part of the original 13 states.

Although Congress had the authority to declare war and make peace and essentially conduct foreign policy, it had no right to collect taxes from the states. It could only ask for voluntary contributions or payments. Also, any action by Congress required the consent of 9 of the 13 states and any amendments had to have unanimous approval. Lastly, the Articles did not establish a national judiciary or system of courts. The fact that the Congress could not raise money for a military rendered it weak and ineffective.

The Constitutional Convention

Due to the weaknesses of the Articles of Confederation, the central government could not guarantee order and stability in the new nation. In 1786, a group of farmers led by Daniel Shays attacked county courthouses hearing the trials of debtors in Massachusetts. Shays' Rebellion demonstrated that the state and central governments could not defend their institutions from armed rebellion. The demand to modify the Articles started to take hold.

 ON THE RECORD

"For God's sake, if they [the rebels] have real grievances, redress them; if they have not, employ the force of government against them at once."

—George Washington

In May 1787, delegates from 12 of the 13 states met in Philadelphia with the main purpose to revise the Articles of Confederation and create a federal government powerful enough to ensure the stability of the nation but still protect individual liberty. Rhode Island did not send delegates because it did not want a stronger central government. However, within a few days of the meeting, it became clear that the delegates would be forming a new government for the United States.

On May 30, 1787, the delegates adopted a proposal put forth by Edmund Randolph of Virginia: "Resolved … that a federal government ought to be established consisting of a supreme Legislative, Executive and Judiciary." The deliberations that followed involved much conflict and compromise.

Who Were the Framers?

Many historians and students of history and politics believe we can better understand the framework of government established by the Constitution if we know who these individuals were and what their motivations were. One school of thought is that the men who gathered in Philadelphia were statesmen who led the fight for independence from Great Britain and were motivated to create a strong future for the new nation. Another school of thought argues that most of the framers were motivated to protect their personal and economic interests. This included the wealthy landholders and slave-owning classes. Yet others see the group as pragmatic politicians who were trying to be problem-solvers and address the critical issues that divided the various factions.

What we know for certain about the 55 men who gathered in Philadelphia in 1787 is that they were all white males, as women and African Americans and other minorities were excluded from this important meeting. Many of the men who attended and who we now call our "Founding Fathers" were lawyers, soldiers, businessmen, bankers, doctors, and large plantation owners. They ranged in age from 26 (Jonathan Dayton of New Jersey) to 81 (Benjamin Franklin of Pennsylvania). Most of the attendees had previously served in the Continental Congress, which governed the nation during the war with Great Britain. One attendee, James Madison (age 36) played such a central role in forming the debate and drafting the final document that he is now called the "Father of the Constitution."

The Virginia Plan

Virginia was instrumental in calling for a convention in Philadelphia and it offered the first plan for a new government, the Virginia Plan. This plan called for a government made up of three separate and independent branches: legislative, executive, and judicial.

The legislative branch would be bicameral—that is, made up of two houses. The number of representatives would be proportional to the state's population. The delegates to the lower house would be elected directly by the people. The upper house would be elected by the individual state legislatures. The legislative branch would elect a national executive and also appoint the national judiciary.

The Virginia Plan clearly envisioned the legislative branch as the dominant branch of government. The large states generally supported the Virginia Plan, as they would form a majority in the national legislature.

The New Jersey Plan

New Jersey, a small state, offered an alternate plan for the new government:

- It called to maintain a one-house—unicameral—legislative branch as in the Articles of Confederation, with each state having one vote.
- The legislative branch would be able to regulate trade and impose taxes.
- The laws of the central government would be supreme over state laws.
- The executive branch would be made up of more than one person.
- The executive branch would appoint the national judiciary.

The Great Compromise

For many weeks the delegates could not reach a consensus on the makeup of the legislative branch, and many threatened to leave the convention. Finally, in July 1787, a plan acceptable to both major factions at the convention was arrived at.

Also referred to as the Connecticut Plan, the Great Compromise resolved the differences between the supporters of the Virginia and New Jersey plans and established the framework for the new government. A bicameral legislature that comprised features of both plans was agreed to:

- The House would be based on proportional representation and would be the larger body.

- The Senate would have equal representation of the states, with each state legislature electing two representatives to the body.

The Three-Fifths Compromise

Once the delegates had agreed to proportional representation in the House, the matter of how slaves should be counted became a major issue. Slavery was legal everywhere in the states except for Massachusetts, but was heavily concentrated in the Southern states. The South wanted slaves to be counted and most of the Northern states largely opposed this. A compromise was reached that stated that "free persons and three-fifths of all other persons should be counted."

Other Issues

The largely agrarian South feared that a Northern majority would jeopardize its economic interests. Therefore, it was agreed that the central government could not levy export taxes on any good produced in the states and sold to other countries. Also, it mandated a Supreme Court but left the power to establish lower courts to the legislative branch.

Lastly, James Madison's system of checks and balances was accepted by the convention. This model creates independent branches of government that can check each other so that no one branch comes to dominate the government and threaten individual liberty. We'll discuss how this actually plays out in subsequent chapters.

 MISINFORMATION

Alexander Hamilton, one of the founding fathers, wanted the president to hold office for life. The Constitution set the president's term at four years. In 1951, with the passing of the Twenty-Second Amendment, the limit of two consecutive four-year terms was implemented.

The Final Document

On September 17, 1787, the delegates at Philadelphia approved the Constitution, which established and embodied certain fundamental principles:

- Popular sovereignty, or control of government by the people

- A republican form of government, in which people choose representatives to make laws and policies for them

- Limited government with written laws and authority given to the government by the people

- Separation of powers and checks and balances among three independent branches of government

- A *federal system* that allows for states' rights and a central government

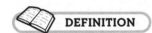 DEFINITION

> In a **federal system,** sovereignty is shared so that on some matters the federal government is supreme and on others the state, regional, or provincial governments retain ultimate authority.

The Constitution established a federal government with specific powers. For example, it gave Congress the power to regulate commerce between the states. It established a president as the chief executive, who would also serve as commander in chief of the armed forces. It also established the Supreme Court. The states were also delegated certain powers and authority. You will read more about the federal system of government in the next chapter.

The Road to Ratification

Each state was to hold a special convention to approve the new government. The delegates decided that the new Constitution should go into effect when it was ratified by popular elected conventions in nine states. This would essentially legitimize the new government because it would receive support directly from representatives the people elected. This would be a government truly founded on the principle, "We the People …." However, two opposing forces quickly emerged over ratification.

The Federalists

Supporters of the new government called themselves Federalists. This group was made up largely of citizens from the seaboard and city regions and included bankers, lawyers, plantation owners, and merchants. They organized themselves quickly to elect delegates to the ratifying conventions. Their most effective tool to make their argument in favor of the new government is known as *The Federalist Papers,* which were printed in newspapers and whose principal authors were Alexander Hamilton, James Madison, and John Jay.

The Anti-Federalists

The Anti-Federalists believed the new Constitution would create a central government that was too powerful and would endanger personal liberty. They were very concerned that the new document did not contain a bill of rights. They also were concerned about the limited power of the sovereign states within the new government structure. Some of the most prominent Anti-Federalists included Samuel Adams and Patrick Henry.

Final Ratification

Most of the small states, satisfied with equal representation in the Senate, ratified the new Constitution. Delaware was the first state to ratify on December 7, 1787, followed by Pennsylvania on December 12, New Jersey on December 18, Georgia on January 2, 1788, Connecticut on January 9, Massachusetts on February 6, Maryland on April 28, and South Carolina on May 23.

By June 21, 1788, with New Hampshire on board, the nine states necessary to put the new government in place were obtained. However, the two largest states, Virginia and New York, still hadn't ratified the Constitution, and it would have been difficult to imagine starting the new government without their consent.

A deal was struck to pass a bill of rights as the new government's first order of business, and with George Washington's support, Virginia ratified the Constitution on June 25, 1788. New York quickly followed on July 26.

With 11 of the 13 states having ratified the Constitution, the new nation—a republic—was born.

 ON THE RECORD

"The United States Constitution has proven itself the most marvelously elastic compilation of rules of government ever written."

—President Franklin D. Roosevelt

North Carolina finally agreed on November 21, 1789, and Rhode Island on May 29, 1790.

The Bill of Rights

The Constitution would not have been ratified by several important states unless there was some guarantee that a bill of rights would be passed to protect individual liberty and rights from a strong central government. Collectively, the first 10 amendments to the Constitution, drafted by James Madison, are known as the Bill of Rights. They were proposed by the first session of Congress in 1789 and ratified by the states in 1791. The Bill of Rights applied initially only to the central government and not to state or local governments.

Amendment I: Religion, Speech, Assembly, and Politics   Congress shall make no law respecting an establishment of religion, or prohibiting the free exercise thereof; or abridging the freedom of speech, or of the press; or the right of the people peaceably to assemble, and to petition the government for a redress of grievances.

Amendment II: Militia and the Right to Bear Arms   A well-regulated militia, being necessary to the security of a free state, the right of the people to keep and bear arms, shall not be infringed.

Amendment III: Quartering of Soldiers   No soldier shall, in time of peace be quartered in any house, without the consent of the owner, nor in time of war, but in a manner to be prescribed by law.

Amendment IV: Searches and Seizures   The right of the people to be secure in their persons, houses, papers, and effects, against unreasonable searches and seizures, shall not be violated, and no warrants shall issue, but upon probable cause, supported by oath or affirmation, and particularly describing the place to be searched, and the persons or things to be seized.

Amendment V: Grand Juries, Self-Incrimination, Double Jeopardy, Due Process, and Eminent Domain   No person shall be held to answer for a capital, or otherwise infamous crime, unless on a presentment or indictment of a grand jury, except in cases arising in the land or naval forces, or in the militia, when in actual service in time of war or public danger; nor shall any person be subject for the same offense to be twice put in jeopardy of life or limb; nor shall be compelled in any criminal case to be a witness against himself, nor be deprived of life, liberty, or property, without due process of law; nor shall private property be taken for public use, without just compensation.

Amendment VI: Criminal Court Procedures   In all criminal prosecutions, the accused shall enjoy the right to a speedy and public trial, by an impartial jury of the state and district wherein the crime shall have been committed, which district shall have been previously ascertained by law, and to be informed of the nature and cause of the accusation; to be confronted with the witnesses against him; to have compulsory process for obtaining witnesses in his favor; and to have the assistance of counsel for his defense.

Amendment VII: Trial by Jury in Common Law Cases   In suits at common law, where the value in controversy shall exceed twenty dollars, the right of trial by jury shall be preserved, and no fact tried by a jury, shall be otherwise reexamined in any court of the United States, than according to the rules of the common law.

Amendment VIII: Bail, Cruel and Unusual Punishment   Excessive bail shall not be required, nor excessive fines imposed, nor cruel and unusual punishments inflicted.

Amendment IX: Rights Retained by the People   The enumeration in the Constitution, of certain rights, shall not be construed to deny or disparage others retained by the people.

Amendment X: Reserved Powers of the States   The powers not delegated to the United States by the Constitution, nor prohibited by it to the states, are reserved to the states respectively, or to the people.

 ON THE RECORD

"Don't interfere with anything in the Constitution. That must be maintained, for it is the only safeguard of our liberties."

—President Abraham Lincoln

Formal and Informal Methods of Constitutional Change

The founders intended that the federal Constitution would be a framework for government that could be interpreted by generations to guide the nation as it developed and continued to grow. In Article V of the Constitution, the framers established the procedures to formally amend, or change in words, the Constitution. The procedures they established do not allow for changes to be easily made. The framers clearly wanted a stable framework to endure; they did not want the Constitution to be easily changed by what James Madison referred to as "a tyranny of the majority"—a majority that could pass amendments to oppress individuals or groups. The process the framers established allows for only those amendments that have wide popular support across both parties and all regions of the country to be approved.

Formal Amendment Process

There are four methods to formally amend the Constitution. The process illustrates the principles of federalism in that the amendment process involves both the federal government and the states.

An amendment may be proposed by a two-thirds vote in each house of Congress and then ratified by three fourths of the state legislatures. This is the process by which most of the Amendments have passed.

An amendment may be proposed by a two-thirds vote in each house of Congress and ratified by conventions held in three fourths of the states. Conventions are comprised of delegates directly elected by the people of the states and are more likely to reflect popular opinion on the amendment. This process was used to pass the Twenty-First Amendment, which repealed the Eighteenth Amendment, which established prohibition.

An amendment may be proposed by a national convention called by Congress when requested by two thirds of the state legislatures. It must then be ratified by the legislatures in three fourths of the states. To date, Congress has never called such a convention.

It is important to note that the President and the Supreme Court have no formal role in the amendment process. Also, the Constitution does not place a time limit on the ratification process, but the Supreme Court has ruled that Congress can specify a time limit on the ratification process as long as it is reasonable.

 REAL-LIFE FACTS

More than 10,000 resolutions calling for amendments have been proposed in Congress since 1789. Only 33 of them have been sent to the states for a vote. And of those 33, only 27 have been finally approved.

Informal Methods of Constitutional Change

The principle, organization, and structure of our government have remained largely unchanged. Yet many changes have been made in our government without formally changing the words of the Constitution. The informal amendment process, by which changes have been made but have not resulted in changes to the Constitution—is a result of the flexibility of the Constitution to adapt itself over time to events and concerns of the citizens.

Congressional legislation   Congress has been an agent of change in that it has passed laws to spell out or clarify provisions in the Constitution and it can define terms that are in the Constitution. For example, Congress has passed many *statutes* to define commerce.

 **DEFINITION**

Statutes are formal, written laws of a country or state, written and enacted by its legislative authority, ratified by the highest executive in the government, and finally published. The president's **cabinet** is the advisory body traditionally made up of the heads of the executive departments and other officers the president may choose.

Executive action   Presidents have used their powers to informally amend the Constitution. Although only Congress has the power to declare war, several presidents, as commander in chief, have made war without a formal congressional declaration.

Judicial review   The federal courts, especially the Supreme Court, have interpreted the Constitution as a result of court cases. When court decisions are applied, this is another example of an informal way to amend the Constitution.

Political parties and customs   The Constitution makes no mention of political parties or the nomination process. The parties have established these rules to nominate and select the president. Custom, not the Constitution, says that the heads of the executive departments—the department of State, Defense, and so on—make up the president's *cabinet*.

 REAL-LIFE FACTS

As of January 2016, President Roosevelt holds the record for the most Executive Orders issued at 3,721. President Reagan issued 381. President Obama has issued 228 so far.

The Least You Need to Know

- English legal traditions and experiments with representative governments in colonial America provided a heritage in limited government in the United States.

- After the War of Independence from Great Britain, the independent 13 **states** established a new government under the Articles of Confederation. This framework of government was too weak for the new nation to grow and succeed.

- The Constitutional Convention in Philadelphia established a federal system of government—a new federal government that is granted power but limited in what it can do. Furthermore, it reserved to the states all the powers not delegated to the federal government.

- The ratification of the Constitution was debated by the Federalists and the Anti-Federalists. The Constitution was adopted by the states in 1788.

- The Constitution has six basic principles: popular sovereignty, limited government, separation of powers, checks and balances, judicial review, and federalism.

- There are both formal and informal methods of amending the Constitution.

Federalism

Ever since the adoption of the Constitution, the nature of the relationship between the federal government and the states has been a major political question and source of conflict. The issue of slavery, the regulation of business, and the social welfare network programs were debated in terms of *national interests* and *states' rights*.

The Constitution structured our federal system of government in a way to deal with political, economic, and social developments. The political history of federalism in the United States is one filled with various shifts of power from the federal government to the states.

In This Chapter

- Defining federalism
- The constitutional structure of federalism
- The powers and relationship of the federal government and the states
- Federalism and the courts
- The politics of federalism

The Federal System

A federal system of government divides authority between a central government and regional governments. In the United States, the federal system consists of the federal government in Washington, D.C., and the sovereign 50 states. The division of authority in a federal system is determined by a written constitution. Each sphere of government has supreme authority within the powers delegated to it by the Constitution. In the United States, the federal government establishes the laws and policies for military service, while the states determine the age at which people can obtain a driver's license or who can obtain a marriage license. There are some overlapping spheres of authority, such as law and order or police powers, which are given to both the federal government and to the sovereign states.

When conflicts arise between the federal government and the states over authority on a particular matter or issue, the federal courts make the final determination over who has constitutional jurisdiction. Since the founding of the republic, Americans have debated what the relationship of the federal government and the states should be. Remember that the Federalists at the Constitutional Convention wanted a strong central government and the Anti-Federalists were concerned that a strong central government would undermine the sovereignty of the states and threaten personal liberty. In the United States today, Democrats argue for a strong central government, particularly on domestic programs, while Republicans want to see the role of big government reduced and most of the federal government's functions returned to the states. This is referred to as a devolution revolution.

 REAL-LIFE FACTS

Although the states are sovereign, they are prohibited from entering into treaties or alliances with other countries according to Article I, Section 10 of the U.S. Constitution.

Why Federalism?

The founders in Philadelphia created a federal system of government in order to protect personal liberty. But they knew from experience that independent sovereign states could not necessarily ensure national law and order. The experiment with the Articles of Confederation proved unsuccessful. So they devised a plan that separates powers between the states and a federal government.

By creating a federal government of unity, while maintaining powers at the state level, the founders created a government that did not concentrate too much power in one authority and offered many advantages to the states and the people.

Unity and Uniformity

Federalism creates a federal government of unity while preserving the unique traditions and culture of the states. For example, the central government provides the nation with defense and foreign policy, among its many functions. The states debate and devise policies on such issues as assisted suicide, same-sex marriage, and capital punishment.

James Madison, in *The Federalist,* No. 10, argues that factional interests working concurrently will check each other. In practical terms, this means that if particular states attempt to infringe on personal liberties, then the federal government can step in to protect the people. Furthermore, if one party were to dominate the federal government and pass laws and policies that the people do not support, the people can elect officials at the state level to counter the federal government.

Experimentation

The states serve as laboratories of public policy and create a training ground for future national political leaders. If one state adopts a policy that fails, the adverse effects are limited. If, on the other hand, the policy is successful, other states can adopt the policy, or the federal government can establish the policy for the entire country.

For example, Georgia was the first state to allow 18-year-olds to vote. In 1971, the passage of the Twenty-Sixth Amendment lowered the legal voting age from 21 to 18 for all citizens of the United States.

Government Close to the People

As you read in the previous chapter, the Federalists wanted a strong central government but were opposed by the Anti-Federalists, who supported strong states' rights. The federal form of government established by the Constitution appealed to both those who wanted to retain state sovereignty and traditions, and those advocating for a strong central government to deal with common national problems.

Government is kept close and accountable to the people in a Federalist form of government because there are numerous venues for decision-making. Because authority is divided at the national and state level, the people are involved directly on many issues. In the United States, citizens serve on or are elected to city councils, serve on school boards and neighborhood associations, and join interest groups. This keeps the people close to the issues and responsive to problems. Citizens also vote for elected officials at the federal, state, and local level.

The Constitutional Structure of Federalism

The Constitution defines the framework of our federal system of government. The basic principles of the U.S. government are as follows:

- The federal government has only those powers delegated to it by the people.

- The federal government is supreme within its scope of authority.

- The state governments retain all the powers not delegated to the federal government by the people, except those powers denied to them by the Constitution or their respective state constitutions.

- Some powers are denied to both the national and state governments, while other powers are denied only to the states or to the federal government.

Powers of the Federal Government

The Constitution delegates legislative, executive, and judicial powers to the federal government. Most of the *expressed powers* delegated to the federal government are detailed in Article I, Section 8 of the Constitution. These are also referred to as the enumerated powers, and include the power to coin and print money, regulate interstate commerce, declare war, and appropriate funds.

The constitutional basis for the *implied powers* can also be found in Article I, Section 8 of the Constitution, called the "necessary and proper" clause. This clause gives Congress the right "to make all Laws which shall be necessary and proper for carrying into Execution the forgoing Powers, and all other Powers vested by this Constitution in the Government of the United States, or in any Department or Officer thereof." This clause is also referred to as the elastic clause, because it provides the federal government with flexibility to carry out its powers. For example, Congress has assumed the power to create banks from the expressed power it has over the nation's money.

Special categories of national powers that do not depend on constitutional provisions are referred to as the *inherent powers.* These are powers that the federal government derives from the fact that the United States is a sovereign nation. As such, it has an inherent right to ensure its own survival and to deal with other nation-states. These powers include the right to make treaties, wage war, enter into trade agreements, and acquire new land and territory. For example, in 1803, the federal government made the Louisiana Purchase. It has also grown from the original 13 states to the current 50 and other U.S. territories such as the U.S. Virgin Islands.

Powers of the State Governments

The Tenth Amendment to the Constitution states that "the powers not delegated to the United States by the Constitution, nor prohibited by it to the states, are reserved to the states respectively, or to the people."

This amendment reaffirms the principle of limited government and federalism. These are the reserved powers the federal government cannot deny to the states or the people. However, these powers are not expressly listed. The vagueness of the Tenth Amendment has meant that the powers reserved to the states have been defined differently at various times in history. The current political debate about states' rights in the area of gun control, same-sex marriage, or gambling is based on the fact that the Constitution does not give authority to the federal government on these issues.

 MISINFORMATION

Legally, a city is a municipal corporation or municipality that can be created or abolished by a state. Cities have no independent existence according to the Constitution.

The Concurrent Powers

The federal government and the states share certain *concurrent powers,* most of which are implied rather than specifically stated in the Constitution. For example, both the federal government and state governments can levy taxes on citizens and businesses. However, state governments cannot levy taxes on imported goods, and the federal government cannot tax real estate holdings. Other examples of concurrent powers include the power to establish courts and charter banks.

 **DEFINITION**

Concurrent powers are powers held jointly by the national and state governments.

The Prohibited Powers

Any power not specifically delegated to the federal government by the Constitution is prohibited to it. For example, the federal government cannot create a public school system. This power is retained by the people and the states. Furthermore, the Constitution prohibits the federal government from levying taxes on exports—goods sold to other countries. The states are also denied certain powers by the Constitution. One example is that no state may enter into a treaty with another country.

The Supremacy Clause

The supremacy clause of the Constitution (Article VI, Clause 2) states the following:

> "This Constitution, and the Laws of the United States which shall be made in Pursuance thereof; and all Treaties made, or which shall be made, under Authority of the United States, shall be the supreme Law of the land; and the Judges in every state shall be bound thereby, any Thing in the Constitution or Laws of any state to the Contrary notwithstanding."

This clause establishes the supremacy of the national Constitution over state laws and actions. Essentially, the states cannot use their reserved or concurrent powers to thwart national laws and policies. The ability of the federal government to dominate over the states has been a continuous source of political conflict in the United States.

Interstate Relations

The Constitution establishes some rules on interstate relations. This is commonly referred to as *horizontal federalism*. The three most important clauses require the states to do the following four things:

- Agree to return persons who are fleeing from justice in another state back to their home state when requested to do so (Article IV, Section 2).

- Extend to every other state's citizens the privileges and immunities of its own citizens (Article IV, Section 2).

- Give full faith and credit to every other state's public acts, records, and judicial proceeding (Article IV, Section 1).

- Settle disputes with one another without the use of force and carry their legal disputes to the Supreme Court, or they may enter into interstate compacts. An interstate compact is an agreement among two or more states that must be approved by Congress.

 **DEFINITION**

Horizontal federalism is the activities, problems, and policies that require state governments to interact with one another.

All of these rules among the states are directly taken from the Articles of Confederation. The states don't always consistently follow these constitutional mandates. For example, a state's driver's license is accepted by the other states. However, although some states have started to issue same-sex marriage licenses, other states have passed laws stating that they will not recognize such marriages. This matter will inevitably be settled in the judicial branch. The courts will have to interpret the full faith and credit clause.

Constitutional Powers: The Early Years

The language of the Constitution has some degree of ambiguity, which has left the door open to different interpretations of federalism over the history of the republic. In the early years, the disputes that arose dealt largely with defining the implied powers of the federal government. Ultimately, the Supreme Court decides the final interpretation. As such, the Supreme Court acts as an umpire when disputes must be settled between the federal government and the states.

Chief Justice John Marshall led the Supreme Court from 1801 to 1835. A Federalist and an advocate for a strong federal government, Chief Justice Marshall is credited with giving the Constitution new power. Two important cases decided by the Marshall Court are *McCulloch* v. *Maryland* (1819) and *Gibbons* v. *Ogden* (1824).

McCulloch v. *Maryland* and National Supremacy

In the *McCulloch* case, the state of Maryland imposed a tax on the national bank. Chief Justice Marshall declared that the federal government had the implied power, under the necessary and proper clause, to charter a bank. He went on to establish the doctrine of national supremacy. Marshall argued that no state could use its taxing power to tax any part of the federal government.

This case provided the basis for a strong central government. Today, practically every expressed power of the federal government has been expanded by the use of the necessary and proper clause.

Gibbons v. *Ogden* and the Commerce Clause

The issue in *Gibbons* was the meaning of the commerce clause in Article I, Section 8 of the Constitution, which gives Congress the power to "regulate Commerce with foreign Nations, and among the several states, and with the Indian Tribes."

Marshall defined commerce as all business dealings, and determined that the federal government could exercise the commerce clause within state jurisdictions. Furthermore, he emphasized that the power to regulate interstate commerce was exclusively a federal government power. Marshall's ruling has allowed the federal government to increase its authority over all areas of economic affairs.

REAL-LIFE FACTS

At the funeral of John Marshall in 1835, the Liberty Bell was rung. It was during that event that the Liberty Bell cracked.

States' Rights and Civil War

Most people think that the Civil War was simply a fight to end slavery. But another controversy closely intertwined with it was the issue of national supremacy and states' rights. In many ways, the Civil War can be seen as the violent outcome of the ideological debate between the Federalists and the Anti-Federalists.

During the presidency of Andrew Jackson (1829–1837), a shift to states' rights began. This period is characterized by questions of regulating commerce. The state of South Carolina claimed that a national tariff on imports was beyond the federal government's authority. This is called the *doctrine of nullification*. Furthermore, the business community preferred state regulation or no regulation at all. The Northern and Southern states were divided over the issue of national tariffs. The Northern states were in favor of a strong federal government that could impose tariffs on imports as part of its constitutional role. The tariffs also protected goods manufactured in the North from competition from similar British goods. The Southern states were opposed to the tariff taxation policy of the federal government largely because it was perceived as favoring Northern manufacturing interests and resulting in higher prices for the British goods Southerners favored.

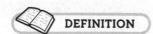 **DEFINITION**

The **doctrine of nullification** suggests that states had the right to void (or nullify) a federal law that, in the state's opinion, violated the Constitution.

On December 20, 1860, South Carolina formally repealed its ratification of the Constitution and withdrew from the Union. On February 4, 1861, representatives from six Southern states met to form a new government called the Confederate States of America.

The end of the Civil War in 1865 not only ended slavery, it also ended the idea that a state can withdraw, or secede, from the Union. The result was an increase in the power of the federal government. Not only did the federal government employ more people to run the war effort, it expanded the budget and passed the first (temporary) income tax to pay for the increased expenses. Furthermore, the federal government curtailed civil liberties in the name of wartime emergency.

Federal-State Relations and the Division of Power

The Civil War firmly established the supremacy of the federal government. Politically, however, the federal government must take into account the fact that the laws and policies it passes must be approved by members of Congress elected from all the states and responsive to their constituents' needs. Several interpretations of federalism and its principles are embraced by Americans across the political spectrum.

Dual federalism is a system of government in which the states and the federal government each remain supreme within their own spheres of authority. This doctrine looks at the federal government and the states as co-equal sovereign powers, maintaining that the acts of states within their reserved powers are legitimate limitations on the powers of the federal government.

The theory of *cooperative federalism* states that the federal government and the states should cooperate strongly in solving problems. This type of federalism describes the Great Depression era when the federal government passed many New Deal programs that required joint action with the states.

Political realities modify legal authority. There is no better example of this than federal grants-in-aid. Even before the Constitution was adopted, the federal government gave grants to the states in the form of land. Cash grants-in-aid began in the early nineteenth century to pay for militias. Grants-in-aid programs funded by the federal government but administered at the state level have grown considerably, especially since the 1960s. Medicaid is an example of such a program. Although these programs are seen as "free" by the states (because they do not have to tax in order to pay for them) they come with many strings and regulations that have considerably increased the influence of the federal government.

Popularized in the 1980s under the Ronald Reagan administration, *block grants* lessen the restrictions on grants-in-aid given to state governments. These give the states more flexibility on how to use the money to solve the problem the grant is intended to address. Rather than issuing a grant for a specific road or bridge, the federal government will issue a block grant for transportation.

The federal government has enacted many laws that require the states to take action in certain areas of public life or policy. For example, the federal government requires states to improve environmental conditions. However, many of these federal mandates are unfunded and pose a serious economic challenge to the states.

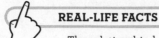

The Politics of Federalism

The structure of our federal system of government, established by the Constitution, has not changed much since the founding of the republic. However, historical and political realities have greatly altered how federalism works.

The Expanding Role of the Federal Government

Since the founding of the republic, power has shifted to the federal government at the expense of the states. This shift came about for a variety of reasons:

- Many local problems became national in scope.

- Industrialization produced powerful interests that placed demands on government.

- The growth of a national, interstate economy and a national rail system changed people's attitudes toward the federal government.

- The Great Depression and World War II stimulated extensive national action.

- The Great Society programs poured billions of dollars into state treasuries.

Today, there is growing political pressure on Congress to reduce the size and scope of national programs. However, many of these social programs, such as Social Security and Medicare, have widespread public support.

The Devolution Revolution

In 1994, Republicans swept elections to the House of Representatives. Many ran on the pledge to return many of the programs now run by the federal government back to the states. One such program was Aid to Families with Dependent Children (AFDC), known simply as *welfare*.

In 1996, President Clinton, in the State of the Union address, declared, "The era of big government is over." Congress and the President then went on to reform welfare and freed the states of certain regulations imposed by the federal government. This shift of programs and jurisdiction back to the states is referred to as the Devolution Revolution. But beyond reforming welfare and allowing the states to set their own speed limits, the devolution revolution has lost most of its support. In fact, after the attacks of September 11, 2001, there has been an increased role by the federal government in homeland security and other efforts to combat terrorism.

Twenty-First-Century Challenges

After the election of 2000, President Bush continued with efforts to continue devolution in the intergovernmental relationship. Faith-based organizations (FBOs) play a major role in delivering services to communities and are funded, in part, by the federal government. President Bush created the White House Office of Faith-Based and Community Initiatives, which was charged with supporting and expanding federal support to organizations that deliver services without legal and administrative obstacles. President Obama renamed the office the White House Office of Faith-Based and Neighborhood Partnerships. Federal funds, totaling more than $2.5 billion annually, are awarded to faith-based and community organizations.

Another initiative that altered the intergovernmental relationship between Washington and the states is President Bush's No Child Left Behind Law. Passed with support from both sides of the aisle, this law expanded the federal government's influence in how local districts run their schools. NCLB mandated that states reform how academic success is measured and required testing standards in order to receive federal funds. Since Washington did not mandate how to reform current standards, the Common Core Curriculum filled that vacuum and was embraced by many states. This controversial approach to education reform continues to divide Americans. In 2015, President Obama signed the Every Student Succeeds Act (ESSA) that replaced NCLB, an attempt to lessen the role of the federal government in K–12 education. Although it does place less emphasis on testing to measure achievement and teacher evaluations, it nevertheless requires school districts to test students between third and eighth grades in math and English language arts.

REAL-LIFE FACTS

According to the Brookings Institute, standardized testing costs the states more than $1.7 billion annually.

Arguably the most significant change in the relationship between Washington and the states is in the area of homeland security. Since the tragic events of September 11, 2001, the federal government has embarked on a campaign to fight terrorism both at home and abroad. State and local governments receive billions of dollars annually for first responder agencies. Additionally, states receive federal funds to protect vulnerable water supplies, improve communication and surveillance, and ensure better security at airports and rail stations.

The federal government has continued to grow under both Republican and Democratic presidents. As long as local and state governments are dependent on federal funds to provide services, it will be difficult to reign in the increasingly large role Washington plays in our daily lives.

Federalism and the Supreme Court

The U.S. Supreme Court generally has the final say on constitutional matters, and, therefore, plays a significant role in determining the interpretation of federalism. Over the history of the republic, the Supreme Court has generally favored the powers of the federal government over the states. Yet there has been an ideological swing back to states' rights.

Since the 1990s, the Supreme Court has reined in federal government powers under the commerce clause. The Court has also sided with the states on matters dealing with the Tenth and Eleventh amendments to the Constitution.

Centralists and Decentralists

Today, the debate over the interpretation of federalism is between the decentralists, who defend the powers of the states and favor action at the local level, and centralists, who favor strong national authority.

Historically, the decentralists were the Anti-Federalists and those who supported states' rights. Today, they are largely found in the Republican Party—President Reagan and both Bushes, as well as Supreme Court justices Antonin Scalia (recently deceased), Clarence Thomas, and Samuel Alito. The decentralists maintain that the Constitution is an agreement among the states to create a central government of limited authority, and there is no justification for the federal government to interfere with the activities or authority reserved for the states in the Tenth Amendment.

Historically, the centralists were the Federalists, Chief Justice Marshall, as well as presidents Abraham Lincoln, Franklin Roosevelt, and Lyndon Johnson. Today, centralists are usually found in the Democratic Party. Centralists reject the notion that the Constitution is a pact among the states. Rather, they embrace it as the supreme law of the land and are strong advocates for national supremacy, even in matters that have been reserved to the states. They would argue that a state government cannot interfere with a federal government representing all the people, including the people of that sovereign state.

Reducing the Power of the Commerce Clause

Several recent Supreme Court cases have placed limits on the federal government's authority under the commerce clause. In 1995, *United States* v. *Lopez,* the Court held that Congress exceeded its authority under the commerce clause when it passed the Gun-Free Zones Act of 1990. It claimed that Congress attempted to regulate something that had nothing to do with commerce.

In *United States* v. *Morrison* (2000), the Court invalidated a section of the Violence Against Women Act of 1994. Again, the Court maintained that regulating violent criminal activity had nothing to do with commerce.

State Sovereignty and the Eleventh Amendment

The Supreme Court has recently ruled in several cases to bolster the authority of state governments. The Court has ruled that states cannot be sued for violations of rights established by federal law without their consent. Essentially, state employees cannot sue the state that employs them without the consent of the state, while employees of the business sector are protected and can sue to enforce federal laws. The cases referred to are *Alden* v. *Maine* (1999) and *Kimel* v. *Florida Board of Regents* (2000).

Tenth Amendment Issues

In *New York* v. *United States* (1992), the Supreme Court held that requirements placed on New York State under a federal law regulating radioactive waste were unconstitutional under the Tenth Amendment. The Court ruled that Congress went beyond the enumerated powers in the Constitution. In 1997, the Court struck down provisions of the federal Brady Handgun Violence Prevention Act of 1993. In *Prinz* v. *United States* (1997), the Court ruled that the federal government could not require the states to check the backgrounds of people wishing to purchase handguns.

 ON THE RECORD

"The ultimate source of the Constitution's authority is the consent of the people of each individual state, not the undifferentiated people of the Nation as a whole."

—Supreme Court Justice Clarence Thomas

The Least You Need to Know

- There are two basic levels of government in the American system: federal and state. The framers agreed on this system of government in order to prevent tyranny.

- The federal government is one of delegated powers, of which there are three types: expressed, implied, and inherent. The states are governments of reserved powers.

- When conflict arises between the two levels of government, the Constitution is the supreme law of the land. The Supreme Court resolves matters between the federal government and the states.

- The federal government provides financial assistance to the states. These financial programs, known as grants-in-aid, can blur the division of power between the two spheres of government in favor of the federal government.

- The Constitution sets forth clear obligations, and prohibits some actions, regarding interstate relations.

PART 2

The Political Process

Many countries have tried to duplicate the formula of the American experiment with democracy, but few have succeeded to the extent that we have. Alexis de Tocqueville, a French observer of American politics in the early nineteenth century, believed that democracy was successful in America because of the abundant land and the economic opportunities it afforded its citizens.

People create political parties to promote their ideas and goals. Parties are an integral part of our political system. Perhaps the most important role parties play is narrowing the choice of candidates in an election. Elections serve to decide who will have political power, and parties are the venue by which people compete to become candidates for election. Parties help stabilize democracy by creating peaceful transfers of power from one candidate to another, and from one party to another.

American Political Culture

The Constitution established the Republic in 1787, but American democracy has endured for more than 200 years for reasons beyond this great framework of governance. Many countries have tried to duplicate the formula of the American experiment with democracy, but few have succeeded to the extent that we have.

Alexis de Tocqueville, a French observer of American politics in the early nineteenth century, believed that democracy was successful in America because of the abundant land and the economic opportunities it afforded its citizens. However, this alone cannot explain the success. After all, many other countries have abundant land and agricultural promise. We need to explore the characteristics that social scientists call political culture.

In This Chapter

- Defining political culture
- Factors that affect the development of political culture
- Similarities and differences in American political culture
- Political efficacy among Americans
- Political tolerance in the United States

What Is Political Culture?

Many cultural differences exist among people. This is especially obvious when one travels abroad. The times of day when people eat vary. Greetings may involve multiple kisses on both cheeks. The use of surnames is often more common than in the United States. In these and countless other ways, we as Americans are culturally different than people of other societies.

A political culture is the unique way of thinking about the political and sometimes economic life among a set of people. In the United States, most people do not judge their political and economic systems the same way. The best example of this is that Americans think it is very important that everyone be politically equal, but they do not believe it is necessary that everyone be economically equal.

The Political System

There are five important elements in the common American political culture:

Liberty   Americans fervently support freedom and individual rights, so long as one doesn't harm other people.

Equality   All Americans believe that everyone should have equal access to the political process, including voting and running for office. Additionally, this includes social equality and equality of opportunity.

Democracy   Americans believe that government should be accountable to the people and that government officials are not above the law. Additionally, Americans believe in majority rule, or government according to the preference of the majority at regular elections.

Civic duty   Americans believe they have a duty to participate in the political process and to help solve problems within the community.

Individual responsibility   Americans generally believe that individuals are responsible for and should be accountable for their own actions and well-being.

These five characteristics, taken together, make up the common American political culture of shared beliefs, values, and norms concerning the relationship of citizens to government and to one another. Americans share many values regarding government and religion. For example, recently more than 60 percent of Americans reported that they "distrust the government." More Americans are distrustful of the federal government than their local government. Also, 85 percent of Americans refer to themselves as patriotic and 87 percent believe in the existence of God.

The Economic System

As in politics, most Americans subscribe to the notion of liberty in the economy. Free enterprise and *capitalism* are highly valued, yet most people support some regulation of business by government in order to protect workers and consumers or correct abuses.

 **DEFINITION**

Capitalism is the economic system characterized by private property, competitive markets, and financial incentives with limited government involvement.

The principle of equal economic opportunity is shared by all Americans, but not the notion that everyone should be economically equal. Americans are more likely to tolerate economic inequality than political inequality. There is popular commitment to economic individualism and responsibility.

This principle of economic liberty is interpreted quite differently by conservatives and liberals. Liberals generally argue that government has a regulatory role to play in our economy to ensure product safety, responsible business practices, environmental and employee protections, and to help bring about an equitable distribution of wealth. Conservatives favor a free and unfettered marketplace with minimal government oversight or regulation, and oppose any mention of redistribution of wealth. Tax policy is the means by which the government can distribute wealth in society. Tax policy funds social welfare and entitlement programs. Without the proper funding, these programs would not exist. Most Americans support some level of social welfare and entitlement programs, but most also oppose increased taxes to support these programs. The challenge for government officials is to find the balance that satisfies the majority of Americans.

The Sources of Political Culture

From the colonial era to the Revolution and the Constitutional Convention, Americans have been historically concerned with preserving their rights and liberty. Americans have a long history of preoccupation with rights and a long-standing distrust of authority and of people wielding too much power. But it would be too simple to say that Americans are hardwired with a common culture. Instead, the common political culture is transmitted in several important venues.

The Family

One of the most important sources of political culture is the family. Children are taught from a very early age what it means to be an American, as seen through the eyes of one's nuclear and extended family. The questions may vary, but the common themes are authority, freedom, equality, and liberty. Families are the most important reference group for transmitting political culture.

Education

Public schools are another important source of American history and political culture. Reciting the Pledge of Allegiance is common in most American schools on a daily basis. Most states mandate a curriculum that teaches American political and economic values. Furthermore, many of these principles are put to action in schools through elections for student government and the publication of the school newspaper. Many states require courses in national and state government.

Religious and Civic Organizations

Americans identify as members of a religious or civic organization in very high numbers. These religious and civic organizations foster a common understanding of freedom of religion, individualism, pluralism, and civic duty. Many of these organizations are involved in major social and political movements. For example, many neighborhoods in the United States have a civic organization that promotes the quality of life. These organizations are vital for democracy because they build social capital, trust, and shared values, which are then transferred into the political sphere and help to hold society together, facilitating an understanding of the interconnectedness of society and the individuals within it. The Palm Beach Civic Association, the Juniper Park Civic Association, the Boy Scouts, and the Rotary Club are examples of civic organizations.

REAL-LIFE FACTS

The Pledge of Allegiance was published in 1892 to celebrate the four hundredth anniversary of Christopher Columbus's discovery of America. It wasn't until the 1950s, during the Cold War, that *under God* was added.

The Mass Media

Young people spend a great deal of their time taking in the mass media today. Television is now a venue for political instruction. For example, MTV's *Rock the Vote* encourages and instructs young voters to participate in the electoral process. Facebook encouraged people to vote by asking its members to post thumbs up, "I voted!" to encourage their friends to vote, too. The internet and social media have transformed how young people today receive and create news. Bloggers circumvent traditional media channels to report personally on stories and issues that are important to them. With politicians and candidates increasingly using social media to reach voters and keep the public on-message, the risks have increased that errors in judgment, inappropriate behavior, or deliberate misinformation can be broadcast immediately to millions of subscribers.

The media influences people's political values through the choices it makes when covering non-political or government news. When selecting which entertainment stories to run, or determine what is "in" or "out" of social fashion, the media influences what people deem to be acceptable or unacceptable in society. These values then translate into attitudes on political issues and often influence how people vote.

 ON THE RECORD

"The media is the most powerful entity on earth. They have the power to make the innocent guilty and to make the guilty innocent, and that's power. Because they control the minds of the masses."

—Malcolm X, African American minister, public speaker, and human rights activist

Political Activities

Americans belong to more groups and organizations than the citizens of almost any other democracy. Americans educate each other about political values through membership in these organizations, as well as in the workplace, on social media, and at various community meetings, such as civic associations or PTA meetings. The Constitution, by creating a federal system of government and dividing political authority between the states and a national government, provided ample opportunity for political participation in organizations that can influence political parties, elections, and public policy.

The American Dream

Historian and writer James Truslow Adams coined the phrase *American Dream* in his 1931 book *Epic of America* (Little Brown & Co., 1931; Simon Publications, 2001):

"The American Dream is that dream of a land in which life should be better and richer and fuller for everyone, with opportunity for each according to ability or achievement. It is a difficult dream for the European upper classes to interpret adequately, and too many of us ourselves have grown weary and mistrustful of it. It is not a dream of motor cars and high wages merely, but a dream of social order in which each man and each woman shall be able to attain to the fullest stature of which they are innately capable, and be recognized by others for what they are, regardless of the fortuitous circumstances of birth or position."

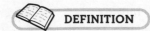

DEFINITION

The **American Dream** is the widespread belief that we live in a land of opportunity and that individual initiative can bring about economic success.

Many of the values of American political culture come together in the notion of the American Dream. This concept speaks to some of the most deeply held hopes and goals of Americans. It is founded on individual freedoms, the enthusiasm for capitalism, the right to private property, and the protection of that right by the government, all of which goes as far back as colonial times. Some people may place monetary gain as their highest goal, and thus strive for this in a very American way, gaining through ability rather than predetermined social status. For others, the American Dream could consist of being free from the chokehold of money and social structure. These two examples of the American Dream are only slices of an ever-expanding spectrum of possibilities.

The Culture War

Americans share elements of a common political culture, yet there is always conflict in American politics over the most hotly debated political issues, which today include abortion, gay rights, drug policy, and school prayer. This conflict can be explained by the two cultural classes that exist in America. Simply put, there are two opposed camps within the culture war: progressive or liberal, and traditional or conservative.

The progressive side of the culture war is made up of people who think that evolving personal freedoms are more important than traditional moral values and rules. These people are often to the left of center on the political spectrum.

ON THE RECORD

"There is a religious war going on in our country for the soul of America. It is a cultural war, as critical to the kind of nation we will one day be as was the Cold War itself."

–Pat Buchanan, American politician, at the 1992 Republican National Convention

The traditional side is made up of people who believe strongly that traditional morality and values are more important than self-expression and individual lifestyles or preferences. These people tend to be right of center on the political spectrum.

The culture war is different from other political disputes because it does not focus on economic or foreign policy matters, but rather on the deep differences in people's beliefs about private and public morality. For example, the Supreme Court has ruled that prayers cannot be conducted at school events, yet many parents and school officials try to reinstate school prayer or "a moment of silence."

Political Efficacy

According to a University of Michigan survey of American voters from 1952 to 2000 (*The National Election Studies*), there has been a significant decline in the extent to which Americans feel the government responds to their needs and beliefs. According to the study, more than 75 percent of Americans believe "politics is too complicated" and nearly 65 percent believe "government officials don't care what people like me think."

Political efficacy is an individual's capacity to understand and influence political activities and policies. One's sense of efficacy has two integral parts: internal and external.

Internal efficacy is the ability of one person to understand and take part in political affairs. Most Americans have a good understanding of what is going on in government even though they report it's too complicated to understand.

External efficacy is the ability of individuals to make the government respond to their needs. In this sense, Americans feel less effective as agents of change today. Perhaps this accounts for the enormous appeal of those candidates who campaign on slogans of change.

Political Tolerance

The success of American democracy depends on all citizens being tolerant of the beliefs, opinions, and actions of others. Perfect tolerance is difficult to imagine and even more difficult to achieve, yet, over time, Americans have become more tolerant of ideas and circumstances that were once unpopular or even unacceptable. For example, biracial marriages were historically seen as controversial in many parts of the country. Today, all laws banning such marriages have been outlawed, and most Americans embrace the freedom of individuals to marry across racial lines.

American political culture allows for the discussion of ideas and selection of leaders with a minimum amount of restriction and oppression. An overwhelming majority of Americans support freedom of speech, the right to vote, majority rule, and the right to petition or protest. Nonetheless, throughout American history, groups or causes have had their liberties restricted or withheld, even though we endorse the notion of liberty for all in the abstract. For example, during World War II, internment camps were established to detain Japanese Americans and Italian Americans.

MISINFORMATION

Although popularly referred to as the "Equal Rights Amendment," it remains a proposal that has never actually been incorporated into the Constitution. It is intended to guarantee equal rights under the law for all Americans, regardless of sex. In 1972, it was passed in the House of Representatives and the Senate, but failed to gain ratification by the state legislatures before the end of the deadline. Its supporters have reintroduced the amendment in Congress every term since without success.

History and American Political Culture

Major historical events have shaped American political culture and the mood of the nation. From the founding of the republic to the present day, national and international events have influenced how the government has evolved. Many unforeseen and unprecedented events have helped shape the role of government and American political culture. Today, the global War on Terror has enhanced the authority of the president to act to protect Americans, but not without limitations. The economic meltdown of 2008 has certainly altered the way Americans regulate free-market capitalism, banks, financial markets, entitlement programs, and the role that Congress and the executive branch must play in ensuring economic security for Americans.

The Civil War: Brother Versus Brother

The Civil War was fought from 1861 to 1865. America suffered the loss of more soldiers than in all of its other wars combined. Nearly all families were affected by the tragedy, but still there was not a large antiwar sentiment. Americans came to view the Civil War as a war for unity, liberty, and equality. The soldiers were typically volunteers who left farms and small towns with groups of recruits from their areas. Many men who enrolled in 1861 and 1862 reenlisted when their terms expired and became the backbones of both the Union and Confederate armies. Local loyalties spurred enrollment, especially in the South; so did ideals of honor and courage. Some soldiers discussed why they enlisted in letters to their families at home. For Southern soldiers, it was usually because they wanted to defend their homes and protect Southern rights and liberty—their Southern way of life, which included slavery. In the North, soldiers were not initially fighting to abolish slavery, but as fighting ensued, some of them helped in the effort to get slaves to the North.

As the war progressed, both the Union and the *Confederacy* dealt with mounting dissent and disloyalty. Within the Confederacy, objection to the war came in two forms. First, from advocates of states' rights such as Vice President Alexander Stephens and the governors of North Carolina and Georgia, who believed that the war had created a government that was increasingly more despotic. Second, loyalty to the Union flourished in a portion of the population who were not slave owners, but small farmers in the Appalachian Mountain region. They viewed the war as a slave-owner conspiracy. On the whole, the Confederate government responded mildly to this opposition. Only rarely did Confederate President Jefferson Davis suspend habeas corpus to put areas under martial law.

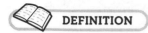 **DEFINITION**

> The **Confederacy** was the government set up from 1861 to 1865 by 11 Southern states that declared their secession from the United States. It was never officially recognized as an independent country.

In the North, President Abraham Lincoln faced the Democratic minority, who opposed both the abolition of slavery and the wartime growth of centralized power. "War Democrats" admitted that the war was necessary to save the Union and "Peace Democrats" called for a truce and a peace conference. Democrats mobilized and held antiwar rallies in several cities in 1863. The most violent antiwar demonstration was the New York City draft riots of July 1863, in which masses of working-class Irish men and women rioted for four days until they were stopped by federal troops. They were against the draft because they did not want to fight a war on behalf of slaves who, if freed, might come north and compete for their jobs. They also objected to the provision in the draft law that allowed for wealthy men to purchase substitutes but conscripted poor immigrants straight into the service. The rioters caused a lot of damage: they lynched at least a dozen blacks, injured hundreds more, and razed draft offices, the homes of wealthy Republicans, and the orphanage for African American children.

President Lincoln suspended the writ of habeas corpus in 1863 nationwide and authorized the arrest of rebels, draft resisters, and others who displayed disloyalty to the Union. As forceful as he was, Lincoln did not seek to destroy freedoms of the press, speech, and assembly. Most people who were arrested during this time were quickly released.

Abolition and Emancipation

Many groups of Americans helped in the emancipation of slaves. Some disagreed on issues surrounding slavery, but all believed slavery should be outlawed in the United States. The abolitionist movement was started early in American history by the Quakers, who had a strong religious objection to slavery. After the Revolutionary War, abolitionists helped persuade slave-holders in the Upper South to free their slaves. In fact, many individuals acting of their own accord freed thousands of slaves. People were moved by their own struggles in the Revolution; wills and deeds cited language about the equality of men in decisions to free slaves.

The abolitionist movement was reinforced by the activities of free African Americans, especially the black church. African American activists and their writings were rarely recognized outside of the black community. Some activists, like Frederick Douglass, were extremely influential to sympathetic whites like William Lloyd Garrison, the first prominent figure in the abolitionist movement. In the early 1850s, the abolitionist movement was divided on the significance of the Constitution in the argument. Garrison and his followers saw the Constitution as a pact with slavery and called for its abolition and replacement. Another group that eventually included Frederick Douglass believed that slavery existed outside the Constitution's jurisdiction and, therefore, should be abolished.

Many abolitionists took an active role in opposing slavery by supporting the Underground Railroad, a network that helped slaves escape slavery and reach the North. After the Emancipation Proclamation on January 1, 1863, abolitionists continued to uphold the freedom of slaves in the remaining slave states. The passage of the Thirteenth Amendment in 1865 officially ended slavery in the United States.

 ON THE RECORD

"I am a believer in that portion of the Declaration of American Independence in which it is set forth, as among self-evident truths, 'that all men are created equal; that they are endowed by their Creator with certain inalienable rights; that among these are life, liberty, and the pursuit of happiness.' Hence, I am an abolitionist. Hence, I cannot but regard oppression in every form—and most of all, that which turns a man into a thing—with indignation and abhorrence."

—Abolitionist William Lloyd Garrison

Western Expansion

American families moved out West with the desire for a better life than they had out East. The earliest whites to venture west were usually trappers. Later pioneers were drawn with the original intent of claiming lands and settling their families. With the promise of more land came the opportunity for farming or ranching success. Life in the West could be a lot different from how it was in the East, but the settlers tried to maintain a sense of their old life. Even before towns sprang up, they met with their neighbors for festivities and games. There was a renewed sense of individualism and self-reliance in the West, especially in those emigrants who ventured to the Far West on the Oregon Trail or to California. To these people, the frontier represented an optimistic future.

The American frontier was generally more democratic and free-spirited than the East because it lacked a lot of organized social and political institutions. Without courts or law officers, settlers developed their own ad hoc systems for establishing rules and resolving disputes. Mining communities had their own rules and often ruled by popular vote, sometimes acting fairly and sometimes exercising vigilantism. These mostly male societies were prone to high levels of violence, drunkenness, and greed-driven behavior, as the miners were isolated from the community, their families, and religious institutions. Gambling and prostitution were central to life in developing western towns, and only later as the female population increased did prostitution fall out of practice. The Gold Rush of 1848 introduced more professionals to the West: precious-metal specialists, merchants, doctors, and lawyers. With these professionals came more organized institutions and the formation of "boomtowns," which helped to make the West more stable politically and socially.

REAL-LIFE FACTS

The Oregon Trail was one of the main overland migration routes, leading from Missouri to the Oregon Territory. The five- to six-month journey spanned more than half the North American continent, about 2,000 miles.

The Labor Movement

The labor movement in the United States centered on the notions of democracy and equality. Forces that helped shape the movement included the evolving authority of the corporation, efforts by employers and private organizations to suppress unions, and federal labor laws. With the expansion of industrialization, workers in the late nineteenth century saw many employment opportunities but often-dire working conditions. Although some Americans were going west to settle on their own land, others stayed in the emerging cities and worked in factories, living in tenements and being exploited by their bosses.

The Knights of Labor was the first effective labor organization in the United States. Its leaders believed in the unity of the interests of all producing groups and sought to enlist all types of laborers. The Federation of Organized Trades and Labor Unions began in 1881, and its goals were to encourage the formation of trade unions and to obtain legislation to prohibit child labor and create a national eight-hour workday. In theory, these early unions advocated for a more democratic America, but in reality, they excluded African Americans, women, and unskilled workers.

The federal government has had a volatile relationship with labor unions. The Sherman Antitrust Act of 1890 led to the prosecution of unions as illegal combinations, but the Clayton Antitrust Act of 1914 reversed this by stipulating that unions could not be construed as "illegal combinations or conspiracies in restraint of trade, under the antitrust laws." The National Labor Relations Act made it illegal for employers to discriminate against workers because of their union membership or refuse to engage in collective bargaining with the union that represented their employees.

In 1947, laws began to set more limits on unions. The Taft-Hartley Act prohibited strikes and secondary boycotts by unions, and authorized states to pass "right to work" laws, which prohibit agreements between trade unions and employers making a membership or payment of union dues a condition of employment. Labor unions peaked in membership after World War II, but membership has been steadily declining for the past 25 years. Although unions have diminished in their popularity, they still hold a strong voice in lobbying to Congress.

Teddy Roosevelt and Turn-of-the-Century Imperialism

At the turn of the twentieth century, new social views of imperialism arose. Rudyard Kipling, for example, urged the United States to take up the "White Man's Burden" of bringing civilization to other parts of the world, regardless of whether or not they wanted it. During this time, the United States expanded at an accelerated pace for a variety of reasons. Having already conquered the entire western frontier, Americans sought to expand their country to the far reaches of the earth. This was partially because of racist attitudes and the desire to promote economic growth and a more aggressive foreign policy.

Theodore Roosevelt responded to these needs by greatly expanding the navy and undertaking a huge construction project: building the Panama Canal. In 1907, he formed the *Great White Fleet*, ships that toured the world, basically to impress other countries, especially Japan. The Panama Canal revolutionized trade and strengthened the navy.

The expansionist, imperialist policies of the United States during this time period, coupled with growing industrial strength, established the United States as a significant world power. The acquired new territories and bases established access to global markets and helped the Republican Party gain dominance politically at home. The business owners and urban workers of the industrial Northeast and Midwest embraced the message of the Republican Party, which emphasized fiscal responsibility and patriotism. In fact, the Republicans would come to control the House of Representatives for 28 of the 36 years from 1894 to 1930.

During this period the pressing political question for Americans was whether a government designed for the needs of a small, agrarian society could serve an industrial nation with global economic ambitions. Still the compelling message of populists during this time, calling for social and economic justice and reform, was particularly popular among farmers, many workers, and immigrant Americans. The populist agenda would help shape the political environment of the progressive movement.

Manifest Destiny and American Exceptionalism

Manifest Destiny is the historical belief that the United States was destined and divinely mandated by the Christian God to expand across North America all the way to the Pacific Ocean. It was used to justify the territorial acquisitions by the government in the 1840s. This idea was first used by the Jacksonian Democrats to promote the annexation of much of what is now the western United States. In the 1890s, this idea was revived by Republican supporters, as a justification for

U.S. expansion outside of North America. During this period, the United States occupied the Philippines, Puerto Rico, Cuba, and Panama. The Polk and Tyler administrations successfully promoted this nationalistic doctrine over sectionalists and others who objected for moral reasons or over concerns about the spread of slavery.

American Exceptionalism is a concept that is a part of Manifest Destiny. American citizens have used it to express that Americans have unique perspectives, different surroundings, and superior political cultures than other nations. This term can also be used as a synonym for the American Dream and the slow, continuous journey of the people of the United States, sharing a nation and a destiny, to build a more perfect union, to live up to the dreams, hopes, and ideals of its founders.

The Great War and Wilsonianism

From 1914 to 1918, a global war had far-reaching consequences for diplomacy. This war, known first as the Great War, then later as World War I, was fought predominantly in Europe, but its scale and intensity affected the entire globe. This historic tragedy is responsible for the participation of more than 65 million soldiers and 40 million fatalities.

Many factors played into the start of this war. Against a backdrop of ethnic tensions, national rivalries, and the proverbial entangling alliances, the spark that led to the wild-fire was the assassination of the heir to the Austro-Hungarian throne, Archduke Franz Ferdinand, by a member of the Black Hand, a secret Serbian-nationalist society. Rumors that the Serbian government was involved with the assassination gave the Austro-Hungarians the opportunity to strike the Serbians by issuing an ultimatum, demanding that the assassins be brought to justice.

Expecting that Serbia would reject the harsh terms of the ultimatum, Austria-Hungary prepared to attack Serbia. This set off a chain reaction that led to the Great War. Russia, bound by a treaty with Serbia, mobilized its army in Serbia's defense. Germany, allies of Austria-Hungary, viewed the Russian mobilization as a threat and declared war on Russia. France, bound by treaty with Russia, therefore found itself at war with Germany and Austria-Hungary. Germany was quick to occupy Belgium, which pulled Great Britain into the war, coerced into defending Belgium by the terms of a treaty and declaring war on Germany to defend France. The military imperative of instant mobilization put these vast armies in motion before any nation could reconsider.

Across the Atlantic Ocean, President Woodrow Wilson followed a policy of absolute neutrality, which summed up his view on foreign policy known as Wilsonianism. This idealism holds that a state should make its internal political philosophy the goal of its foreign policy. In terms of World War I, the war could be interpreted as a reappearance of monarchy and aristocracy, and Wilson held to a modernist, democratic peace theory. Even as the United States was in pandemonium due to a German submarine that sank the British ocean liner *Lusitania,* killing 128 U.S. citizens, President Wilson remained neutral. The United States maintained its stance despite protests from citizens who wanted the administration to take more of a merciless attitude. Not until the German submarines directly endangered American lives, as well as the livelihood of the country, did President Wilson declare war.

Although the United States was instrumental in defeating the Central Powers in the Great War, it shied away from its leadership role in the postwar period and once again embraced the posture of neutrality it maintained before the war. At the Versailles Peace Conference, the United States and its victorious allies laid out the peace agreement that ended the Great War. Part of that agreement was the creation of a new international organization, the League of Nations. This new organization embodied Wilson's vision of a new world order of peace and justice. However, the sentiment among most Americans was isolationist. Many believed the new organization would entangle the United States in the bickering affairs of Europe, and it would furthermore oblige member states to preserve the political integrity of other member states. Many in Congress felt that this provision limited American sovereignty and infringed on Congress's power to declare war.

Additionally, in the aftermath of the Russian Revolution in 1917, postwar antiradicalism resulted in a Red Scare. This brought about the arrest of hundreds of suspected radicals and communists, as well as many labor leaders and organizers. The House of Representatives went as far as denying a seat to a representative elected from Milwaukee who won on the Socialist ticket in 1919.

The Great Depression

The Great Depression of 1929 was the longest and deepest economic depression the United States and the world have ever faced, and most historians say that it began with the stock market crash of October 29, 1929. No one was immune to the devastating effects as international trade plummeted, wealth and investments were wiped out, farming areas suffered, and industries halted. In relation to the economic recession, circulating theories could be characterized into three main views:

- The classical economics theory, which focuses on the supply of money in an economy as the primary means by which the rate of inflation is determined.

- The structural theory, which aims at lack of consumption and overinvestment, the misconduct by bankers, and the ineffectiveness of the government.

- The Marxist point of view, which emphasizes how capitalism generates large accumulations of wealth that settle in risky, speculative investment bubbles.

American economist Irving Fisher argues that the Great Depression was triggered by too much borrowing and deflation. He states that nine factors created conditions of debt that led to the crash:

1. Debt liquidation and distress selling

2. Contraction of the money supply as bank loans are paid off

3. A fall in the level of asset prices

4. A greater fall in the net worth of businesses

5. A fall in profits

6. A reduction in output, consumption, and employment

7. Hoarding of money

8. A fall in nominal interest rates and rise in deflation adjusted interest rates

9. Loss of confidence and pessimism

Modern economic and political liberals believe that the profit system became too concentrated in the hands of a small number of financiers and industrialists who made certain choices that obviously had detrimental consequences. The majority of people failed to benefit from this wealth and the expansion of manufactured goods were too expensive for the average person to afford. Those who controlled and owned the resources of production had acquired too much economic power, allowing them to influence and manipulate the competition and hinder the flow of natural reform and mobility.

Conservatives felt their power being threatened as the government tried to revive the economy after the stock market crash by tightening credit and keeping tabs on government spending.

World War II

After suffering defeat at the end of World War I, Germany signed the Treaty of Versailles, which resulted in a loss of its territory, limited the size of its forces, required payment for the war damages, and placed upon it the blame for the conflict. Despondent about the terms of the treaty and their subsequent economic collapse, the German people were dissatisfied with the government, factionalized and divided politically, and eventually voted into power a man who would radically rise to become one of the most notorious faces of tyranny, Adolf Hitler.

Hitler became the chancellor of Germany in January 1933 and secretly began to develop Germany's army. He quickly gained control and influence and worked on efforts to take back the land that Germany once claimed. Hitler occupied Rhineland and then proceeded to move his troops to Austria and Czechoslovakia as well. Neville Chamberlain, the prime minister of Great Britain, and Hitler signed the Munich Agreement, which stated that Hitler could take control of the Sudetenland region of Czechoslovakia as long as he did not invade the rest of the nation. Chamberlain returned home and famously declared that he believed he had secured "peace in our time." Hitler led his troops to invade the rest of Czechoslovakia in 1939.

On September 1, 1939, Hitler invaded Poland, initiating the start of World War II. France and Great Britain declared war on Germany but provided limited military support. The Soviets, who signed an armistice with Japan, launched their own attack on Poland. As the war progressed, Germany invaded France and prepared for the invasion of Great Britain.

Meanwhile, the United States continued to be neutral. Having sustained losses in World War I and slowly coming out of an economic depression, Americans wanted to improve America, not be occupied with what was again happening overseas. The Roosevelt administration maintained neutral status even with an increase in aid and matériel to England and mounting anti-Western sentiments stirring in Japan as the United States enacted tariffs that affected the Japanese economy. The Japanese attack of the naval base at Pearl Harbor prompted the United States to declare war on Japan and Germany on December 8, 1941.

After nearly four years of battle, the United States and her allies declared victory in the war against the Axis Powers of Germany, Italy, and Japan. The postwar period ushered in many changes. National policies and institutional practices as they related to race relations came under fire. Many local and state governments started to pass laws barring discrimination on the basis of race, and the struggle to end racism in America was underway.

The alliance between the United States and the Soviet Union that was crucial to the defeat of Germany and Japan in World War II was replaced by antagonism, misperception, and misunderstanding following the war. A new international rivalry called the Cold War pitted the former in an adversarial battle where each sought to undermine the objectives of the other while avoiding direct military conflict. This rivalry would last for 45 years and embarked the United States in a global campaign to contain the spread of communism.

The Cold War

The Soviet Union considered its military presence in Eastern Europe as essential to its security given the two violent invasions from Germany earlier in the century. The Soviet Union essentially installed puppet governments and supported the communist regimes that came to power in such countries as Poland, Bulgaria, Hungary, Romania, Albania, and Yugoslavia.

The United States opposed Soviet domination as an enemy of democratic principles and self-determination. President Harry S Truman, a Democrat, emboldened by the economic and military supremacy of the United States, embarked on a policy of containment to halt the spread of Soviet communist domination. George F. Kennan, the author of America's containment policy, wrote that U.S. policy toward the Soviets should be "long-term, patient but firm and vigilant containment of Russian expansive tendencies." Thus, the United States embarked on the Cold War, what some have also labeled World War III.

The struggle against global communism had consequences at home and abroad. The United States entered into military and security arrangements with many countries around the world. Furthermore, the United States greatly expanded military and intelligence-gathering forces. Additionally, President Truman's plan to assist the rebuilding of Japan and Germany, as well as helping the disadvantaged at home, helped spur one of the largest economic expansions in U.S. history.

At home, the Cold War had chilling effects. Many conservatives feared domestic treason and subversion. This led some on the extreme right to denounce the New Deal as a communist agenda. Furthermore, investigative committees of Congress subjected millions of Americans to security investigations and loyalty oaths. This obsession with subversion and communism silenced the left in American politics for many years. Perhaps one of the most notorious consequences was the Red Scare accusations of Senator Joseph McCarthy and the hearings held by the House Un-American Activities Committee. Prominent conservatives during this period included two future presidents, Richard Nixon and Ronald Reagan. Nixon led congressional hearings against suspected American communists, and Ronald Reagan, as president of the Screen Actors Guild, exposed suspected communists who worked in Hollywood.

Liberals still maintained an opposition to both conservatism and communism. Among policies for which they advocated:

- Support for a domestic economy built on a balance of power between labor and management

- A foreign policy focused on containing the Soviet Union and its allies

- The continuation and expansion of New Deal social welfare programs

- An embrace of *Keynesian economics*

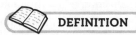 **DEFINITION**

> **Keynesian economics** is the policy that advocates building government surpluses during economic expansions and government spending in downturns as the key to recovery. The basic premise is for government to expand existing programs and create new ones that will spur job growth and demand for goods and services. Additionally, government should offer tax incentives in order to spur job growth and overall demand.

The Vietnam War

At the heart of America's involvement in Vietnam, unfortunately, was a fundamental misunderstanding that it was a proxy war with communism (China and the USSR), rather than a war for independence from colonial powers—first France, then the United States. The North Vietnamese certainly took opportunistic advantage of communist aid and ideology, but they were no more interested in becoming part of the communist bloc than they were in being a colony of the West.

Conservatives supported the war effort in Vietnam and later criticized the *détente* policies of the Nixon and Carter administrations. Conservatives claimed that in the aftermath of the Vietnam War there was a risk that the public of the United States would oppose all future U.S. military interventions. Intense social divisions emerged between 1968 and 1973 due to the controversy in the United States over the Vietnam War, the failure of the United States to achieve its political goals in Vietnam, and the massive number of U.S. and Vietnamese casualties.

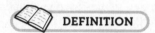

DEFINITION

Détente is a French term meaning a relaxing or easing. The term has been used in international politics since the early 1970s. Generally, it may be applied to any international situation where previously hostile nations not involved in an open war deescalate tensions through diplomacy and confidence-building measures.

From Watergate to 9/11 and the War on Terror

The Vietnam War cast a long shadow for conservatives, but both parties shared much of the blame politically. What triggered a far greater domestic political crisis was the cluster of corruption and scandal in the Nixon administration that was grouped under the name Watergate. The break-in at Democratic National Headquarters at the Watergate complex in Washington, D.C., resulted in a cover-up of criminal activity that led directly to the White House and to President Richard Nixon himself. Americans' faith in their public servants and government was shattered and tainted. The Watergate scandal revealed to Americans that their representatives believed themselves to be above the law and acted in ways that not only broke the law but also the commitment to uphold and protect the Constitution.

The Oil Embargo of the 1970s and the capture of American hostages in Iran in 1979 further diminished Americans' confidence in their government. With our citizens and economy held hostage, Americans of all political persuasions agreed that the course of our government must be changed. Not everyone agreed on how best to achieve strengthening American stature in the world and at home, but a majority felt that Ronald Reagan would be the best choice to get us back on the road to recovery and strength and out of the malaise President Carter spoke of. However, Reagan also would further diminish Americans' faith in their government.

The Iran-Contra Scandal could have brought down the American president—and might have done so if Watergate not been in the so near past. The Iran-Contra Scandal involved secretly selling arms to Iran, in defiance of a Congressional ban and public support to punish Iran for the hostage crisis less than 8 years previously. The money from these arms sales was funneled to support the forces fighting the Nicaraguan government in Central America. Support of the Contras was also banned by Congress.

When this information came to light, many Americans felt the government was once again acting in its own self-interests and not as representatives of the people. This diminished confidence in government and government officials was damaged further during the Clinton presidency when it came to light that Bill Clinton had a sexual relationship with a White House intern named Monica Lewinsky. The president lied under oath when questioned about it and was impeached by the House of Representatives by a highly partisan vote. Clinton was ultimately acquitted of the charges by the Senate.

Another recent and important event that contributed to a growing lack of confidence and respect for the government was the 2000 presidential election between Al Gore and George W. Bush. This election, in which Al Gore received more popular votes, was decided by a Supreme Court decision to stop the recount in Florida while George W. Bush was still in the recount lead. That decision delivered Florida's Electoral College votes to Bush and thereby made him the forty-third president.

The Supreme Court's decision to insert itself in the election outcome was controversial then and continues to be today. Whatever one thinks of the outcome, what is clear is that the outcome raised the question: "How can the candidate who received the most popular votes not win the election?" While the *Bush* v. *Gore* case upheld the principles of the Electoral College and judicial review, it raised for many the need to reform the election process. All these events together, along with many others not mentioned here, contributed to a loss of faith in government and government officials and raised the level of support for diminishing the role of government on many levels.

All this would change on a late summer day in September 2001.

The desire to maintain a strong national defense was bolstered when the terrorist attacks of September 11, 2001, took place. The terror group al Qaeda took responsibility for flying planes into the World Trade Center and the Pentagon, international symbols of American economic and military power. The group's leader, Osama bin Laden, issued a strong rebuke of the United States and called for an international jihad against it before going into hiding.

For many conservative and liberal Americans, finding those responsible and bringing them to justice was the only concern in 2002. It was a uniting factor. Americans of every political stripe rallied around President Bush as he built an international coalition in what would later become the War on Terror. When he decided to invade Afghanistan to root out the Taliban government, which was harboring bin Laden, Bush received wide support. Within months the unpopular Taliban suffered defeat and was relieved of power in Kabul, but bin Laden reportedly escaped into the hills of Tora Bora, which borders Pakistan.

In 2003, arguing that Saddam Hussein had harbored al Qaeda fugitives and was hiding weapons of mass destruction (WMDs), Bush embarked on what many Americans now see as the controversial invasion of Iraq. There were quick successes in the initial phases of the war, however, the American media and antiwar movement began to focus on the questionable motivations for the war, the United States' failure to keep order when Saddam's government collapsed, the decision to disband the Iraqi military, the failure to predict or quickly respond to the insurgency, the failure to discover any WMDs, and the increasing death toll in Iraqi civilians and Americans both in the private sector and the military. Opponents of the war also focused on the Abu Ghraib prison scandal, which involved photographic evidence of U.S. war crimes against Iraqi prisoners.

Starting in December 2001, the United States sent captured terrorism suspects to the U.S. naval base at Guantanamo Bay in Cuba. Many of the detainees have been held for years without any formal charges or scheduled hearings or trials. The extent to which these prisoners have rights has been passionately debated in the United States. In June 2008, the Supreme Court of the United States ruled that the detainees are entitled to rights of habeas corpus. In January 2009, newly elected President Barack Obama signed an order closing the detention center at Guantanamo within 12 months; however, as of January 2016, the detention center remains open as relocating detainees poses security concerns.

The War on Terror continues to divide Americans. Although there have been many successful attempts to combat individuals and organizations that promote terrorism, new groups and organizations emerge to fill in the shoes of defeated radical jihadists. On May 2, 2011, nearly 10 years after the September 11 attacks, the leader of al Qaeda, Osama bin Laden, was killed by U.S. Navy Special Forces in Pakistan. In early 2014, a group known as ISIS (the Islamic State in Iraq and Syria) came to world attention as it captured Iraqi and Syrian territory due to weak Iraqi security forces and the Civil War in Syria. ISIS envisions establishing a new *caliphate*, with its capital in the Middle East. Exploiting social media with videos of beheading captured civilians, ISIS has refocused the War on Terror globally.

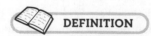 **DEFINITION**

A **caliphate** is an Islamic state led by a political and religious leader who is a successor of the Muslim prophet Muhammad.

Mistrust of Government

For the last several decades, there has been a decline in the proportion of Americans who profess trust in the government. Americans are angry with our elected officials for many reasons. One reason is the inability of the government to respond to the needs of ordinary citizens. Too often, government officials are seen as doing the work of special interests. The Watergate scandal, the Clinton impeachment, the War on Terror, and general overreach by the government, has led to a level of disenchantment that has not been seen in many decades. This level of mistrust in the institutions of government is one reason that nonincumbent major party candidates do well and appeal to voters. As Americans lose trust in their democracy and engage less with organizations that promote social capital, some scholars fear this may give rise to radical candidates and policies.

The Least You Need to Know

- Political culture is the set of beliefs that people share about politics, and sometimes economics.
- The political culture shared by Americans has five important elements: liberty, equality, democracy, civic duty, and individual responsibility.
- Although most Americans embrace the notion of the American Dream, they disagree on many hotly debated issues. This is referred to as the "culture war."
- The degree of political efficacy—the notion that the government is responding to the needs of citizens—has greatly diminished in the United States.
- Americans are generally tolerant of the beliefs, opinions, and actions of others compared to most other nations, even though there have been historical exceptions.

American Ideology and Public Opinion

The term ideology refers to a person's beliefs about political values and the role that government should play in people's lives. Ideology links our fundamental values to the day-to-day operations of government and the policies that a government enacts. Two major schools of political thought dominate American politics: liberalism and conservatism. However, many other schools of thought define the spectrum in American political ideology. These political labels sometimes have different meanings across state boundaries and certainly have evolved over time. It's important to keep in mind that political ideology can both cause events and policies to emerge and can be affected by them as well. People and politicians will address major economic events or foreign-policy crises based on ideology, but ideology may also cause people to reconsider the role of the national government.

In This Chapter

- Political ideology and attitudes toward government
- Political ideology and the American people
- Ideology and tolerance
- Political elites
- Public opinion and public policy

Diversity and the Origins of Political Attitudes

The United States is different from most other countries in the degree to which it is made of people from all over the world. Unlike other nations in which a common people share a long history with a common language and common beliefs, the United States is known and celebrated for its *diversity*.

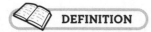 **DEFINITION**

Diversity is the quality of being different, varied, or changeable.

Most Americans, as you read in Chapter 4, share a belief in the American Dream. However, some elements of this diversity have political significance. Most Americans continue to identify with their ethnic roots even after many generations. People's political attitudes are formed by a process of political socialization, by which parents and others teach us our political values, beliefs, and attitudes.

The Role of the Family

Studies have shown that a majority of young people identify with their parents' political party. According to a study by M. Kent Jennings and Richard G. Niemi, 91 percent of high school students knew their parents preference in the presidential election. By the time most children are in fifth grade, they identify with either one party or the other or as independents, in line with their parents' preference.

Still, children will differ with their parents on specific social or economic issues due to changes over time. For example, older Americans are much more vigilant about protecting Social Security than younger Americans.

Religion

Religious traditions and differences influence political attitudes. Catholics tend to be more liberal on economic issues than most Protestants. Jews tend to be more liberal on both economic and social issues. Christian evangelicals tend to focus more on social issues than economic issues.

These differences are largely related to the social status of groups who identify as religious and the extent of orthodoxy among the individual. The more orthodox the individual, the more likely he or she is to be conservative on economic or social issues, or both.

The Gender Gap

Increasingly, men identify with the Republican Party and women with the Democratic Party. This difference in political views is known as the gender gap. Since the election of Ronald Reagan in 1980, women have voted in larger numbers for Democratic candidates while men have voted in larger numbers for Republican candidates.

One reason political scientists give for this gender gap is that male voters tend to be more conservative on social issues such as spending programs for the poor, gun control, and the size of government than female voters. Women are more likely to oppose violence in any form and studies show women are more compassionate than men. Women tend to favor a government that provides more services in health care, education, family leave, and environmental protection. These "gender issues" are becoming increasingly more important in national elections.

 REAL-LIFE FACTS

According to the Center for American Women and Politics, women have voted in higher numbers than men in every election since 1964. Nationally, the gender gap is approximately 10 percent.

Education

Studies have shown that there is a correlation between one's level of education and one's political attitudes and likelihood of participation in the political process. A college education makes a person more likely to be liberal and participate in politics at a higher rate than those who have not attended college. Still, age also is a factor, since most 18- to 25-year-olds with a college degree have relatively little interest in political affairs and often vote in very low numbers compared to their older counterparts with college degrees.

Cleavages in Public Opinion

Many divisions in society cut across demographic categories and influence one's politics, opinions, and position on issues. Political scientists call these cleavages in public opinion.

These cleavages overlap and crosscut in complex ways. If, for example, the United States was made up of only one religious group, there would still be political conflict because many within this group would have differences in income, education, and employment.

Politics is sensitive to public opinion. Today, the most significant crosscutting cleavages are based on race, ethnicity, region, income, occupation, age, and sexual orientation. All of these factors affect the development of an individual's political opinion.

Racial and ethnic differences are an important source of political cleavage. African Americans are overwhelmingly Democrats, while whites are more likely to identify as Republicans. Latinos identify more with the Democratic Party, particularly on issues of immigration and bilingual education programs. Asian Americans tend to identify more with the Republican Party. Generally, Latinos are more socially liberal than Asian Americans or whites, but less liberal than African Americans. It is important to note that the differences between some of these groups narrows or disappears depending on the issue.

A region, or the geographic part of the country in which a person lives, is an important crosscutting cleavage. The most consistent support for Republican candidates can now be found in the South, and the Northeast is now overwhelmingly in favor of Democratic candidates. Democrats also draw their strength from big cities, while Republicans tend to do well in suburban areas, and even stronger in rural areas.

Although Americans have no formal class structure, they do identify as part of a social class based on income or wealth levels. Classifications such as *middle class, upper class,* and *working class* are closely linked with income and are important cleavages. Generally speaking, the greater someone's income or wealth, the more likely they are to support the Republican candidate. Conversely, lower income Americans tend to support the Democratic Party.

 ON THE RECORD

"The most common and durable source of factions has been the various and unequal distribution of property."

—James Madison, *The Federalist,* No. 10

Unskilled or blue-collar workers are more likely to support Democrats and to have liberal economic views, but also to have conservative social views. White-collar or skilled workers lean toward the Republicans, but they may also be more socially liberal. It is also important to remember that education greatly affects one's career choice and subsequent earnings potential. Therefore, many medical professionals tend to be among the ranks of liberal voters, even though they are among some of the highest income earners due to their choice of occupation.

Younger voters are more likely to support the Democratic Party than older voters. Studies have consistently shown that as a person gets older they tend to move to the right politically. This does not mean that Democrats become Republicans as they get older, but rather that they become less liberal. Having children, for example, is one of the most "conservative" influences many people will encounter!

Differences in sexual orientation have become an important cleavage in American politics. Homosexual and bisexual voters overwhelmingly support Democratic candidates. The gay community is especially important politically because of their size in large urban centers.

Ideology and Tolerance

Whether voters identify as liberal or conservative influences their position on many issues. These cleavages in political thinking have important consequences and often cause groups to take action. Some argue that conservatives are less tolerant than liberals on issues relating to civil liberties. This is largely because liberals are perceived to be more tolerant of dissent and of views and opinions that are not considered orthodox. Yet liberals can be equally intolerant of abortion foes or those who oppose gun-control laws.

Liberals are strongly opposed to crime and law-breaking, just as conservatives are. Yet they are more concerned about the punishment of criminals and the causes of crime. Conservatives tend to take a much harder line against criminals and are more concerned with the victims of crime and punishing perpetrators than protecting the rights of the accused or addressing the roots of crime in poverty and social injustice.

These differences in ideology have played out in American politics in several important ways. The Right to Work movement believes people should have a right to work without being forced to join a union as a condition of employment. Currently, 25 states have laws that ban mandatory union membership where unions have historically existed. Policy fights among liberals and conservatives play out between the Congress and the president, most especially during confirmation hearings of judicial nominees. The American political spectrum is somewhat vast and adversarial.

 ON THE RECORD

"The uncontested absurdities of today are the accepted slogans of tomorrow. They come to be accepted by degrees, by dint of constant pressure on one side and constant retreat on the other—until one day when they are suddenly declared to be the country's official ideology."

—Ayn Rand, Russian born and American writer and novelist

What Is Liberalism?

The term *liberalism* has changed significantly since it came into existence in the seventeenth and eighteenth centuries. Historically, liberals stressed individual rights and sought to minimize the role of government, which they believed threatened liberty. Over time, liberals have maintained their emphasis on personal rights and liberties but their perception of the role and need for government has changed. Contemporary liberals believe individuals may be denied equal opportunity by the current economic and social structures, and want an active government that will regulate the economy, create social programs, and bring about justice and equal opportunity—even if such programs require more spending and higher taxes.

On a philosophical level, liberals believe in progress. They hold optimistic views on human nature and trust government programs to help people overcome obstacles. President Harry Truman said, "We have rejected the discredited theory that the fortunes of the nation should be in the hands of the privileged few …. Every individual has a right to expect from his government a fair deal." Today, equality of opportunity is seen as essential by liberals, and they believe the government must take an active role to see this realized.

What Is Conservatism?

Contemporary conservatism is centered on the belief in free enterprise and the right to private property. Conservatives differ from liberals in that they believe the best way to guarantee individual liberty is by keeping the government as small as possible, except in the area of military defense. They also believe that government should maintain order through strong leadership and strict moral codes. Conservatives believe that individuals are responsible for their own success or failure, and that individuals must bear the responsibility for the outcome of their actions or decisions.

Conservatives support government policies that are pro-business. They support lowering corporate taxes and resist almost any new taxes on income, interest earnings, and dividends. They strongly support abolishing the estate tax that is levied on inheritances greater than $6,000,000. In general, conservatives believe that the market should provide social services rather than government. Human needs should be met by families, places of worship, and charitable organizations.

Political Consistency

People have a political ideology even without necessarily labeling themselves liberal or conservative. As was noted in Chapter 4, Americans share a political culture and place a great deal of importance on the American Dream. Yet they may have inconsistent opinions on a wide range of issues and categories, which makes it difficult to label them as only liberal or conservative, let alone Republican or Democrat. Many combinations of views on important issues make up the American political spectrum.

Pure liberals are liberal on both economic and social issues. They want the government to regulate the economy and provide the broadest possible degree of social support, labor and environmental regulation, and individual expression and choice. They overwhelmingly oppose Republican candidates.

Pure conservatives are conservative on both economic and social issues. Pure conservatives want to see the New Deal and Great Society programs drastically reduced or abolished outright. They are opposed to unlimited sexual and reproductive rights, as well as laws and entitlements designed to offset discrimination against minorities. Like pure liberals, this group makes up only a small portion of the electorate.

Libertarians cherish individual liberty and freedom, and they insist on sharply reducing the size of the government, including the military. Libertarians oppose nearly all government programs and regulations, especially those governing personal behavior, such as mandatory seatbelt laws. This also makes them socially liberal, and they do not support laws governing personal morality.

Populists are usually liberal on economic issues and conservative on social ones. They support government programs that regulate business and seek to end economic inequality. Populists favor strong unions and legislation that protects workers. However, they are conservative on social and moral issues such as gay rights and abortion.

Socialists advocate for government ownership of most sectors of the economy while maintaining democratic political institutions. They would place much higher taxes on the wealthy and greatly reduce the defense and military budget. This group is even further to the left than pure liberals.

Usually members of the Green Party, environmentalists are intensely concerned with the environment and related issues. In areas such as social justice, equal opportunity, and diversity, environmentalists are not much different than liberals, but their distinct focus on ecology sets them apart. When there is no candidate running on their party ticket, they tend to support the Democratic candidate.

 MISINFORMATION

Although the United States is a two-party democracy, Bernard Sanders, a self-described socialist, was elected to the U.S. Senate from Vermont in 2006.

Who Are Political Elites?

There is one group made up of members from all the groups we have just discussed; they are political elites: people who have a disproportionate amount of power and influence in politics. These people are activists who run for political office, work on campaigns, lead interest groups, and speak out on public issues. Political elites tend to be more consistent in their political beliefs than the general voting public. They are generally better informed about politics and the issues, and they tend to associate with people of similar politics.

Political elites are more ideological than the general public, which may help explain the *political polarization* that has taken place in American politics. Candidates for office, and elected officials, are far more likely to be either liberal or conservative in their views on policy matters. This makes compromise on many social and economic issues much more difficult to achieve.

Public Opinion and Public Policy

A central component of American politics is the role of political elites in shaping American public opinion and the policy process. Political elites and the general voting public see politics through very different lenses. The public tends toward the political center, while elites on both sides are much more ideological in their views. Yet political elites influence *public opinion* in significant ways.

> **DEFINITION**
>
> **Political polarization** is the process by which public opinion divides and goes to the extremes. **Public opinion** is the distribution of individual preferences of a given issue, candidate, or institution in a population.

First, political elites raise and set the agenda of issues to be addressed. Elected officials and policy-makers are very responsive to the issues that are important to elites. The issues that are debated and the policy options considered are generally driven by the preferences of political elites. Secondly, political elites "frame the debate": they set the standards that determine what the policy options will be. For example, the use of medicinal and recreational marijuana is currently being debated in American politics.

Still, political elites have little influence over many areas of public life. The economy is the primary example. When the economy is not doing well, most Americans can see that for themselves. Elites might continue to frame the policy options to deal with the economy, but they do not define the problem.

How Polls Work

Public-opinion surveys are as old as the republic itself. The first poll asked more than 500 male voters walking in the streets of Wilmington, Delaware, for whom they planned to vote in the 1824 presidential contest. The first scientific opinion poll was developed in the 1930s by George Gallup, the founder of the famous Gallup Poll company. Gallup, along with his partner, Elmo Roper, was able to measure public opinion accurately by taking many of the factors discussed previously: gender, ethnicity, race, social class, and region. Pollsters select their participants using *random probability sampling*. Since 1936, this method of polling the public on presidential preferences has accurately called the winner of each presidential election except two—the 1948 and 2012 elections.

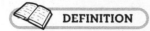 **DEFINITION**

Random probability sampling is a method by which pollsters choose interviewees based on the idea that the opinion of individuals selected by chance will be representative of the population at large.

Another common type of poll is referred to as the straw poll. Straw polls rely heavily on convenience samples and are highly inaccurate and unreliable. This is largely due to the fact that many groups representative of the broader population are often not included. Polls are important to media outlets and campaigns. For the media, a poll result can be an important story to report on. For campaigns, polls are necessary to strategize, allocate campaign resources, and develop opinions and positions on issues important to constituents.

A good and reliable poll must carefully and scientifically select the sample participants, ask good questions, and measure how well people are informed about the subject of the survey. Polls help citizens in a democracy make sense of the political process and can help them make more informed decisions.

The Paradox of Public Opinion

In the 1950s and early 1960s, Americans had very optimistic views of their government and government officials. The nation was experiencing a growing and expanding economy and was the leader of the free world on the international stage. However, since the 1970s, Americans have lost confidence in their government officials. This decline in trust of government has occurred as cynicism among Americans is on the rise, especially about the behavior and actions of their elected officials. Trust and confidence in Congress has been less than 15 percent for many years now. Still, members of Congress are reelected at very high rates due to gerrymandering. (I discuss this more in Chapter 8.)

Yet even with confidence so low and cynicism so high, Americans still believe that no other country in the world provides better opportunities to succeed than the United States. And although most Americans believe the system is broken, a nearly equal amount believes that the problems with government can be fixed.

The Least You Need to Know

- American political attitudes are formed by many factors, including family, gender, religion, and education.
- Many crosscutting cleavages influence political ideology, such as race, ethnicity, region, income, occupation, age, and sexual orientation.
- The two main political ideologies in America are liberalism and conservatism. However, the American political spectrum includes libertarians, populists, socialists, and environmentalists, too.
- Most Americans are politically tolerant and are not extremists. Instead, they are at the center of the political spectrum.
- Political elites are those Americans who wield an extraordinary amount of political power and are the most activist in politics. They are very consistent in their political beliefs.
- Political elites set the public agenda and influence public opinion on policy matters.

Political Parties

People create political parties to promote their ideas and goals. Parties have many functions in a democracy, but perhaps the most important role parties play is narrowing the choice of candidates in an election. Elections serve to decide who will have political power, and parties are the venue by which people compete to become candidates for election. Parties help stabilize democracy by creating peaceful transfers of power from one candidate to another, and from one party to another. As we have seen in the 2016 nomination contest of both major parties, the lead-up to the nomination can be very competitive and divisive.

In This Chapter

- The nature and functions of U.S. political parties
- The history of the two-party system
- The nature and role of minor parties
- The structure of the two major parties
- The presidential nominating process

What Political Parties Do for Democracy

Political parties are a group of persons who seek to control the government by winning elections, holding public office, and determining public policy. They share common principles and policy goals. When a party controls government, they attempt to make their policy goals and solutions to the nation's problems into law and policy.

The two major parties in the United States, the Republican and Democratic parties, are more election oriented than policy oriented, as they are made up of many different groups. It is best to think of them as umbrella parties, or *coalitions*. Each party includes groups that are diverse economically, racially, religiously, and regionally. As such, the parties serve to bring conflicting but loosely allied groups together, tempering and modifying the different views within their party. Thought of this way, parties serve to lessen the possibility of extremism in politics.

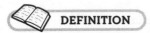 **DEFINITION**

A **coalition** is a union of many persons of diverse interests who have come together to get its candidate elected.

Political parties perform many important functions to facilitate democracy. They are a link between the people and the government. Political parties organize the competition by nominating candidates for election, selecting qualified candidates through caucuses, conventions, or primaries, then presenting them to the voters. Candidates must present themselves to the party for selection and are judged on their record and their ability to win in the general election.

Parties work out the differences within their party through the nominating process and then unify to seek the votes of those outside their party and win elections. This helps unify the electorate, at least into two large national parties. Political parties try to inform the public and stimulate interest and support for their position on the issues that are important to them through advertisements, conventions, and rallies. Parties constantly seek to balance their principles with positions that will attract the most voters.

Once their candidates are in office, parties are important when it comes to organizing government in the United States. Congress is organized along party lines. The political party with the most votes in the House and Senate controls the leadership positions and the committees that formulate laws and public policy. (This is covered in more depth in Chapters 10 and 11.) The party not in power closely monitors and comments on the actions of the party in power, serving as "watchdogs" for the people and attempting to convince voters that the party in power should be replaced.

The Two-Party System

The United States has many political parties, but practically speaking we only have two major parties that have a chance of winning elections. Multiparty systems tend to be found in parliamentary democracies, in contrast to our presidential democracy. The United Kingdom, however, is an exception. It is both a parliamentary system and a two-party system of government.

The two parties—Republican and Democratic—dominate in American politics for several important reasons. Americans share a political culture based on the same democratic principles. Although we are a diverse society, there is a consensus on fundamental matters of government. Since the founding of the republic, the nation is rooted in a two-party system; in the early days there were the Federalists and the Anti-Federalists. Americans accept the idea of a two-party system because there has always been one and the republic has worked with this system in place.

Winner Take All

The two-party system has prevailed for so long largely due to the system of elections. In the United States, elections at the national, state, and local levels are based on a plurality, winner-take-all method. The *plurality system* means that whoever wins an election for senator, president, governor, state legislator, or mayor simply received the most votes cast in that election. In many other nations, if a candidate fails to get a majority, there is a run-off election between the top two candidates. Because our political system is dominated by the two parties, a plurality system ensures that one of the major parties will almost always win an election.

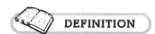 **DEFINITION**

The **plurality system** is an electoral system in which the candidate with the most votes wins. A majority is not necessary to win.

State Laws

The U.S. Constitution says nothing regarding political parties and, therefore, it is left to the states to create laws that define what a party is and the rules and regulations that govern political parties. Since Republicans and Democrats dominate the legislatures in all 50 states, they have created laws that make it difficult for third-party candidates to get on the ballot. State laws have helped the two-party system to prevail and survive for so long.

The Role of Minor Parties

The many minor parties in the United States include the Libertarian, Socialist, Right to Life, Conservative, Liberal, and American Independent parties. These parties have very little chance of winning elections, particularly national elections, yet they serve an important role.

Minor parties have helped establish political traditions. For example, in 1831, the Anti-Mason Party held a political convention to nominate its candidate for president. Ever since then, the Democrats and Republicans have used national political conventions to nominate their candidates for president and vice president. Minor parties have also run strong third-party candidates in elections. Although they do not win the election, they have a spoiler role. In 1948, a group of southern Democrats that opposed the racial integration policies of the national Democratic Party broke off to form the States' Rights Democratic Party. This group coined the term *Dixiecrat*. The Dixiecrats nominated South Carolina Governor Strom Thurmond, who would later go on to serve in the U.S. Senate. Although Strom Thurmond would eventually win four southern states with 39 electoral votes, Truman still won the general election by defeating Republican Thomas Dewey.

In 1968, Alabama Governor George Wallace entered the presidential campaign as a candidate for his own American Independent Party. He ran on an antifederal government, anti–civil rights agenda, arguing that there was not a "dime's worth of difference" between the two main candidates, Richard Nixon and Hubert Humphrey. Wallace competed successfully and won more than 13 percent of the nation's popular vote, and 46 electoral votes, but Nixon won the election.

Independent candidates also played a significant role in 1980, 1992, 1996, and 2000 elections. John Anderson was a moderate Republican who opposed the Republican nominee, Ronald Reagan, in 1980. Although Anderson won 6.6 percent of the vote in the general election, Ronald Reagan still defeated incumbent Democrat President Jimmy Carter. In 1992 and 1996, Texas billionaire Ross Perot won nearly 19 percent and 8 percent of the national vote, respectively. In both elections, Democrat William Jefferson (Bill) Clinton won the presidency. In the very close 2000 presidential election, the Green Party candidate, Ralph Nader, pulled enough votes away from the Democratic ticket to result in a Republican win for George W. Bush.

Minor parties are also important in their roles as critics and innovators. Their members feel that the two major parties do not sufficiently represent their views or positions on issues. Yet the major parties try to compromise with them, incorporate their positions, and bring them under their umbrella, to improve their own chances of electoral success. There are four distinct types of minor parties.

Ideological parties embrace a view of American society and government that is substantially different from the two major parties. The Communist Party has been in existence in the United States since the 1920s and advocates for a Marxist framework. Ideological parties seldom win many votes, yet they endure.

Single-issue parties focus on only one public policy issue. Their name usually incorporates their primary concern. For example, the Right to Life Party strongly opposes abortion. These parties are sometimes absorbed by the major parties when they take on the issue as their own.

Economic-protest parties are usually born in times of economic discontent and tend to be regional. These parties also do not have a clear ideological base. They tend to disappear as economic conditions improve. The Populist Party of the late nineteenth century is an example. They advocated for the public ownership of railroads and other innovative industries of the time, in response to the great wealth amassed by the so-called Robber Barons.

Splinter or factional parties are usually formed by a split in a major party over a philosophical position or a party's candidate. Most of these parties form around a strong personality. For example, Theodore Roosevelt broke from the Republican Party and formed the Bull Moose Progressive Party in 1912. Roosevelt maintained that President Taft had allowed fraudulent seating of delegates at the Republican convention in order to capture the presidential nomination from progressive forces within the party. Republican progressives reconvened in Chicago and endorsed the formation of a national progressive party. When formally launched later that summer, the new Progressive Party chose Roosevelt as its presidential nominee and Hiram Johnson of California as his running mate. Questioned by reporters, Roosevelt said he felt as strong as a "bull moose." Labeled the "Bull Moose Party," the Progressives promised to increase federal regulation and protect the welfare of ordinary people.

In 1968, Alabama Governor George Wallace broke with the Democratic Party to form the American Independent Party in response to the counterculture and mass social movements of the 1960s and what he believed was a northern liberal bias in the party.

 REAL-LIFE FACTS

In the election of 1912, Theodore Roosevelt, running as the candidate for the Progressive Party, won the most votes of any minor party in U.S. history, and almost certainly denied the Republican William Taft the election. Roosevelt garnered 4,118,571 popular votes (27.4 percent) and 88 electoral votes. He is the only third-party candidate to come in second in a presidential election.

The Rise and Decline of the Political Party

The founders of the American republic were against factions and parties because they feared that bigger and better organized groups threatened free government. Benjamin Franklin was concerned about the "infinite mutual abuse of parties, tearing to pieces the best of characters." George Washington famously warned the country against the "baneful effects of the Spirit of the Party." And Thomas Jefferson added, "If I could not go to heaven but with a party, I would not go there at all."

Our nation began without parties, and at no time in our nation's history have political parties been weaker than they are today. After the founding, parties were created, rose in prominence, and became very powerful, establishing the two-party system. Parties have reformed themselves and have ultimately declined in stature and effectiveness. They have evolved and changed over time.

The Founding Period

From the onset of George Washington's administration, the hostility between Alexander Hamilton (Federalist) and Thomas Jefferson (Anti-Federalist) made the development of parties all but inevitable. Jefferson organized his followers to oppose Hamilton and formed the first organized political party, calling themselves Republicans.

Federalists supported the new Constitution, and favored the strong central government it created. Federalists believed the Constitution would provide a better balance between the national government and the state governments. Anti-Federalists feared that the new Constitution would create too powerful a national government. Anti-Federalists believed that only small governments close to the people could ensure rights and liberties. Many differences arose between the Federalists and the Anti-Federalists concerning social issues. The Anti-Federalists were supported by the poorer classes, while the Federalists were supported by the higher, more aristocratic classes.

The Democratic-Republicans, as they came to be known, opposed the Federalists, and thus began the party system in America. The party of Jefferson was so successful in defeating Federalists that by 1800 the Federalists had almost ceased to exist. Democratic-Republicans went on to dominate national politics for the next 24 years.

 MISINFORMATION

Jefferson's party is the party of the present-day Democrats. The modern Republican Party did not emerge until the Civil War.

The Jacksonians

In 1824, Andrew Jackson made his first bid for the presidency. Although he won more popular votes, he lost in the Electoral College to John Quincy Adams. Soon after, new laws were passed that enlarged the number of eligible voters and in 1828, nearly one million votes were cast and Andrew Jackson won the election. This period is known as Jacksonian Democracy. During this period of *realignment*, the Democrats became a large, nationwide party. The opposition party that emerged was the Whig Party.

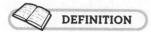 **DEFINITION**

Realignment occurs in an election during periods of expanded suffrage and major social or economic change in the society, shifting the way voters identify with parties.

The Civil War

Slavery and the issue of states' rights gave birth to the modern Republican Party, which started as a third party with the Democrats and the Whigs. When Lincoln was elected the sixteenth president, the Republican Party became a major party and has held that position ever since. The Republican Party garnered its support from a coalition of those opposed to slavery, Northern industrialists and merchants, and a large number of urban workers and farmers. The Democratic Party survived with a very strong base in the South, but the Republicans would dominate national politics for the next 50 years.

The Reform Era

After the election of 1896 and through the election of 1932, the two major parties went through a period of reform. During this period, primary elections were established to replace nominating conventions, lessening the power of party leaders to select candidates for office. Also, stricter voter-registration laws were passed to reduce voter fraud. In 1932, a new realignment of voters took place in American politics, largely in response to the Great Depression. Democrats maintained their stronghold on the South and added union workers, immigrant citizen workers, and people hurt by the Great Depression.

 ON THE RECORD

"The old parties are husks, with no real soul within either, divided on artificial lines, boss-ridden and privilege-controlled, each a jumble of incongruous elements, and neither daring to speak out wisely and fearlessly on what should be said on the vital issues of the day."

—Theodore Roosevelt

The Decline of the Political Party

By the 1960s, there was substantial evidence of party decline in the United States. First, increasing numbers of Americans voted a split ticket, voting for one party's candidate for president and the other party's candidate for Congress. Previously, people tended to vote a straight ticket. This ushered in a phenomenon known as *divided government*.

Secondly, party leaders continued to lose influence over nominating candidates as primaries became more important to winning nominations, and the parties become more decentralized.

Before primaries were widely adopted in the twentieth century, powerful state and local party leaders—the so-called political bosses—controlled the selection of nominees at political conventions. The bosses had the power to select delegates to the convention, so they could extract political favors from candidates and, in exchange, ensure that delegates would support that candidate.

Lastly, the rise of independents in a large segment of the population lessened the identification with parties and more to candidates themselves.

The National Party Organization

Despite the decline in influence of political parties, the two-party system remains strong in the United States. Most registered Democrats and Republicans continue to vote for the candidates from their party. The president serves as the leader of his or her party when in office, and the party not in office usually has several high-profile leaders.

Federalism also contributes to the decentralization of the national party as many elections are held at the state and local level. Although the two parties are quite different in philosophy and focus, they are similarly organized at the national level, with a national convention, national committee, national chairperson, and congressional campaign committees.

The National Convention

Both parties hold national conventions every four years to nominate their candidates for president and vice president. At the convention, the parties also adopt a *platform* of issues on which to campaign.

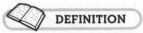 **DEFINITION**

A party **platform** is the official statement of party policy on a wide range of issues.

The National Committee

In between conventions, the party's business is conducted by the Republican National Committee (RNC) and the Democratic National Committee (DNC). The committees are made up of members from each of the states and several of the *territories*. On paper, the national committee appears to be a very powerful organization, but it functions mainly to stage the convention every four years.

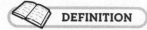 **DEFINITION**

Territories of the United States are one type of political division of the United States, administered by the U.S. government but not part of any U.S. state.

The National Chairperson

The national chairperson is the leader of the national committee, usually selected by the presidential nominee and approved by the national committee. They serve four-year terms, focusing on the convention and the campaign during presidential election years, and promoting party unity, raising money, and recruiting new voters during the off years.

 REAL-LIFE FACTS

In 1972, the Democrats elected Jean Westwood to be the first woman to lead a national party. The Republicans elected Mary Louise Smith in 1974. Ron Brown was the first African American national chairperson when he was selected by the Democrats in 1989.

The Congressional Campaign Committees

The congressional campaign committees for each house of Congress raise money for three main purposes:

- To help reelect the *incumbent*
- To ensure that seats given up by retiring officials stay within the party
- To select campaigns to unseat incumbents from the other party

 **DEFINITION**

An **incumbent** is the current office holder.

State and Local Party Organizations

At the national level, party organization is not governed by federal laws but rather through tradition and rules adopted at the national party convention. At the state and local level, however, party structure is determined by state laws. At the state level, each party has a state chairperson who is usually appointed by the governor of the party in power or a U.S. senator from that state or by some other powerful leader in state politics. The state party organization attempts to further the state's interest within the national party.

Local party structures vary considerably in the United States. Local party organizations are often broken down into smaller units called wards. In large cities, wards are further broken down into precincts. Local party structures are an important vehicle for getting voters to the voting booths on Election Day.

The Road to the Party Presidential Nomination

The road to the presidential nomination confronts the major parties with two conflicting forces: one is the need to keep voices of dissent from leaving the party and forming a third party with their own candidate, and the second is the need to select a candidate who will appeal to a majority of all voters and win the presidency in November. At times, these contrary forces result in party compromises that hurt their nominee in the general election.

When political parties had greater influence and presidential nominees were selected by party leaders and brokers, it was much easier for the party to ignore dissent within the party and select the candidate who could more easily win. The electoral objective of the party was the important consideration. Today, however, political parties have declined in their dominance over the selection process because the nominee is selected by delegates through the caucus and primary process.

Who Are the Delegates?

Delegates to the national convention are the most ideological and activist of voters. They are also made up of party officials and elected leaders. Delegates to the party conventions are political elites. They also tend to be more liberal, for the Democrats, and more conservative, for the Republicans, than the general voting public.

Who Votes in Caucuses and Primaries?

Delegates are probably not representative of the larger population of Democrats and Republicans because they are chosen at caucuses and primaries by the most ideologically active members of each party. According to voting statistics, only half the number of general election voters participates in caucuses and primaries. Thus primary and caucus voters greatly influence the choice for president for the general electorate. Independents, who are not able to vote in most Democratic and Republican venues, are essentially left out of the nominating process. However, their votes are crucial to victory in November.

The Least You Need to Know

- Political parties join together to elect candidates to public office. Parties serve key functions in our political system and are instrumental to our government.

- The two-party system in the United States is a result of history and tradition. Furthermore, the American electorate is largely in the center of the political spectrum and there is little room for more parties to flourish.

- Minor parties have enjoyed little success in national American politics; however, they have had a significant impact on the two major parties. There are four types of minor parties: ideological parties, single-issue parties, economic-protest parties, and factional parties.

- The organization of the major parties on the national level is similar. State and local parties look after their interests within the national party structure. Delegates to the national conventions are party elites and more ideological than the general voting public.

Campaigns and Elections

Anyone who wants to get elected to Congress or become president must first get his or her name on the ballot. In other words, he or she must receive a party's nomination for office to campaign and compete in elections for office.

In the United States, an individual who wants to win a nomination must decide to run for office, raise money, collect the necessary signatures to get on the ballot, and ultimately appeal to the voters. As you read in Chapter 6, the nominating process is a major function of political parties and is a critically important part of the electoral process.

In This Chapter

- How candidates are nominated
- Similarities and differences with presidential and congressional campaigns
- Similarities and differences with primary and general election campaigns
- Campaign finance rules
- The role of the electoral college

The Nominating Process

Those who decide who is nominated have a great deal of influence on the choices all other voters will have in the general election. In the early years of the republic, *nominations* were made at private meetings by influential figures in the community. Once political parties emerged, these meetings—or caucuses—also nominated individuals for state government offices. However, this process collapsed with the emergence of the convention as the main venue to nominate individuals.

 **DEFINITION**

Nomination is the process of candidate selection in an electoral system.

There are significant differences in the nominating process for candidates for Congress and candidates for president. Candidates for Congress are selected at state conventions and presidential candidates are selected at national conventions. For example, only Republicans from New York select their party's candidates for the U.S. Senate and the House of Representatives, but the Republican nominee for president is selected by delegates from all the states. Furthermore, states have different methods of selecting candidates and delegates.

Why Do People Run for Office?

People decide to run for public office for myriad reasons. Most observers would agree that the three main reasons people enter a political campaign are public service, policy goals, and personal ambition. These factors explain why so many politicians climb the political ladder starting at the local level, then moving onto the state level, and finally the national level, with the presidency being the crown jewel of the journey. Political scientist Joseph A. Schlesinger refers to this as the opportunity structure.

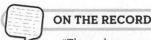 **ON THE RECORD**

"The stakes are too high for government to be a spectator sport."

—Congresswoman Barbara Jordan

The Closed Primary

A closed primary is limited to registered members of that party. Nearly half the states conduct closed primaries. Some states allow individuals to register on the same day as the election in order to participate.

The Open Primary

In an open primary, any qualified voter may participate in the nomination process for a party's candidate. Half the states hold open primaries to nominate a party's candidate. Voters, however, must choose on Election Day which party nomination process they want to participate in. They receive and vote on only one party's ballot.

The Runoff Primary

In most states, a candidate only needs to win a plurality of the votes in order to get the nomination. However, several states require a majority of the votes. A runoff primary is held between the two top vote-getters in the first primary race in order to determine a nominee. The runoff election is usually held several weeks after the initial primary election.

The Blanket Primary

The blanket primary is a variation of the open primary. Voters do not have to choose which party nominating process they want to participate in. Rather, voters receive a ballot with all the candidates and they can participate however they choose. For example, they could switch between party primaries as they go down the ballot.

REAL-LIFE FACTS

In 1902, Wisconsin Governor Robert La Follette called for the nomination of each party's candidates directly by the voters through the primary system.

The Presidential Primary

Unlike the aforementioned primaries, the presidential primary is not a nominating device. Rather, the presidential primary is an election that is held as part of the process of nominating a candidate for president. The presidential primary takes place to elect some of the delegates to the party's nominating convention. Presidential candidates must compete in all state primaries and caucuses in order to win delegates who will vote for them at the convention.

The Caucus

The caucus is a nominating device where a group of people gather together to select a candidate, or in the case of a presidential caucus, vote for their preference. Caucuses are generally open to all members of the party and tend to resemble a town-hall meeting. People must vote publicly for a candidate. It does not have the privacy of the primary voting booth. Caucuses select delegates who then attend the national convention to select the party's nominee for president and vice president. In order for a candidate to "win" delegates, he or she must have a minimum number of votes from the people in attendance. Democrats and Republicans from each state have different rules governing how caucuses are conducted and what numbers are necessary to obtain delegates. Caucus gatherings are among the most fiercely partisan events in American politics and are equally as important as the primary in the nominating process.

REAL-LIFE FACTS

Iowa has held caucuses since 1846, but it is only since 1972 that the Hawkeye State has held the first-in-the-nation status.

Presidential and Congressional Campaigns

Presidential and congressional campaigns differ in many important ways. Presidential campaigns are national in scope, while congressional campaigns are limited to the district the candidate is running to represent in Congress. There are other important differences to note:

Presidential races are much more competitive than races for Congress, especially for the House of Representatives.

Presidents are limited to two terms, or 10 years. If a vice president succeeds a president due to death or resignation, he or she could run for election and serve two additional terms as long as it would not exceed the 10-year limit. Lyndon Johnson, for instance, finished the term JFK was elected to in 1960, then ran for reelection in 1964. He was eligible to run again in 1968 but declined. Gerald Ford would have been eligible to run again in 1980 had he won in 1976 as well.

Members of Congress do not have term limits.

Fewer voters participate in elections in years when there is no presidential contest. Candidates for office must appeal to the more partisan base that tends to vote in these elections.

Candidates for Congress can take credit for bringing federal funds to local projects. Candidates for president do not have the same local appeal.

Incumbent members of Congress enjoy what are called *franking privileges*, which means they can send mailings to their constituents at government expense highlighting their achievements. Presidential candidates do not have this privilege.

Incumbent presidents running for reelection cannot run away from national issues. Candidates for Congress can often run against Washington, D.C., and embrace their local roots.

Presidential and congressional campaigns can sometimes help or hinder each other. When a popular president is running for reelection in good economic times, congressional candidates from his party may be able to ride his *coattails* to victory.

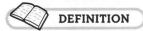 **DEFINITION**

Coattails refer to riding into office on the popularity of a better-known candidate for office.

Conversely, when an unpopular president is running for reelection, it can result in voters not turning out or turning against the president's party in Congress as well.

Running for President

Anyone considering running for president must first get on the national radar as someone who is sufficiently qualified for the office. The media plays a key role in mentioning potential candidates for office. One way people considering running for president can get mentioned in the national press is by alerting reporters.

Another way to get coverage is by going around the country and giving speeches to large audiences in popular venues or early election states. Elected officials can propose important legislation or run for a leadership position in Congress. Governors of big states can also easily get mentioned in the press as eligible possibilities.

 **ON THE RECORD**

"All politics is local."

—Former Speaker of the House Tip O'Neill

Once a potential candidate has succeeded in getting mentioned as a possible candidate for president, they must start the daunting task of raising money, organizing a team to run a national campaign, and determining a strategy for winning.

In order to run for president, a candidate must build an organization of many followers who are willing to contribute money to the campaign. As you will see later in the chapter, laws restrict the amounts of money individuals can contribute to a campaign. Candidates must also fulfill certain rules in order to qualify for federal matching grants for a campaign.

Running a successful campaign requires many professionals, specialists, advisers, and volunteers. These include lawyers, consultants, accountants, advertising experts, pollsters, travel planners, and press spokesmen. Additionally, a cadre of volunteers is necessary to register voters, staff phone banks, and help with mass mailings.

Every candidate must have a strategy and theme for their campaign. A candidate can run against an incumbent as an agent of change. An incumbent can run on the theme of experience. Candidates must also decide on the tone of their campaign. Should it focus on the positive attributes of the candidate, or attack the opponent? Campaigns must focus on issues and positions, trust factors, competence, or a combination of these.

Candidate-Centered Campaigns

Many candidates for public office use the media, private campaign consultants, and independent polls to run their political campaigns. They bypass the political parties to perform many of these roles. Candidate-centered campaigns run to receive the nomination of one of the two major parties but the candidate does not come through the traditional party landscape. In the 2016 Republican presidential nomination race, Donald Trump is an example of a candidate-centered campaign. In fact, Mr. Trump's campaign often challenges the establishment of the Republican Party.

Who Gets Nominated?

Traditionally, the nominees of both major parties have been male, white, wealthy, and Protestant. There have been some exceptions, however. The barrier against Catholics was broken by the Democratic nomination of Al Smith in 1928 and the election of Democrat John Kennedy in 1960. Most nominees have previously held elected office, be it governor, senator, or vice president. Many nominees have also been war heroes. The last military leader to win a major party nomination and win the presidency was General Dwight D. Eisenhower in 1952.

Many women, Jews, and African Americans are challenging the historical barriers to the nomination and to the presidency. The Democratic Party nominated the first woman vice presidential nominee in 1984, New York Congresswoman Geraldine Ferraro. In 2000, the Democrats nominated Senator Joseph Lieberman of Connecticut, the first Jewish VP nominee on a major party ticket. In 2008, Senator Barack Obama became the first African American nominee for President and went on to win the election and was reelected in 2012. In 2008, Sarah Palin, governor of Alaska, was the first female Republican candidate for vice president. As of this writing, in 2016 the Democrats are poised to nominate the first female presidential candidate, former First Lady, Senator, and Secretary of State Hillary Clinton, or the first Jewish presidential nominee, Senator Bernie Sanders of Vermont.

Running for Congress

Because Congress does not have term limits, a candidate for congressional office has a good chance of running against an incumbent. Incumbents are overwhelmingly reelected, so the chances of an opponent winning the election are slim.

The Power of Incumbency

Incumbents tend to run very personal rather than party-oriented campaigns. They stress their record and experience and the benefits they've brought home to their district. They tend to cater to their constituent's requests. Furthermore, they are able to use some of the privileges of their office to develop a good opinion of themselves among their constituents. One of the most frequently employed techniques is *franking*. Incumbents also make frequent trips to their home districts to meet with voters.

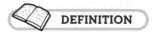 **DEFINITION**

Franking is the privilege of free mailings by members of Congress.

The Importance of the Primary

A candidate who wants to win the party's nomination for office must gather enough signatures to get on the ballot for the primary election. Political parties have very little influence in restricting the ability of an eligible citizen from meeting the ballot requirements. Still, it is quite unusual for an incumbent to lose a primary. Election data shows that nearly 98 percent of congressional representatives are renominated in primary elections, and 94 percent of incumbent senators are nominated again. Winning the nomination in a primary in a congressional district dominated by your party almost certainly means winning in November.

The Map Advantage

Each state has two senators and at least one representative. The number of representatives depends on a state's population; California has the most with 53, while seven states—Alaska, Delaware, Montana, North Dakota, South Dakota, Vermont, and Wyoming—have only one. States that have more than one representative have their district lines drawn up by their respective state legislatures, and are usually, logically, drawn to favor whichever party has a majority in the statehouse. Traditionally, congressional districts are redrawn every 10 years, following the national census.

District boundaries affect election outcomes. Some boundaries are created in such a manner that they favor one party over the other. This is referred to as *gerrymandering.* Districts can be drawn to have a majority of voters from one party. Anyone considering running for the House of Representatives must consider the dominant party affiliation of the voters in that district. This serves to enforce more extreme partisan positions, because representatives in "safe" districts have more to fear in the primary, in the form of a challenge from within their party, than they do in the general against the other party.

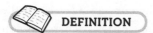 **DEFINITION**

> **Gerrymandering** is the process of drawing congressional district boundaries in bizarre or unusual shapes that favor one party over the other in a general election.

Candidates for the Senate, because they compete in the entire state, are not as restrained by local party preferences among the voters. Still, some states do lean more heavily Democratic or Republican, so a candidate for the Senate from one party might have an advantage going into a general election.

Primary and General Campaigns

Candidates for president are essentially entering two elections. The first is the road to the nomination, which consists of primaries and caucuses. The second is the general election in November. As you have read in prior chapters, voters in primary elections are much more ideological than general election voters. To motivate and mobilize these voters, a candidate must usually run a campaign that is more liberal for the Democratic nomination, and a more conservative one for the Republican nomination. In fact, data suggests that voters in the Iowa Caucus, the first presidential contest in the nomination process, generally do not represent all the members of the national party. Yet they have enormous influence in propelling a candidate to national prominence.

In the 2008 election cycle, a one-term U.S. senator from Illinois, Senator Barack Obama, won the Iowa Caucus and went on to win the Democratic nomination for president in a long, tight race against Senator Hillary Clinton of New York. Candidates lock up the nomination with activist support, then, in order to win a general election, presidential candidates must move back to the ideological center. The candidate's positions on campaign issues also affect election outcomes. There are two types of issues in election campaigns: position issues and valence issues. A position issue is one in which candidates for the nomination or for office have different or opposing views on matters that divide voters. For example, in the 2008 presidential contest, Republican nominee John McCain and Democratic nominee, Barack Obama, had opposing views on the war in Iraq.

Valence issues are matters on which the public is not divided; however, they look to see which candidate is more strongly aligned with the public view. For example, everyone wants a strong defense, but not all candidates agree on how to achieve that goal, or are perceived to be the best to handle the matter.

Money in Politics Today

Running for public office costs lots of money. In the 2012 electoral contests, candidates spent a total of more than $7 billion. It is estimated that more than $5 billion will be spent by candidates and political parties in the 2016 presidential primaries and election alone. Some say this figure might be too low depending on whether there is a significant third-party candidate running.

The need to raise so much money in politics raises some concerns. The first is that wealthy individuals can be seen as trying to buy their way into office. The other, of course, is that special interests raise money for candidates in exchange for special favors, influence, and consideration once in office. Parties and candidates must have money and the ability to raise money. Without financial resources, they cannot campaign, compete, or win elections.

Much of the rise in campaign spending has to do with the complex organization that it now takes to run a campaign and the high cost of media advertising. Of course, more is spent on presidential campaigns, followed by Senate and House races, and then by state and local races. Campaigns require radio and television ads. In major markets, the cost of running an advertisement on the air is astronomical. In addition, campaigns must have a staff of speechwriters, pollsters, consultants, and advertising professionals that make up a big portion of the spending budget.

Candidates and political parties draw their campaign resources from two basic sources of money. As you will read later in the chapter, money from public treasuries—the U.S. Treasury and state and local treasuries—is now an important source of presidential campaign money. Public funds, sometimes referred to as subsidies, are grants from the government to run a campaign.

 ON THE RECORD

"You have to be loaded just to get beat."

—Will Rogers

Private contributions have always been the largest source of campaign funds in American politics. There are five categories of private contributors:

- Small contributors who donate less than $250.

- Wealthy individuals and families, often referred to as "fat cats."

- Wealthy candidates who spend their own money.

- Nonparty groups, especially political action committees (PACs), which are the political arms of groups and organizations that have a stake in the election.

- Temporary organizations created for the immediate purpose of the campaign, especially fundraising.

Individuals are motivated to make private contributions for many reasons. Some simply believe in the candidate or the party. Others seek access to government in order to influence public policy or benefit themselves or their interests. Still others are motivated by potential appointments to public office, especially ambassadorships. Some do it simply for social recognition—to get their name on the White House or congressional guest list.

The Federal Election Commission

Congress started to regulate money in federal elections as far back as 1907. The first act Congress passed was the ban on campaign contributions by banks and corporations to candidates running for federal office. Congress passed significant legislation regulating the use of money in presidential and congressional campaigns in 1971 with the Federal Election Campaign Act. This act replaced all prior laws dealing with money regulations and was an attempt to strengthen enforcement of the laws. This act was amended twice, in 1974 and 1976.

The 2002 Bipartisan Campaign Reform Act sought to close the loophole in soft-money contributions left in the 1974 and 1976 amendments. The 1974 act also set up the Federal Election Commission (FEC). It is an independent agency of the executive branch and it administers all federal laws dealing with campaign finance. The six members of the commission are appointed by the president and confirmed by the Senate for five-year terms. The president designates one of the commissioners to serve as chairperson. Only three commissioners can be from the same political party. Commissioners can be appointed to fill a term of a vacant seat and then renominated to a full five-year term.

The FEC is charged with the responsibility of enforcing federal laws regulating campaign contributions. However, the task of the agency is difficult. Many of the laws are strongly worded and detailed—however, the FEC is usually underfunded and understaffed. Congress has made it difficult for the agency to enforce laws that would directly affect their ability to raise funds for campaigns, and it has become hopelessly deadlocked, with nearly every issue brought before it resulting in a 3–3, Democrats versus Republicans stalemate.

The laws the FEC is charged with enforcing cover four main areas:

- Timely disclosure of campaign finance data
- Limits on campaign contributions
- Limits on campaign expenses
- Public funding for part of the presidential election

MISINFORMATION

Although the FEC was established to regulate laws dealing with campaign finance, it is limited to federal laws dealing with federal elections. The FEC has no jurisdiction when it comes to contributions to state and local elections.

Disclosure Requirements

Disclosure requirements are so detailed that all campaigns have professional accountants to handle the work. No individual may make a contribution in the name of another person. Cash contributions are limited to $100. All contributions or loans that exceed $200 must be identified by the source and date. Any person or organization receiving money due to campaign spending that exceeds $200 must also be identified. Any contribution that is greater than $5,000 must be reported to the FEC within 48 hours. Additionally, during the last 20 days of a campaign, any contributions that exceed $1,000 must be reported within 48 hours.

Limits on Contributions

Corporations, unions, and banks may not contribute directly to a federal campaign. Individuals are restricted as follows:

- Maximum of $2,100 to any federal candidate in a primary election, and $2,100 to any federal candidate's general election campaign
- Maximum of $5,000 in any year to a PAC
- Maximum of $26,700 to a national party committee

Essentially, an individual's total contributions are limited to $101,400 in any one election cycle, or every two years.

PAC Contributions

Although corporations and unions are prohibited from contributing to campaigns, their political action committees (PACs) are free to do so. PACs are interested in influencing public policy and, therefore, they have an interest in election results. There are several thousand PACs registered in the United States. PACs are limited to contributing $5,000 to any candidate in an election, or $10,000 to any one candidate in an election cycle. PACs can give the maximum amount to as many candidates as they like. Furthermore, PACs are limited to $15,000 annual contributions to national political parties. PACs are relatively easy to form and individuals may become members to as many PACs as they wish. PACs contributed more than $600 million in the 2004 federal elections.

Limits on Expenditures

Congress has made several attempts to limit federal campaign spending. In the landmark 1976 case, *Buckley* v. *Valeo*, the Supreme Court found most limitations were unconstitutional. The court maintained that the restrictions violated the First Amendment right to freedom of expression. However, the court did rule that any presidential contenders who accept FEC matching funds could be regulated.

Currently, candidates are limited to spending $37.5 million in the preconvention period and no more than $74.6 million in the general election if they accept federal funds. In 2008, Senator Obama became the first party nominee to reject federal funding so his general-election campaign could exceed the historical limit.

In 2010, the Supreme Court, citing the First Amendment to free speech, ruled in *Citizens United* v. *FEC* "that corporations [and unions] may spend freely to support or oppose candidates for President and Congress" essentially overturning any limits that unions and corporations can spend, as long as they do not coordinate their efforts with a candidate's campaign. The long-term impact of this decision will take some time to determine, but it has already increased the amount of money being spent on campaigns.

Public Funding of Presidential Campaigns

Congress first provided for public funds for presidential campaigns starting in 1971. Citizens can check off on their tax returns if they want tax money (currently $3 per person) to go to this fund. The FEC administers the public subsidy process. The FEC matching fund limits are set up in such a manner as to discourage frivolous candidates or minor party candidates. Additionally, the FEC gives each of the major parties public monies toward their national convention and the $74.6 million subsidy to a national presidential candidate, if they choose to accept it.

The Electoral College

Most voters who vote for president and vice president think that they are voting directly for a candidate. Instead, citizens vote for electors who will cast their ballot in the Electoral College. Article II, Section 1 of the Constitution specifies that the selection of president shall be made by electors, not directly by the people. Each state's electors are selected in the presidential election year. This process is governed by state laws and by state party rules. After the national conventions, the electors are pledged to the candidates chosen. The number of electors from each state equals the number of senators (two) plus its number of representatives in the House. Additionally, three electors are chosen from the District of Columbia.

If a plurality of voters chooses one slate of electors on Election Day, then those electors are pledged to cast their ballot for the candidate for president and vice president of the winning party. The Constitution, however, does not specify that electors act in this manner. It is possible that the electors could overturn the choice of the people. In this way, it is the ultimate check on the choice made by the people. Remember, the founders were very wary of passions that might cause citizens to select someone who would be harmful to the republic.

If no one receives the votes needed for election, or there is a tie in the Electoral College, then the House of Representatives decides from among the candidates with the three most votes, and the Senate decides the selection of vice president from the two highest candidates. The House votes by state delegation, with a plurality of each delegation deciding on a candidate, and in the Senate each senator is given one vote.

In the history of the republic, Congress has selected the president only twice: first in 1801, with the selection of Thomas Jefferson, and second, in 1825, when it selected John Quincy Adams. There have been times, however, when the winner in the Electoral College did not have a majority of the popular vote. Most recently this occurred in the 2000 election between George W. Bush and Albert Gore. The Electoral College process was heavily criticized as undemocratic. Yet it was the founders' intention that the electors would select the best person for the job. However, electors do not debate the merits of a candidate and instead vote for the candidate to whom they are pledged.

Besides the possibility that a candidate can become president without winning the popular vote, the other concern that people have today is that winner-take-all is unfair to candidates who receive substantial votes. Some people feel that the Electoral College should be reformed, or perhaps even abolished so that the president and vice president are elected directly by the people. But changing the way the president and vice president are selected would require a constitutional amendment. The chance of such an amendment passing is, at present, remote.

REAL-LIFE FACTS

The president who won the most electoral votes was Ronald Reagan in 1984 with 525 electoral votes.

The Least You Need to Know

- Candidates for Congress are selected at state conventions, while candidates for president are selected through a process of primaries and caucuses, and then nominated at the national party convention.
- Campaigns for federal office require complex organizations and lots of money. Most funds for political campaigns come from private contributions.
- The Federal Election Commission (FEC), an independent agency of the executive branch, enforces the laws regulating campaign finances.
- The president and vice president are selected by the Electoral College and not directly by the citizens of the United States, as prescribed in Article II of the Constitution.

Political Participation and Voting

The right to vote is often considered the fundamental right of an individual in a democracy. Many groups have had to fight for this right, including African Americans, women, and young people over 18 years of age. In the United States, three basic criteria determine a person's eligibility to vote: age, citizenship, and residence. The Constitution does not give the federal government the authority to determine suffrage qualifications. Therefore, it falls under the jurisdiction of the states. The Constitution does restrict how the states can use this power. These restrictions come in the form of the Fifteenth, Nineteenth, Twenty-Fourth, and Twenty-Sixth Amendments.

About 215 million people meet the criteria to vote, yet only a little more than half tend to show up on Election Day. The people who do vote are strongly influenced by their sociological backgrounds and party identification. The candidates and issues at stake in an election have become increasingly more important and often cause voters to cast their ballot outside of their normal political party.

In This Chapter

- The American electorate
- Qualifications of American voters
- Who are the nonvoters?
- Factors affecting voter behavior

The History of Voting Rights

The first group of people with the right to vote in the United States was white male landowners. In 1789, that excluded 93 percent of even white men. *Suffrage* has been extended to the majority of Americans over a period of 200 years of struggle. In the early 1800s, religious restrictions were removed from voters. States also began to eliminate tax and property ownership requirements. By the middle of the 1800s, almost all white adult males could participate in elections in every state.

After the Civil War, the Fifteenth Amendment was approved, which was intended to protect any citizen from being denied *franchise* because of race. However, it took another 100 years for African Americans to express that right because state governments disenfranchised them by other means, which included voter-qualifying tests, discriminatory enforcement on voting regulations, poll taxes, and violence and terror against those who tried to register and vote.

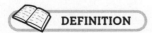 **DEFINITION**

Suffrage and *franchise* are synonyms for the right to vote.

The Nineteenth Amendment was ratified in 1920 and extended suffrage to women. This movement had started earlier on a state-by-state basis, but was made a nationwide requirement with this amendment.

The Voting Rights Act of 1965 finally enacted the Fifteenth Amendment and ensured racial equality in the right to vote.

The Twenty-Third Amendment, passed in 1961, gave residents of the District of Columbia the right to vote in presidential elections.

Voter Qualifications

Voter qualifications are based on three factors: age, citizenship, and residence. The Twenty-Sixth Amendment declared that people age 18 and older have the right to vote. States cannot set a minimum age higher than that. The wording of the amendment does permit states to lower the voting age if they would like. In a growing number of states, 17-year-olds can vote in primary elections if their eighteenth birthday is between the date of the primary and the general election.

People born outside the United States who have not become citizens are typically not allowed to vote. The Minnesota constitution requires a person to have been an American citizen for at least three months before he or she can vote. The Pennsylvania constitution calls for a one-month requirement.

States have also adopted residence requirements to vote. In order to vote in most states, a person must have lived there for a period of time determined by state law. States have adopted these laws in order to discourage bribing outsiders in order to alter the outcome of local elections and to allow new voters some time to get accustomed to the candidates and issues in a particular area. In the Voting Rights Act Amendments of 1970, Congress banned any requirement of greater than 30 days for voting in presidential elections. Nearly every state prohibits transients, people living in a state for only a short period of time, from gaining residence there.

REAL-LIFE FACTS

As of the 2010 census, the average population per district is 710,767 people. The state with the most districts is California, with 53. The states with only one district are Alaska, Delaware, Montana, North Dakota, South Dakota, Vermont, and Wyoming. The district with the greatest area is Alaska. And the district with the smallest area is New York's thirteenth district.

Voter Registration

All states except North Dakota require that most or all voters be registered. Registration is a procedure designed to prevent fraudulent voting. Some states, like Wisconsin, only require voters in urban areas to be registered. To register, voters must submit their basic demographic information. People remain registered until they die, get convicted of a felony, or get admitted to a mental health institution. Over the years, states have made it easier to register to vote by sending the applications through the mail and making application forms available at the department of motor vehicles (when people apply for their driver's licenses) and other state offices.

REAL-LIFE FACTS

The United States is the only democratic nation where each person chooses whether or not he or she will register to vote. In other countries, it is mandated by law that public officials enter the names of all of those eligible to vote on registration lists. In 2002, the federal government passed the Help America Vote Act (HAVA). This law requires all voters to either provide the last four digits of their Social Security number or their state's driver's license number to register to vote.

Literacy Tests

Literacy tests were once used to discourage the participation of African Americans, American Indians, and Latinos in elections. They required that voters know how to read, write, or sometimes "understand" some printed text, often taken from the state or federal Constitution. These tests were outlawed in 1970 by the Voting Rights Act Amendments.

Taxes

In the past, some states required that people pay a poll tax in order to vote. This was used as another means to disenfranchise African American and other minority voters. In 1964, the Twenty-Fourth Amendment outlawed this practice in federal elections. The Supreme Court extended this to all elections with *Harper* v. *Virginia Board of Elections* in 1966 as a violation of the Fourteenth Amendment's equal protection clause.

Congressional Districts

There are 435 congressional districts. The Constitution mandates that the population be counted at least once every 10 years in order to set the number of members from each state to the House of Representatives and by extension to the Electoral College. The Census Bureau within the Department of Commerce conducts a census to determine the number of districts in each state. Census data also affect how the more than $300 billion (roughly) per year in federal and state funding is allocated to communities for services in schools, public health, transportation, and much more.

The process of changing the borders of the districts is known as redistricting. The procedures vary by state. In 36 states, the state legislature has primary responsibility for creating a redistricting plan, which is typically subject to approval by the governor. Five states (Arizona, Hawaii, Idaho, New Jersey, and Washington) use independent, bipartisan redistricting commissions to reduce the effect party politics might have on the process. Two states (Iowa and Maine) give independent organizations the power to propose a redistricting plan, but defer the right to confirm the plan to the state legislature. The remaining seven states only have a single representative due to their low populations.

Each state has its own standards for creating congressional and legislative districts, but they must comply with federal requirements. Some of the criteria include: attempting to create compact, adjacent districts; venturing to keep political units and communities within a single district; and avoiding the drawing of boundaries to create demographic advantages for partisans or incumbents.

 REAL-LIFE FACTS

In *Wesberry* v. *Sanders* (1964), the Supreme Court ruled that U.S. Congressional districts must be drawn to be approximately equal in population. This requirement does not limit the legislature from carving out districts to include similar constituents from different parts of the state.

The latter is known as gerrymandering, and in states where the legislature controls the process, the possibility of this occurring often makes the process controversial, especially where the governor and the majority of the state legislature are from different parties. Many times state and federal court systems get involved to resolve issues regarding possible gerrymandering and the execution of timely, lawful redistricting.

Partisan power in state legislatures has created districts that divide voter groups and pack opponents into as few districts as possible, leading to district maps that are skewed toward one party. In this manner, many states such as Texas, Michigan, and Pennsylvania have successfully eliminated competition for most House seats. Other states, such as New York, New Jersey, and California, have chosen to protect the incumbents of both parties by reducing the number of competitive districts.

In 2004, the Supreme Court essentially ruled, in *Veith* v. *Jubelirer,* that elected officials have the right to choose their constituents, as partisan gerrymandering claims were unconstitutional because there was no discernible or manageable standard for "adjudicating political gerrymandering claims." Therefore, the majority of control of Congress is determined by a small number of competitive districts in a small number of states. So-called "safe" seats are also highly partisan because the only threat to incumbents is from a more extreme member of their party.

In 2013, the Supreme Court overturned a portion of the Voting Rights Act in *Shelby County* v. *Holder.* The court held that Section 4 of the Voting Rights Act imposes burdens that are no longer responsive to the current conditions in the voting districts in question. The court essentially argued that voting barriers African Americans historically faced in southern districts no longer existed and, therefore, the VRA infringes on state sovereignty to regulate elections.

Why People Vote the Way They Do

Most political scientists would agree that voters all consider the candidate they support to be the best one. But what influences their choice? How did they decide who to choose to be president in 2012? How will they choose in 2016? And how do they decide which candidate to support for Congress? A number of important factors inform voter choice.

Party identification provides a sense of how a candidate stands on various policies and issues, but the diverse factions that make up the major political parties are complex and often adversarial. This can be misleading as a candidate can have different viewpoints on certain issues that are important to the voter. Still, the party identity serves as an indication of where the candidate stands on most issues. The Democratic Party label, for example, alerts voters to policy solutions that usually involve government programs or regulations. The Republican Party label usually signifies a candidate's tendency to support more individual or local state choice and an opposition to public programs and the taxes to fund them.

ON THE RECORD

"Lincoln said you cannot be president without spending some item on your knees. I have repeated that and a bunch of atheists got all over me. ... Does that mean that you cannot be president if you are an atheist? I say yeah that does mean that."

—President George H. W. Bush

The personal qualities of a candidate play a significant role in how voters cast their ballots. Leadership qualities, as well as honesty and trustworthiness, have become increasingly important to voters as they consider whom to elect to the nation's highest office. In local elections, candidates must exhibit qualities that are consistent with a large majority of constituents.

American voters focus on many issues when deciding on a candidate, but with so many issues to confront, not every issue can be most prominent all the time. During times of war or international crisis, voters look for candidates who will project strength and keep the county safe. When the economy is weak or in decline, voters look for candidates who will best promote economic growth. Incumbent candidates always run, or are challenged, on their record. Challengers tend to focus on what they will do and propose policies that contrast with the incumbent.

Why People Do Not Vote

In the 2012 presidential election, an estimated 219 million people were eligible to vote. Only 126.1 million (57.5 percent) actually did. Why does this happen in the United States? That has been the subject of much study and debate.

People most likely to vote are usually of higher income, education, and occupational levels. They tend to be people who have lived in an area for a long time and are members of the community. They usually identify with a party and believe that voting is an important right. Women are more likely to vote than men. Nonvoters are likely to be under age 35, unmarried, and unskilled. More nonvoters live in the South and in rural areas than in suburban or urban areas.

Of the 95 million people of voting age in 2004, 10 million of them were resident aliens who are not permitted to vote. About 7 to 9 million Americans were ill, disabled, or traveling on Election Day and could not vote. Other people, some 100,000 in 2004, do not vote because their religion deems it equivalent to worshipping idols.

Even taking those groups into account, close to 80 million people could have voted but did not. They are referred to as nonvoters. Some of them feel that it makes little difference how they vote or who wins an election. People in this group are either satisfied with the way government is being managed and would be happy with either candidate, or are alienated by what they perceive as an untrustworthy political system. Another large group of nonvoters consists of people who do not have political efficacy, which means that they lack any feeling of influence or effectiveness in politics. They do not believe that they or their votes can have any effect on the government.

Other factors that affect turnout are election procedures like inconvenient registration requirements, long ballots, and long lines at the polls. Bad weather also decreases voter turnout. Long lines at the polls can be attributed to a number of factors. Many polling locations are simply not equipped to handle the volume of voters on Election Day—they do not have enough voting machines or poll workers, their machinery malfunctions, or they have issues with the paper or electronic ballots. Voters might also be unfamiliar with the voting process because it is their first time voting, or the technology might have changed.

Another notable fact is that, even among voters, there are nonvoters. That is, people who show up on Election Day do not always vote in every race on the ballot. This might be due to fatigue, as some ballots can be very long, or not enough knowledge about all the elections. Also, turnout is usually greater in presidential election years than in off year or midterm elections, when congressional, state, and local leaders are elected.

 MISINFORMATION

Not all American citizens over 18 can vote. People who have been convicted of a felony and people in prison or mental institutions do not have the right to vote. In the 2012 election, this accounted for about 5.8 million otherwise eligible voters.

Voters and Voter Behavior

Even though millions of people in the United States choose not to vote, millions more do. What makes them vote the way that they do? Most of what is known about voter behavior comes from the results of past elections, research and polls, and studies of political socialization. Political socialization is the process by which people acquire their political attitudes and opinions that continues throughout life.

 ON THE RECORD

"The ballot is stronger than the bullet."

—President Abraham Lincoln

There are both sociological and psychological factors that affect voter behavior. The sociological factors affecting voters' behavior are their personal characteristics and their group affiliations. Among these are age, race, income, occupation, education, religion, family, co-workers, and friends. The psychological factors that decide voter behavior include a voter's perception of politics. The ways a person views the political and economic system, the candidates, and the issues are very much a product of a person's sociological background.

Income and occupation   Voters in low income-tax brackets tend to vote for Democrats. Voters in higher income-tax brackets tend to vote for Republicans. Professional and business people, and others with higher incomes, also tend to vote for Republicans. Manual workers tend to vote for Democrats.

Education   College graduates vote for Republicans in higher percentages than do people who graduated high school. High school graduates also vote for Republicans in higher percentages than voters who graduated from middle school.

Gender   Men and women vote differently, a phenomenon known as the gender gap. Typically women tend to vote Democratic more than Republican, while men are more likely to vote for a Republican than a Democrat. Men and women are also more likely to differ on issues such as abortion, health care, and military actions abroad.

Age   Younger people tend to vote for Democrats and older people tend to vote for Republicans. This has held true in almost every presidential election except for Ronald Reagan in 1984 and George Bush in 1988.

Religious and ethnic background   Historically, Protestants have voted with the Republicans. Jews and Catholics have been more likely to vote Democrat. African Americans have historically supported the Democratic Party. Latinos, which includes people from Cuba, Mexico, Puerto Rico, and other Latin American countries, tend to show up in smaller numbers than African Americans. Mexican Americans and Puerto Ricans usually vote Democratic, while Cuban Americans tend to vote for Republicans.

Geography   Generally, the Democrats draw strength from the big cities in the Northeast and West Coast. Republican voters dominate the suburbs, rural areas, and the smaller cities of the south.

Family   Typically, members of a family vote similarly. Nine out of ten married couples identify with the same political party. Approximately two out of every three voters vote the same way as their parents.

Party identification   Party identification is the single most important predictor of how a person will vote. In recent years, split-ticket voting has increased, and there has also been a significant increase in the number of people who call themselves independents, not considered part of the Republican or Democratic Party.

Candidates and the issues   These are considered short-term issues. The impression that a candidate makes on the electorate is clearly a factor in how people will vote. The role that issues play also varies, depending on what issues are facing the United States at that time.

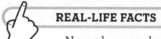

November was chosen as the month for elections in the United States because work on farms was completed by that time and farmers could vote. Tuesday was chosen because it allowed for a full day of travel between Sunday and voting day.

Other Forms of Political Participation

Voting is by far the most prevalent form of political participation. Donating money to a candidate and being a member of a political organization are other ways people are involved in the political process.

About 20 percent of the population is completely inactive in politics; that is, they do not vote, donate, get involved in organizations, or talk about politics very much. The opposite of this group is known as political activists. They make up approximately 11 percent of the population and participate in all forms of government.

In between these two groups are voting specialists, who vote but do little else. Campaigners are a type of political activist. They vote and get involved in campaign activities during election years. They tend to be better educated than the average voter and have a strong party identification and desire to defend their party's beliefs.

Communalists are similar to campaigners in social background, but reserve their passions for more nonpartisan causes such as organizations that deal with community issues. Finally, parochial participants are members of the population who do not vote or participate in organizations but are willing to contact local government officials regarding specific issues.

The Least You Need to Know

- The right to vote has been a struggle for many groups of people including African Americans and women, most importantly.
- The Constitution allows for states to control the voter qualifications, which include American citizenship, residence in a particular state, and age of 18 years or older.
- The most important factors are party identification, the candidates, and the issues at stake in the election. These factors often trump economic or social status.
- There are millions of nonvoters in the United States. Most of these people don't vote because they don't believe their vote has any significant impact on the government.
- Political participation is most commonly achieved by voting, but can also include donating to campaigns and being a member of a political organization.

The Legislative Branch

The Congress of the United States is made up of the House of Representatives and the Senate. The House and Senate are organized into various committees and caucuses that focus on different issues such as the budget and national defense. The founders thought the Congress to be of paramount importance in our government structure.

Every year, thousands of measures, or bills, are introduced in the House of Representatives and the Senate, yet fewer than 10 percent typically become laws. Where do all these bills come from? Why are so few passed into law? What is the process to create laws? The basic steps in the lawmaking process are the same, but there are some critical differences.

Congress

We are a representative democracy. In the United States, the elected representatives and their appointees handle the day-to-day business of government. The U.S. Congress is the leading example of our form of government. It is the legislative branch of the national government.

In This Chapter

- The role of Congress in democracy
- How Congress has changed
- The scope of congressional powers
- Congress's expressed and implied powers
- The nonlegislative powers of Congress

The National Legislature

The framers clearly intended for Congress to have the paramount function in our government because they made the first, and the longest, of the articles establishing our government about the legislative branch. Article I, Section 1 of the Constitution reads:

> "All legislative powers herein granted shall be vested in a Congress of the United States, which shall consist of a Senate and House of Representatives."

The Constitution established a bicameral legislature to enact the laws of the land.

Bicameralism

Bicameralism—a legislature made up of two houses—was very familiar to the founders. The British Parliament had been a two-house legislature since the early 1300s. In the U.S. colonies, most of the legislatures were bicameral. So it appears logical in hindsight that the founders would decide on a bicameral legislature for the national government. Also, bicameralism embodies the ideals of federalism. Each of the states is represented equally in the Senate and proportionately in the House. Also, each house of Congress acts as a check on the other, an important underpinning of our checks-and-balances system.

Terms and Sessions of Congress

Each term of Congress lasts for two years and is numbered consecutively. Currently, every term of Congress starts and ends on January 3 after the November elections every two years. There are two sessions in each term, each for one year. Congress can adjourn as it sees fit after its business is completed. Congress can also meet in special session. This is a special meeting called by the president to deal with a pressing problem.

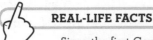

REAL-LIFE FACTS

Since the first Congress, 27 special sessions have been held. The last was called by President Truman in 1948 to deal with economic measures.

The Evolution of Congress

The founders placed the legislative powers of government in the hands of Congress. The Great Compromise struck a deal between the interests of the small states and the large states by creating a bicameral legislature. The House of Representatives is based on population while the

Senate gives the states equal representation. Although Congress is given primacy in legislative matters, laws that it passes are signed by the president and must withstand Supreme Court review if challenged.

Congress has gone through several periods of important change. Sometimes the leadership in Congress is so strong that individual member interests are overwhelmed. This is generally when congressional power is mostly centralized. During other periods in congressional history, the power has been mostly decentralized.

Evolution of the House

The House of Representatives has always been a powerful government institution and has changed more than the Senate in the way it is organized and led. The House faces some fundamental challenges because it is both big and powerful. The House currently has 435 members and its members want to be powerful as individuals and as a group. The problem has been finding a balance between these two goals.

The historical shifts in power in the House of Representatives can best be summarized as follows:

The powerful house   During the first three administrations, the House was the dominant institution of the legislature and of government.

The divided house   From the 1820s to the post–Civil War era, the rise of powerful presidents and the issue of slavery diminished the power of the House. It lacked clear leadership during this period.

The speaker rules   From the late 1880s to early twentieth century, powerful Republican speakers and chairmen ruled the House with a near iron fist.

The house revolts   From the 1920s to the 1960s, the speaker lost many of his powers as party caucuses gained strength.

Members rule   During the 1960s to 1980s, power was decentralized further from committee chairmen to members. Chairmen were no longer selected on seniority basis. Individual members were given larger staffs.

Leadership returns   1990s to the present. With the Republican takeover of the House in 1994, power reverts back to speaker and committee chairs.

Although the Democrats controlled the House from 2007 to 2011, the structure and power in the House of Representatives has remained the same since 1994. With the election of Paul Ryan as speaker in 2015, it remains to be seen if more power will be given to members or remain in the hands of the leadership.

Evolution of the Senate

The Senate does not face the same power dilemma as the House. Because it only has 100 members, it can run effectively without having to give too much power to the leaders or any group within the institution. Also, until the twentieth century, senators were elected by their state legislatures, so they were not directly accountable to the voting public. Instead, they owed their ability to serve to state party organizations that were mostly interested in getting Washington to send money for local jobs and other economic development projects. In 1913, the Seventeenth Amendment to the Constitution was passed, changing the way senators were elected. Since then, all members of the Senate are selected through popular elections.

Another issue that should be highlighted in the development of the Senate is the filibuster. Senators have almost unrestricted speaking rights, and a filibuster is a prolonged speech or series of speeches made to delay or obstruct Senate action. It had become a common feature in the Senate by the late 1800s. Several attempts to restrict the filibuster have been proposed, but ultimately they all fail.

According to a 2003 report for Congress, Senate Rule XXII, the rule to end speeches and debate known as the cloture rule, enables senators to end a filibuster. In order for a cloture measure to take effect, a minimum of 16 senators must petition to end debate. Once a motion is made to end debate, the Senate must wait one extra day before voting on the matter. An affirmative vote from at least 60 senators is needed to invoke cloture. Today, even the threat of a filibuster by a senator can essentially prevent a bill from coming to the floor for a vote.

 REAL-LIFE FACTS

Filibusters were sixteenth-century English and French pirates who raided Spanish treasure ships. The term originates from the Dutch word *vrijbuiter,* meaning "freebooter."

The Limits of Congressional Power

Although Congress is in session most of the year, there are very real limits on what Congress can do. The U.S. Constitution is a framework for limited government, and the federal system divides responsibilities between the national government and the states. The Constitution places real limits on the federal government and on Congress.

Many areas of power are denied to Congress because the Constitution is silent on these matters. For example, the Constitution does not give the national government or Congress the power to create public schools, determine the age for drivers licenses, criteria for marriage licenses, and many other things. Congress does, however, have the power to do many things, specifically in three different ways:

- The expressed powers, those powers given it expressly in the Constitution

- The implied powers, those powers inferred by the expressed powers

- The inherent powers, those powers bestowed to it as the national government

As you have already read, the debate over the role and power of the national government is as old as the republic itself. The conflict between the Federalists and the Anti-Federalists in the early years is mirrored today by the debate among strict and liberal constructionists. The strict constructionists argue that Congress should only exercise its expressed powers and those implied powers necessary to carry out the expressed powers. They want the sovereign states to retain all other government powers.

Liberal constructionists favor a broad interpretation of the Constitution and a broad interpretation of the powers given to Congress. Over time, liberal constructionists have succeeded, because the growth of the federal government has advanced tremendously, particularly in areas of transportation and communication. Also, the demand for more from the national government, as well as the current security demands of most people, has contributed to the growth of federal power and authority.

The Expressed Powers

Congress is given 27 explicit powers in 18 separate clauses in Article I, Section 8 of the U.S. Constitution. The Constitution is rather brief in the description of these powers, however. The power Congress has exercised has developed over time and has given rise to many Supreme Court cases.

The third clause, also known as the Commerce Clause, gives Congress the power to regulate commerce with foreign countries, among the states, and with Native American tribes. This clause alone has resulted in profound debates in our nation's history. The words are brief, but broad in scope. What is the meaning of *commerce?* Does it include all means of transportation? Can Congress regulate banks? What about airwaves? The nation is still debating the meaning of this clause, and Congress and the Courts are still developing a meaning of commerce. Some argue that this is the strongest case that our Constitution is a living document for our times.

The language the founders used in the Constitution allows courts today to interpret the powers of government so that Congress can act with relevance and still maintain the principle of limited government.

The Power to Tax

Taxes are charges levied on people, businesses, and property by government to meet public needs. Congress is given this authority in Article I, Section 8, Clause 1. However, it is not without limits. Congress may not tax churches and exports.

The Power to Borrow

Congress has the power to borrow money to finance projects or government expenses that cannot be paid from current revenues. This is also known as *deficit spending.*

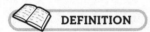

Deficit spending is when government spends more than it takes in each year, and it borrows to make up the difference. The accumulating amount borrowed is the national debt.

The Commerce Power

The power to regulate interstate and foreign commerce is one of the most powerful tools given to Congress. This power made it possible for the government to build a strong union of states. It is largely from this power that the national government has built all of its implied powers. Congress cannot, however, tax exports, or favor the port of one over another when regulating trade.

The Power to Print and Coin Money

The Constitution gives Congress the power "to coin money and regulate the value thereof." Only the national government has this power. The responsibility of providing the nation with a single, stable money system is one of the most important powers granted to Congress.

Bankruptcy Law Powers

Congress has the power to establish the laws governing *bankruptcies.* A bankrupt individual or business is unable to pay his or her debts in full.

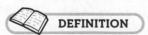

Bankruptcy is the legal proceeding in which the bankrupt's assets are distributed among the individuals or businesses to which a debt is owed.

Foreign Relations Powers

The Constitution grants the federal government more powers in the area of foreign relations. Congress shares these powers with the president. The states are forbidden from taking part in foreign relations. Only the federal government can enter into treaties with other nations. Congress can regulate foreign commerce. Security and economic alliances are negotiated by the president and must be approved by Congress.

War Powers

In Article I, Section 8, Congress is given eight expressed powers that deal with war and national defense. In these areas, Congress also shares its powers with the president. Only Congress may declare war, yet the president is the commander in chief. Only Congress has the authority to fund war efforts and our armed forces. Starting in 1973, with the passage of the War Powers Resolution, Congress claimed the power to restrict the president in combat where a state of war does not exist. However, this has been difficult for Congress to enforce in practical terms.

Once Congress has authorized the president to act militarily, it is very difficult for Congress to cut off troops to support the war effort they previously authorized, such as in Vietnam and in Iraq. The U.S. Congress passed the Gulf of Tonkin Resolution on August 10, 1964, in direct response to a minor naval engagement known as the Gulf of Tonkin Incident. It is of historical significance because it gave President Lyndon B. Johnson authorization for the use of military force in Southeast Asia without a formal declaration of war by Congress. The Johnson administration subsequently cited the resolution as legal authority for its rapid escalation of U.S. military involvement in the Vietnam conflict.

 REAL-LIFE FACTS

The first treaty of the new nation under the Constitution, the Jay Treaty, also known as the Treaty of London of 1794, between the United States and Great Britain, averted war, solved many issues left over from the American Revolution, and opened 10 years of largely peaceful trade.

In response to the perceived notion that Iraq was concealing and developing weapons of mass destruction, the U.S. Congress passed a joint resolution authorizing force against Iraq in October 2002. This law authorized the president to use force "as he determines to be necessary and appropriate" in order to "defend the national security of the United States against the continuing threat posed by Iraq; and enforce all relevant United Nations Security Council Resolutions regarding Iraq."

Naturalization Powers

Naturalization is the process by which immigrants become citizens of the United States. You will read more about this in the chapter on civil rights. Only Congress has the power "to establish a uniform rule of naturalization," as stated in Article I, Section 8, Clause 4 of the Constitution.

Postal Powers

Article I, Section 8, Clause 7 gives Congress the exclusive authority to "establish post office and post roads." This power gives the federal government jurisdiction over mail delivery and costs, as well as the authority to prevent the use of mail for fraud or other illegal activities.

Copyright and Patent Powers

In Article I, Section 8, Clause 8, Congress has the power "to promote the progress of science and useful arts, by securing, for limited times, to authors and inventors, the exclusive right to their respective writings and discoveries." A copyright is the exclusive right of ownership of an author of a creative work. A patent gives ownership over the production or use of a machine.

Copyrights are good for the life of the author plus 50 years. At that time, the copyright expires. Patents are generally good for 17 years and can be renewed indefinitely.

Weights and Measures Power

Congress has the power to establish the standards of weights and measures throughout the United States according to Article I, Section 8, Clause 5 of the Constitution. Congress established the National Institute of Standards and Technology to maintain and test all measures in the United States.

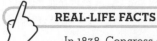

REAL-LIFE FACTS

In 1838, Congress established the English system of measurement that includes pound, ounce, mile, foot, gallon, etc. In 1866, Congress also legalized the metric system.

Territorial Powers

Congress has jurisdiction in federal areas that are not part of the states. These areas include the District of Columbia, Puerto Rico, Guam, and the U.S. Virgin Islands. It also covers all military and naval installations, post offices, and federal parks. Congress may also acquire lands by admitting new states, purchasing lands from foreign states, or by discovery of unclaimed territory.

Eminent Domain

Congress may exercise the right of eminent domain—the inherent power to take private property for public use. Although highly controversial, this power has allowed Congress to implement national programs, such as the Interstate Highway System. States also have the power of eminent domain within their jurisdiction.

Judicial Powers

Article I, Section 8, Clause 9 gives Congress the power to establish all federal courts inferior to the Supreme Court. This is an important aspect of the principle of checks and balances that underlies the U.S. Constitution. Congress also has the authority to define federal crimes and provide for guidelines and mandates for punishment for those found guilty of federal offenses.

The Implied Powers

The Constitution grants Congress many important expressed powers. The Constitution also gives Congress a number of important powers that are not outlined specifically but are covered in one of the most important clauses of Article I, Section 8. Clause 18 gives to Congress the power "to make all laws which shall be necessary and proper for carrying into execution the foregoing powers, and all other powers vested by this Constitution in the Government of the United States, or in any department or officer thereof."

Many of the expansive powers assumed by the federal government can be traced directly to this clause. Both Congress and the Supreme Court have relied heavily on a far-reaching interpretation of this clause to interpret laws and decide cases. The necessary and proper clause is often referred to as the "Elastic Clause" because it has been stretched very far over many years.

Today, the necessary and proper clause is, practically speaking, the "convenient and useful" clause. Still, the federal government does not have blanket authority to do anything it deems desirable or preferred in order "to promote the general welfare." The implied powers of Congress must be drawn from the expressed powers:

- The power to establish the Federal Reserve System is drawn from the expressed power to borrow money.

- The power to make tax evasion a crime is based on the taxing authority the Constitution grants Congress.

- The power to establish federal aid programs is implied from the commerce power of Congress.

- The power to draft citizens into the military is based on the power of Congress to raise armies and a navy.

- The power to establish the minimum wage is based on the commerce clause.

The Nonlegislative Powers

Congress performs a number of functions that are beyond its legislative mandate. Some of these functions are purely political. Individual members of Congress are expected to act as intermediaries between their constituents and the federal government. Members of Congress and their staffs spend a considerable portion of their time providing service to the voters back home, including resolving matters with the Social Security Administration, promoting local business initiatives, or interceding with an agency on behalf of a constituent.

Senators and representatives benefit in elections when they are seen as advocates for the people whom they represent and maximize opportunities for the communities that send them to Congress. Still, other nonlegislative functions are enumerated specifically in the Constitution.

Constitutional Amendments

Congress plays a key role in the process of amending the Constitution. Congress can propose an amendment to the Constitution by a two-thirds vote in each house. Congress can also call a national convention to propose an amendment.

Electoral Duties

Congress has several very important electoral duties to perform, but only in very rare and special circumstances. If no single candidate receives a majority of votes in the electoral college, the House of Representatives is called to elect the president. The House of Representatives, voting by states, must decide the issue.

Similarly, the Senate must choose a vice president. In the case of the election of the vice president, the vote is not by state but rather by individual senator.

 MISINFORMATION

Although Congress is the national legislature, it cannot amend the Constitution on its own without ratification by three-quarters of the states' legislatures.

Impeachment and Removal from Office

The Constitution gives the House of Representatives the sole power to impeach—or bring charges against—the president, the vice president, and all civil officers of the United States for "treason, bribery, or other high crimes and misdemeanors." The Senate has the sole authority to conduct a trial and convict or acquit.

The Chief Justice of the Supreme Court must preside over the trial in the Senate for the removal of the president. The House can impeach—or press charges—with a majority vote. The Senate, however, needs a two-thirds vote to convict and remove an official from office.

 REAL-LIFE FACTS

Only two presidents have been formally impeached by the House of Representatives: Andrew Johnson (1865-1869) and William Jefferson Clinton (1993-2001). Neither was convicted by the Senate or removed from office.

Executive Powers

The Constitution gives two executive powers exclusively to the Senate. This is commonly referred to as the "advice and consent" function of the Senate. The president makes many appointments that require Senate approval:

- Secretaries of the 15 Cabinet agencies, deputy secretaries, undersecretaries and assistant secretaries, and general counsels of those agencies: more than 350 positions

- Certain jobs in the independent, nonregulatory, executive-branch agencies, like NASA and the National Science Foundation: about 120 positions

- Director positions in the regulatory agencies, like the Environmental Protection Agency and the Federal Aviation Administration: 130 positions

- U.S. attorneys and marshals: about 200 positions

- Ambassadors to foreign nations: 150 positions

- Presidential appointments to part-time positions, such as the Board of Governors of the Federal Reserve System: 160 positions

Additionally, the president can negotiate a treaty, but it must then be approved by two-thirds of the Senate.

The People's Investigator

Congress has the power to investigate any matter that falls within its jurisdiction. These inquiries are generally held for the following reasons:

- To gather information useful for upcoming legislation

- To promote particular interests of Congress

- To oversee various operations of the executive and judicial branches

- To focus public attention on a pressing matter

- To expose the questionable or illegal activities of public officials or private persons

Congressional hearings have resulted in some of the most dramatic and colorful moments in American political history.

 ON THE RECORD

"My faith in the Constitution is whole, it is complete, it is total. I am not going to sit here and be an idle spectator to the diminution, the subversion, the destruction of the Constitution."

—Congresswoman Barbara Jordan (D-TX) during the House Judiciary Committee hearings to impeach President Richard M. Nixon

The Least You Need to Know

- The Constitution grants to Congress a large number of specific powers called the expressed powers.

- Besides the powers expressly given to Congress in the Constitution, Congress has the power to make laws "necessary and proper" to execute its expressed powers. This is known as the elastic clause.

- Congress has several important nonlegislative functions, including electing a president and vice president in the event of a tie in the Electoral College. Congress may also impeach and conduct a trial to remove from office the president, vice president, and other important federal officials.

- The Senate has the power to accept or reject presidential appointees and treaties negotiated by the executive.

CHAPTER 10

The House of Representatives

The House of Representatives is the larger of the two chambers of Congress. It is currently comprised of 435 voting members. The entire membership of the House is up for election every two years. The House is the more partisan chamber. The members are elected from smaller districts whose citizens generally are demographically similar. The two-year term means members are more immediately accountable to the electorate than senators, who serve six years, or the president, who serves four. The House is organized by a complex system of committees and caucuses to conduct the business of the nation. The leader of the House is called the Speaker of the House, and is elected by its members.

In This Chapter

- The historical legacy and exclusive powers of the House
- Terms and qualifications to serve in the House
- Party politics and leadership in the House
- The role of committees and caucuses
- The role of staff agencies

Legacy and Unique Aspects

The House of Representatives is often considered to be the "lower house" of Congress. This notion stems from James Madison's Virginia Plan, which called for a bicameral Congress with a lower house that would be "of the people," elected directly by the people of the United States and, therefore, more closely representing public opinion. The number of representatives from each state is chosen based on population, while each state is represented in the Senate by an equal amount of senators.

Although the main function of the House of Representatives is to put forth legislation, it also holds three exclusive powers: the power to initiate revenue bills, impeach officials, and elect the president in an Electoral College deadlock.

The Distribution of Representatives

Each state receives representation based on its population but is entitled to at least one representative. The total number of representatives is not defined by the Constitution; rather, Congress sets it. A particular number of representatives is delegated to each state according to its share of the national population, which is determined by a census every 10 years. The District of Columbia, Guam, the Virgin Islands, Puerto Rico, and American Samoa each elect an official to represent them in the House. These delegates participate in debate and vote in committees but cannot vote when their votes would be decisive.

REAL-LIFE FACTS

The Three-Fifths Compromise was a movement by slave-holding states to count three-fifths of the slave population in their overall population to increase their voting power in the House.

Malapportionment and Gerrymandering

States are divided into districts that then elect members to represent them in the House. Some states are proportionately entitled to only one representative. States that have more than one district may construct the districts proportionate to the population. The individual state legislatures are responsible for this task. *Malapportionment* is unconstitutional, and districts must have approximately the same number of constituents. States may only redistrict every 10 years, after the U.S. Census has been conducted.

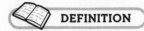

DEFINITION

Malapportionment is drawing the boundaries of political districts so that districts are very unequal in population.

Gerrymandering refers to when district lines are manipulated for political advantage. The Voting Rights Act was passed to prohibit states from gerrymandering districts to decrease racial minorities' voting power. Gerrymandering's goal is to create as many "safe districts" for the party in power as possible in order to maximize that party's number of representatives in the House.

REAL-LIFE FACTS

In 2003, Representative Tom DeLay of Texas spearheaded a mid-census redistricting effort in order to gain more Republican seats in the state legislature. This was considered controversial, and in 2006, the Supreme Court issued an opinion that upheld all the redistricting except for one district that was found to be egregiously and noncontiguously drawn in violation of the Voting Rights Act.

Power to Elect the President

If no presidential candidate receives a majority vote in the Electoral College, the House of Representatives has the power to elect the president. This power and procedure is described in the Twelfth Amendment. The House of Representatives has twice elected the President of the United States. The first time was in 1800, when a tie in the Electoral College between Thomas Jefferson and Aaron Burr resulted in 35 ballots before Jefferson was elected the third president. The second time was in 1824, when there were 10 candidates for president. The House selected John Quincy Adams over the first place popular vote winner Andrew Jackson.

Power of Impeachment

The Constitution empowers the House to impeach federal officials for "treason, bribery, or other high crimes and misdemeanors." The House may approve impeachments by a majority vote.

MISINFORMATION

Many people think Richard Nixon was impeached, but in fact, he resigned prior to the House vote on the Judiciary Committee's articles of impeachment against him.

Power to Initiate Revenue Bills

The Constitution states that "all bills for raising revenue shall originate in the House of Representatives." Therefore, any laws relating to taxes originate in the House. The Senate can amend these bills before it decides to pass the bill.

Qualifications of Members

The Constitution states that a member of the House must be at least 25 years of age, have been a U.S. citizen for at least 7 years, and live in the state that he or she represents.

The House is the "judge" of its own members, meaning that it has the power to refuse to seat a member-elect by majority vote. Historically, the House has used this power to impose additional standards on its members. For example, the House refused to seat Brigham H. Roberts of Utah in 1900 because he was a polygamist. A Supreme Court decision in 1969 ruled that the House must seat any elected official who meets the three criteria set forth by the Constitution.

Elections are held every even-numbered year on the Tuesday after the first Monday of November. Off-year elections are those congressional elections that occur in the nonpresidential election years. Representatives and delegates serve two-year terms. There are no term limits described in the Constitution.

Compensation and Privileges

The Constitution allows for Congress to decide its own salary. The current salary for both senators and representatives is $174,000. The Speaker of the House earns $223,500 and majority and minority leaders earn $193,400. Representatives are also eligible for lifetime benefits after serving for five years, including a pension, health benefits, and Social Security benefits.

Representatives receive a number of fringe benefits. Each member gets a special tax deduction designed to compensate for the maintenance of a residence in Washington, D.C., and one in their home constituency. They are given an office in the Capitol building and funds for hiring a staff. The franking privilege allows them to mail letters and other materials postage-free. They are also given generous travel allowances. To circumvent the president's veto power and public scrutiny, instead of increasing their salary, members of Congress will vote on providing extra fringe benefits. The president is less likely to veto these types of changes to members of Congress's benefit plans as they are often financed by various sources (such as lobbyists and other interest groups) and not taxpayer money.

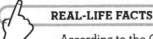

REAL-LIFE FACTS

According to the Congressional Research Service, franking privileges of House members cost the American taxpayers $6.2 million in 2014.

Members of Congress have certain privileges outlined by the Constitution. They cannot be arrested (except for treason, felony, or breach of peace) while they are attending, going to, or returning from Congress. The speech or debate clause also protects representatives and senators from suits for libel or slander originating from a speech or their work done in floor debate or in committee. This was designed to limit the restraint members of Congress might feel when discussing certain controversial issues.

Party Structure of the House

The House is made up of a majority and minority party. Because the United States is a two party political system, the Democrats and the Republicans are always either in control or in opposition. The majority party controls who will serve as the speaker and assigns the committee chair roles. Every Speaker of the House has been a member of the majority party in power. The role of the speaker is not spelled out in the Constitution. Rather, it has evolved through years of practices and traditions.

The Speaker of the House

Nearly all of the speaker's powers are centered on two duties: to lead and keep order. The speaker directs discussion on the floor of the House by choosing the order in which members of the House speak. The speaker also appoints other presiding officers to debates in the House.

ON THE RECORD

"I had set out to do a very unusual job, part revolutionary, part national political figure, part speaker, part intellectual."

—Republican Representative Newt Gingrich

The Speaker of the House wields extraordinary powers:

- The power to select which members will serve as chairs of the various steering committees

- The power to appoint the majority party's steering committee

- The power to appoint a majority of the members to the Rules Committee

- The power to appoint all members of conference committees

The speaker is the de facto head of his or her party in the House of Representatives. The speaker is second in the line of succession to the presidency after the vice president. No speaker has ever succeeded to the presidency, although James Polk is the only former speaker to later win election as president.

REAL-LIFE FACTS

Nancy Pelosi, Democratic representative from California, was elected the first female Speaker of the House in the 110th Congress on January 4, 2007. Pelosi served until 2011, when the speaker role reverted to the GOP after the 2010 election.

Other House Officers

The House has several important officers called floor leaders elected along party lines. The majority leader is the floor leader of the controlling party and the minority leader is the floor leader of the opposition party. The minority leader is the highest-ranking official of the minority party, while the majority leader is number two, after the speaker, for the majority party.

Each party also elects a whip, who works closely with the leaders to gather votes for particular pieces of legislation. Representatives usually vote as their leaders decide because it is those same leaders who choose the committee chairmen, a position many representatives seek. Because members of Congress tend to vote along party lines, it is essential that a majority of the quorum is present to vote on a given day in order to express the power of being the majority party in Congress. The whip is responsible for making sure that this happens on votes for important and controversial issues, such as economic policies. A whip in the U.S. House of Representatives manages his or her party's legislative program on the House floor. The whip keeps track of all legislation and ensures that all party members are present when important measures are voted upon.

Committees in the House of Representatives

The most important organizational feature of the legislative branch is the committee structure of Congress. Committees are where the real work of proposing and working out the details of bills happens. The chairmanship of these committees (held and selected by the majority party) and their subcommittees is where most of the power in Congress lies. The number and authority of these committees are of the greatest concern to members of Congress. Because committees are organized around certain issues, the members who sit on a committee get to deliberate legislative proposals, review the workings of agencies of the executive branch, and direct investigations.

Although the members of the majority party could occupy all the seats of the committees, usually the ratio of Democrats to Republicans corresponds to the ratio in the House as a whole. On occasion, the majority party will try to take extra seats on the more important committees such as the Appropriations or Ways and Means Committees. Chairmen traditionally dominated the committees and often did most of their work behind closed doors. Over the years, the House has set some rules in order to democratize the system. These changes were made by the Democratic caucus and are regarded as a "bill of rights" for representatives, especially those with little or no seniority. These rules include:

- Committee chairmen are to be elected by secret ballot in party caucus.

- A member can chair only one committee.

- All committees with more than 20 members must have at least 4 subcommittees.

- Committee meetings are to be public unless the members agree to close them.

These changes gave greater power to individual members of the House and lessened the power of the party leaders and chairmen. This "decentralization" made it much harder for chairmen to block legislation they did not approve. It also made way for much more debate and amendments to legislation. But these changes also made it harder for business to get done in the House. Many times only one person, the chairman, attended subcommittee meetings. To regain some order, Democrats began to limit debate and amendments. Committee chairmen began casting proxy votes, which are written authorizations to cast another person's vote. In this way, chairmen could once again control the results of committee deliberations.

When Republicans took control of the House in 1995, they announced some changes to the rules. They banned proxy voting. They limited committee and subcommittee chairmen's tenure to three terms and the speaker's to four terms. They allowed more frequent floor debate under open rules. They reduced the number of committees and subcommittees.

More open meetings and easy amending processes may have opened up the system to individuals, but the real beneficiaries are lobbyists. When the House operates under closed rules and powerful chairmen, it is easier for it to get business done. These rules put the House in a favorable bargaining position with the Senate and president. It also makes it easier to reduce the number of special interest groups with legislative influence. But it keeps the individual members of the House weak. The endless arguments about the rules illustrate a fundamental problem that the House faces and underlines the importance and power of partisan politics in Congress.

"Congress in session is Congress on display. Congress in committee is Congress at work."

—President Woodrow Wilson

Standing Committees

Standing committees are permanent bodies with specified legislative responsibilities. A list of the standing committees is provided in a later section. The most important standing committees are the Rules and the Ways and Means committees for the work they do in controlling the inner workings of the House itself.

The Rules Committee

The House Rules Committee controls the time of floor debate for a particular bill and limits the amount of amendments on that bill. The members decide whether a bill will go by *closed rule* or *open rule*. By refusing to grant a rule, which describes the parameters of a debate, the Rules Committee can delay the consideration of a bill. The Rules Committee also has the unusual power to meet while the House is in session, to have its own resolutions reviewed immediately on the floor, and to institute legislation on its own.

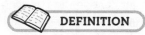

DEFINITION

A **closed rule** prohibits amendments of a bill or permits only members of the committee reporting the bill to make changes. This usually occurs with tax and spending bills. On the other hand, an **open rule** permits amendments within the time allotted to the bill.

The Ways and Means Committee

The Ways and Means Committee is the primary tax-writing committee in the House. The committee has control over all taxation and social programs such as Social Security and Medicare. Before the official roles as floor leader were established, the chairman of Ways and Means was considered the majority leader.

Standing Committees of the House of Representatives

Exclusive Standing Committees (Members may not serve on any other committee except Budget.)

Appropriations

Rules

Ways and Means

Major Committees (Members may only serve on one.)

Agriculture

Armed Services

Education and the Workforce

Energy and Commerce

Financial Services

International Relations

Judiciary

Transportation and Infrastructure

Nonmajor Committees (Members may serve on either one Major and one Nonmajor committee or two Nonmajor committees.)

Budget

Government Reform

House Administration

Resources

Science

Small Business

Standards of Official Conduct

Veterans Affairs

Select Committees

Select committees are groups appointed for a limited purpose and usually lasting for only a few sessions of Congress. They rarely create any original legislation.

Joint Committees

Joint committees are those on which both representatives and senators serve. An especially important kind of joint committee is the conference committee, made up of representatives and senators appointed to resolve differences in the Senate and House versions of the same bill prior to final passage.

Caucuses

A caucus is a group of members of Congress that meets to pursue a shared legislative interest. There are the broad Democratic and Republican caucuses, but there are also more focused caucuses that can be bipartisan or even contain members of both the House and Senate.

Some examples include the Congressional Black Caucus, the Liberty Caucus, the Congressional Human Rights Caucus, and the Congressional Climate Caucus. The diversity of these caucuses also demonstrates the fragmentation of interest groups, as there is a caucus for nearly every business and public interest issue.

Staff Agencies

In addition to increasing the number of staff members, Congress has also created a set of staff agencies that work for Congress as a whole. The Congressional Research Service (CRS) is part of the Library of Congress. As a politically neutral organization, it does not endorse policy but it will look up facts and indicate the arguments for and against a piece of legislation. CRS also keeps track of the major bills and summarizes them. This information is available to members of Congress digitally at their offices in the Capitol. This agency employs approximately 900 people and responds to about a quarter of a million inquiries per year.

The General Accounting Office (GAO) performs audits of money spent in the executive branch. It also investigates agencies and policies. The head of the GAO is called the Comptroller General and is appointed by the president. The Comptroller General serves a 15-year term. The GAO employs about 5,000 people who work with various congressional committees.

The Congressional Budget Office (CBO) advises Congress on the likely economic effects of different spending programs and provides information on the costs of proposed policies. This office prepares analyses of the presidential budget and other programs that are sometimes different from the administration, opening up more topics for debate on the House floor.

The Least You Need to Know

- The House of Representatives has distinct constitutional roles including the power to initiate revenue bills, to elect the president in a tie, and the power to impeach federal officials.

- The House of Representatives is organized into committees. The highest-ranking official is the Speaker of the House, followed by the majority and minority leaders.

- The most important standing committees are the Rules and Ways and Means committees. The chairmen of these committees have a powerful role in controlling which bills are voted on and how Congress will spend money.

- Caucuses are informal committees centered on a specific issue or commonality. Members can be of either party or either house of Congress.

- Congress employs special staff agencies that have many important functions, including auditing the finances of the executive branch and providing economic analysis on the federal budget and spending laws.

The Senate

The Senate is generally referred to as the "upper" house of Congress. It has this unique and elite distinction because of the patrician history associated with the chamber. Nearly one third of all senators once served in the House of Representatives—however, no one in the House has ever served in the Senate. House members generally look forward to the day when they can join the exclusive club of 100 senators.

In This Chapter

- The Senate's historical legacy and distinctiveness
- Terms and qualifications to serve in the Senate
- Party organization and leadership in the Senate
- The role and importance of committees in the Senate
- The role of caucuses

Legacy and Uniqueness

The Constitution says that the Senate must be comprised of two senators from every state. When the first session of Congress first opened in March 1789, there were only 22 senators. By the end of that session of Congress, all 13 states had representation in the Senate for a total of 26 senators. Today, the Senate is comprised of 100 members, two from each of the 50 states.

For the first nearly 125 years, senators were chosen by state legislatures. However, in 1913 the Seventeenth Amendment was ratified, changing the way senators were selected. Since then, senators have been elected by voters in each state in November elections. Every two years, one third of the Senate seats are up for election. Two thirds of the Senate remains intact in every election, unlike the full body of the House, which is up for election every two years. In this way the Senate is referred to as a continuous body. Senators have larger constituencies than their House counterparts since they are elected by voters from the entire state. Also, senators tend to be older than representatives.

 ON THE RECORD

"He took pride in belonging to the world's most exclusive club: the United States Senate."

—Margaret Truman, referring to her father, Harry Truman, senator from Missouri and thirty-third president of the United States

The Senate is given the responsibility of "advice and consent." In addition, the Senate has several exclusive powers within the legislative branch that include the consent and ratification of treaties entered into by the United States, and consenting to appointments made by the president. The appointments include nominees to the various cabinet positions, executive branch agency leaders, and federal judges and Supreme Court justices.

Individual senators who object to a measure being considered can prevent it from reaching the floor for a full vote by placing a hold on it. A hold is essentially the veto power every senator has to block legislation.

Speech in the Senate among members is very formal. Anyone who takes the floor to speak must address themselves to the presiding officer of the session. Presiding officers are always called "Mr. President" or "Madam President." Members are required to refer to colleagues in the third person and never directly by name. The tradition is to refer to a colleague by the state they represent and by their rank. For example, Senator Schumer would be referred to as "the senior senator from New York."

Senators can defeat legislation through the use of the filibuster. The filibuster allows senators to talk a bill to death by debating without end; however, Senate culture has evolved such that currently the mere threat of a filibuster can essentially kill any legislation that does not have the support of at least 60 members. A filibuster can only be halted by invoking cloture, the rule to end debate and bring a matter to the floor for a vote. Cloture requires a three-fifths vote, or 60 votes.

Terms and Qualifications of Members

Each senator is elected to a six-year term. In the event a senator cannot complete his or her term in office, the governor of the senator's home state shall appoint someone to fill the term. Senators are elected for terms three times longer than their counterparts in the House. The founders intended for the Senate to be less subject to public pressure and special interests. Since senators are not up for election every two years, they are intended to focus more on the national interest than on local interests. Indeed, senators are more likely to be viewed as national leaders than their counterparts in the House, with the exception of the speaker.

In order to be elected to the Senate, an individual must meet higher qualifications than those running for the House of Representatives. A senator must be at least 30 years old when they are sworn in. A senator must also have been a U.S. citizen for at least nine years. A senator must be a resident of the state from which he or she is elected. The Senate may judge the qualifications of a member-elect, and by majority vote may exclude the person. The Senate may also punish a member for disorderly conduct by majority vote, and with a two-thirds vote, expel the member from the Senate.

REAL-LIFE FACTS

Fifteen members of the Senate have been expelled since the founding of the republic: 1 in 1797 and 14 during the Civil War, all from the Confederate States.

Compensation and Privileges

The Constitution gives Congress the power to set its own pay and benefits package. Currently senators are paid the equivalent of their House counterparts: $174,000 per year. The president pro tempore of the Senate, the Senate majority leader, and the Senate minority leader each earn $193,400 per year. In addition to salaries, members of the Senate, along with their House counterparts, receive many special benefits. Senators are allowed a tax deduction to help keep up two residences, one in Washington, D.C., and another in their home state. Senators are given very generous travel allowances to cover the costs of round trips between their home state and the

Senate. Additionally, members of Congress have among the best health-care and life insurance coverage in the nation. The average retirement pension of a senator exceeds $125,000 per year, in addition to any social security benefit they may be entitled to.

Each member of the Senate is also given a generous allowance to maintain an office in the Capitol building as well as offices in their home state. Each office is funded to include a full staff and services. Each senator is also given free mailing privileges, free parking, free gym memberships, and access to restaurants. In all, the nonsalary benefits of a senator exceed $300,000 per year.

REAL-LIFE FACTS

Until 1855, members of Congress were paid on a per diem basis. In 1790, congressional salaries were set at $6 per day. By 1855, the figure had risen to $8 per day. The first annual salary was set at $3,000 per year. When adjusted for inflation, that's the equivalent of about $83,000 in 2015 dollars. Congress has been very generous in awarding its members raises.

Party Organization

The Democrats and Republicans in the Senate are organized by party leaders. The key leaders are elected by the full party membership in the Senate. The majority party chooses one of its members—usually the senator with the most seniority—to be president pro tempore of the Senate.

According to the Constitution, the president of the Senate is the vice president of the United States. The president of the Senate does not have the usual powers of a presiding office; in fact, compared to the Speaker of the House, the president of the Senate is very weak, tedious, and largely ceremonial. The vice president, as a member of the executive branch, cannot take the floor to speak or debate. In fact, the only time a vice president can vote in the Senate is in the event of a tie vote. The Senate elects a president pro tempore to serve as the presiding officer in the absence of the vice president.

Majority and Minority Leaders

The real leadership in the Senate rests with the majority and minority leaders, elected by the members of their parties. These leadership roles are not official positions, yet these senators wield a considerable amount of power.

REAL-LIFE FACTS

The first president of the Senate, John Adams, cast 29 tie-breaking votes, the most of any vice president in the history of the republic.

When the president and the Senate majority leader are from the same political party, the president serves as the party's national spokesman. However, when the Senate majority leader is from the opposition party, he or she becomes the de facto national spokesperson for the party. Also, as the Senate's power broker, the majority leader has the right to be the first senator to speak on the floor. The majority leader, in consultation with the minority leader, establishes the agenda of the Senate. A piece of legislation cannot come up for a vote without the support of the majority leader. The majority leader recommends committee assignments for members of the majority party.

The Whip

The two party leaders in the Senate are each assisted by a *whip*. In effect, they are assistant floor leaders. The whip is responsible for ensuring that his or her party's senators vote in line with the party leadership's goals. The whip is chosen by a vote of senators from within the party, and almost always at the recommendation of the majority or minority leader. The whip often goes on to serve as party leader once that position becomes vacant.

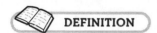 **DEFINITION**

A **whip** is a party leader who ensures party members are present for votes and vote the way the party wishes.

Committee Chairpersons

Most of the work in Congress is done in committee. Therefore, the committee chair holds a prominent position of power in the Senate, just as in the House. The chair of a steering committee (discussed later in the chapter) is chosen from the majority party. The committee chair decides when the committee will meet, which bills they will consider, if public hearings are necessary, and whom to call should public hearings be held. When a bill is delivered to the entire Senate for consideration, the committee chair usually manages debate on the floor. Senators commonly serve upon between three and six committees, but no senator may hold more than one chair.

Seniority Rule

Leadership positions, especially powerful committee chairmanships, are given to senators based on their years of service. Thus, the longest serving member of a committee serves as the committee chair when his or her party is in the majority.

MISINFORMATION

Although seniority provides a predictable means of assigning positions of power in the Senate, each party caucus can determine their own rules. When the Republican Party gained the majority in 1995, it altered its rules to allow Republicans to vote by secret ballot for their committee's chairman, irrespective of seniority. This was a logical consequence of the party's decision to place a six-year limit on the service of its chairmen and, when in the minority, its ranking members. The Democratic caucus in the Senate does not abide by these rules.

Committees in the Senate

The number of committees, and their respective jurisdiction, is of great interest to members of Congress, and especially to senators. Since there are fewer senators, each individual member has a more important role to play. Committee actions are rarely overturned on the floor of the Senate, so a committee and its chairperson exercise considerable control over legislation within their committee's jurisdiction.

There are three types of committees in the Senate: *standing committees,* select committees, and joint committees. The ratio of Democrats to Republicans on a committee usually corresponds to the ratio of Democrats to Republicans in the Senate. For example, in 2001, when the Democrats and the Republicans were evenly divided in the Senate, each committee had the same number of members from each party. Generally speaking, standing committees are the most important committees in the Senate. They are the only committees that can propose legislation. Most senators serve on two committees. Certain committees allow senators to help formulate important national policy while others help senators serve their constituents' interests.

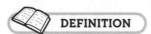

DEFINITION

A **standing committee** is a permanent committee in the Senate that considers bills within a certain jurisdiction.

The Importance of the Standing Committees

Standing committees are established by the rules of the Senate and continue from session to session. Most standing committees have several subcommittees to help carry out their work. Each standing committee is given a specific area of jurisdiction and all legislative proposals are considered by the appropriate committee.

Among the most important Senate standing committees are the Senate Appropriations Committee, the Senate Finance Committee, the Senate Foreign Relations Committee, the Senate Committee on Homeland Security and Governmental Affairs, and the Senate Judiciary Committee.

Select Committees

A select committee is created for a specific legislative purpose and generally for a limited period of time. Select committees generally disband once they have reported to the Senate. Current select committees in the Senate include the Committee on Indian Affairs, the Select Committee on Ethics, the Select Committee on Intelligence, and the Special Committee on Aging.

Joint Committees

A joint committee is formed by the concurrent action of both chambers of Congress. A joint committee has members from both chambers as well. Lastly, joint committees may be permanent or temporary. The current joint committees of Congress are the Joint Committee on Printing, the Joint Committee on Taxation, the Joint Committee on the Library, and the Joint Economic Committee.

A conference committee is a special type of joint committee. It is a temporary joint body formed for the sole purpose of achieving agreement between the House and the Senate versions of a bill. No bill may be sent to the president for approval unless it is in identical form from both chambers. Because of its special role in resolving legislative disputes, the Conference Committees are sometimes called the "third house" of Congress.

Caucuses

Caucuses are committees that are not mandated with a specific legislative goal. Instead they are best seen as informal organizations that allow individual members to promote shared legislative interests. There are caucuses exclusively for House members, those exclusively for senators, and also caucuses for members of both chambers. The wide range of caucuses reflects the diverse interests of the American public. The diversity also parallels the growth of interest groups.

The party caucus is comprised of each member of the Senate from each party. Sometimes the party caucus is called the party conference. This caucus deals primarily with party organization in the Senate, the selection of floor leaders, and questions of committee membership. In addition to the party caucus, there are six types of caucuses in Congress.

An intraparty caucus is made of members who share a similar ideology, such as the Conservative Opportunity Society or the Democratic Study Group. A personal-interest group caucus is formed around a common interest regarding a particular issue. Examples of this type of caucus are the Military Reform Caucus, the Arts Caucus, and the Senate Children's Caucus.

Finally, there are four types of constituency caucuses: those concerned with national issues, those concerned with regional issues, those concerned with state issues, and those concerned with industry issues.

The Least You Need to Know

- The Senate has unique constitutional roles in our democracy in addition to its legislative role. This is known as the "advice and consent" role it plays in conjunction with the president.
- The Senate is organized along party lines, just as the House of Representatives is. However, power in the Senate rests with the majority and minority leaders, and not the president of the Senate.
- Committee chairs wield extraordinary power in the Senate. Committees are very important because it is there that most of the Senate's business is conducted.
- Individual senators can block legislation by placing a hold on a vote, or by threatening a filibuster.
- The growing number of caucuses in the Senate reflects the diversity of the American public and the growth of interest groups in American politics.

How Laws Are Created

Congress is given the important function in our democracy of passing legislation. Every year, thousands of measures, or bills, are introduced in the House of Representatives and the Senate, yet fewer than 10 percent typically become laws. The myriad rules and procedures to pass a law often favor opponents to the legislation. Where do all these bills come from? Why are so few passed into law? What is the process to create laws?

The basic steps in the lawmaking process are the same in each body, but there are some critical differences. We will explore all this and more in this chapter, which will guide you through the process of how a bill becomes a law.

In This Chapter

- The process in the House of Representatives
- The process in the Senate
- Different types of bills
- How differences in bills are reconciled
- Final passage of legislation

The First Steps in the House

According to the Constitution, only Congress has the authority to pass legislation. But before a law can be enacted, it must of course be signed by the president and eventually stand up to judicial review. Article I, Section 7, Clause 1 of the Constitution states, "All Bills for raising Revenue shall originate in the House of Representatives; but the Senate may propose or concur with amendments as on other Bills."

In short, either chamber of Congress can propose a bill to become a law, but all bills dealing with money, taxes, the budget, and so on must originate in the House of Representatives. This goes back to the earliest concern of the founders regarding "no taxation without representation."

A bill is a proposed law presented for consideration to the House or Senate. However, most bills do not originate with members of Congress. Instead, most bills are a result of measures drafted by interest groups and the executive branch. Business, labor, and agriculture interest groups, as well as private citizens draft measures that they propose to their elected officials. The executive branch, especially the various departments, draft legislation to implement policies. Still, members of Congress draft legislation as part of the work of standing committees. Only members may introduce bills in the House of Representatives. In order to do so, a member must drop off a bill for consideration to the clerk of the House by placing it in the *hopper.*

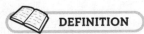 **DEFINITION**

All bills originating in the House must be placed in the clerk's **hopper,** which is a box hanging on the edge of the clerk's desk.

Types of Bills

Congress considers two types of bills in each session. There are public bills, which apply to the nation as a whole, such as a tax bill, or a change in trademark laws. The second type is called a private bill, which applies to a certain group or location rather than the whole nation. An example of this is compensation for losses due to some federal act or regulation.

Types of Resolutions

In addition to bills, Congress can pass resolutions, which vary in the degree to which they have the force of law.

Joint resolutions are most similar to bills and have the force of law when passed by the House and Senate. They are generally used to appropriate money or for special matters. The president must approve or disapprove of the measure before it can be enacted. Only joint resolutions may be used to propose amendments to the U.S. Constitution.

Concurrent resolutions are statements of position on an issue, adopted by the House and the Senate acting jointly, usually on foreign policy matters. These do not have the force of law.

Resolutions are measures dealing with some issue in either chamber. These do not have the force of law.

Most bills and resolutions deal with a single subject; however, members of Congress can attach riders to a bill that are unrelated to the bill or resolution at hand. A rider is a provision (not likely to pass on its own) attached to an important bill. For example, many members of Congress will attach riders to important spending bills knowing that both Congress and the president will accept the riders if they want the major provisions passed.

MISINFORMATION

Christmas trees, in political terms, are not what you might think. Instead this is the term given to a bill that has had many riders, or "decorations," attached to it by members of Congress. In 2015, Congress passed a budget bill with more than $620 billion in "presents" for interest groups and constituents. That is equivalent to giving every American more than $1,900.

The First Reading

The clerk of the House must assign a number to each bill that is introduced. In the House, all bills are assigned the prefix *H.R.* and all bills originating in the Senate are assigned the prefix *S.* For example, H.R. 1234 would be the 1,234th measure introduced in the House during that term, and similarly, S. 123 would be the 123rd measure introduced in the Senate that term. The clerk also assigns a descriptive title to the bill. It is then formally entered into the House *Journal* and the *Congressional Record*. Members have five days to make any changes before the first reading is conducted. After the first reading, the speaker of the House refers the bill to the appropriate committee for debate and review.

REAL-LIFE FACTS

All bills must go through a process of three readings before final passage. This is intended to ensure careful consideration of a bill along the way. They are also read aloud because, in the early days of the republic, some of the members of Congress were illiterate.

The Bill in House Committee

After the first reading, the speaker refers the bill to the appropriate standing committee for debate and review. The Constitution makes no mention of standing committees, but Congress has created them in order to sift through the many proposed bills and do most of the work on behalf of the entire legislative chamber. In fact, whether a bill is referred to the whole body for a vote depends on how successful it is in the standing committee. Most bills that are proposed are sent to committee and then *pigeonholed*—that is, they die in committee and are never acted upon.

 **DEFINITION**

A bill that is **pigeonholed** is introduced only because some constituent or special interest group has asked for it, and then it is left to die because it has little broad support.

On occasion, a special or select committee is created to deal with a single bill. In 2002, President George W. Bush requested the creation of the Department of Homeland Security. Since this new department included consolidating functions from many different security agencies, the bill would have had to be referred to several committees, resulting in delays at a time when there was urgency to act. In response, the House created the Select Committee on Homeland Security to propose legislation to establish the Department of Homeland Security. After the work of the committee was complete, the select committee was dissolved.

If, however, a committee tries to bury a measure that has support from a majority of the House, members can force the bill to the floor for a vote by issuing a discharge petition. A discharge petition must have the support of at least 218 members of the House. The committee then has seven days to report on the bill to the entire House. This maneuver almost never occurs, as it is rare that a majority of members challenge the prerogatives of the House leadership. Still, in 2002, this process was successfully used to bring the Bipartisan Campaign Reform Act of 2002 to a full vote by the House, where it had been buried in committee for several years. A bill that a committee wishes to consider, or at least the powerful chair of the committee wishes to consider, has to go through an information gathering process. This is usually done through their several subcommittees.

Subcommittees exist to address specific issues that come before a committee. There are nearly 80 subcommittees in the House. Their main functions include holding hearings, inviting members of the president's administration, representatives of special interest groups, citizen advocacy groups, and other members of Congress to testify. The House can force witnesses to testify if necessary, and conducting research by looking at an issue or condition in question. This usually requires the subcommittee to travel to conduct investigations. These trips are called junkets and are paid for by public funds. After this work has been completed, measures go through a mark-up phase, when members offer amendments to the bill. Amendments to a bill often deal with specific language that will ultimately foretell whether a bill will have enough support to move on, or whether it will die in this phase. Most legislation referred to a subcommittee does not make it to the full committee. As President Woodrow Wilson noted, "As a rule, a bill committed is a bill doomed."

Once a subcommittee has completed its work, the measure goes to the full committee. The committee has five options at its disposal:

- Report the bill favorably with a "do pass" recommendation to the full House. Debate must then be scheduled before a full vote.

- Refuse to report the bill, essentially pigeonholing it again.

- Report the bill in amended form. This usually combines several bills on the same subject into a single bill.

- Report the bill with an unfavorable recommendation. This does not happen often, but occasionally the House leadership will want the entire House to vote a measure down for the record.

- Report a committee bill. This is an entirely new bill the committee has substituted for the one that was originally referred.

Scheduling Floor Debate in the House

Before a bill can be voted on by the entire house it must be placed on one of several calendars that determine the order in which bills will be taken up by the entire body. There are five calendars in the House:

- The union calendar, formally known as the Calendar of the Committee of the Whole House on the State of the Union

- The house calendar

- The private calendar

- The corrections calendar

- The discharge calendar

Under House rules, bills are taken from each of these calendars at regularly scheduled times for consideration. However, these procedures are not as simple as they appear. Remember, the powerful Rules Committee plays a critical role in the legislative process in the House. It must approve rules for almost every bill before they can reach the floor for consideration. The committee may apply the *closed rule*, which would prohibit amendments to the bill from House members from the floor of the chamber.

By not granting a rule for a bill, the Rules Committee can essentially kill any bill it is not in favor of. Or the Rules Committee can set special rules on a bill for consideration, which can help or hinder its chances of passage by the entire House. Some bills, however, are privileged and are not subject to this process. These include major spending bills, bills dealing with taxes, and conference committee reports. These procedures have developed over time to help House members manage their business and heavy workload.

The Bill on the Floor of the House

When a bill reaches the floor of the House, it receives its second reading. Most minor bills are called from a calendar and then get their second reading by title only. Nearly all major bills are considered in the Committee of the Whole. This committee includes all the members of the House, but only requires 100 members to be present in order to conduct business.

When the House operates as the Committee of the Whole, the speaker removes himself or herself from presiding over the House and another member presides. The rules of the Committee of the Whole are less strict than the rules for the House and it is much easier to conduct business in this manner. General debate is limited to five minutes per member and amendments may be offered. Votes are taken on each section and each amendment that is proposed. Once the Committee of the Whole has completed its work, it dissolves and the speaker resumes his or her role and the House adopts the work that has been completed.

Controversial bills that will not be approved by unanimous consent, and all bills that deal with spending, are scheduled by the powerful Rules Committee. This committee is considered very powerful because it determines the time allowed to debate the bill and decides whether any amendments may be added to the bill. In so doing, the Rules Committee can either ensure that a bill survives or dies on the floor of the House.

Limits on Debate

Due to its size, the House has placed strict limits on floor debate, rules that were first adopted as far back as 1841. Since 1880, the speaker has had the authority to have any member cease debate after his or her allotted time is up. Debate on a bill is usually predetermined by the majority and minority leaders. Bills are debated usually only for a period of one hour. However, any member may move that a vote be taken, and if it is adopted, debate ends and a vote on the measure itself takes place. This is a very important tool used in the House to limit debate.

Voting on a Bill

A bill is usually subjected to several votes. If amendments are offered to a bill, every amendment must be voted on. Several motions can be made on a bill, such as setting the bill in question aside and all these motions must be voted on, too. These votes usually indicate whether a bill is likely to pass the entire House or not. The House has four different methods it uses for taking floor votes:

- Voice votes are registered by a chorus of "ayes" (yes) and "nays" (no). The speaker announces the result.

- If a member believes the speaker has misheard the count, then they can demand a standing vote. Members stand and are counted by the clerk either in favor or opposed.

- In a teller vote, the speaker assigns one member from each party to serve as a teller. Members pass the tellers and are counted either for or against a measure. This method is rarely used.

- In a roll-call vote, members are individually called and their vote recorded. This is now done electronically.

Once a measure has been approved, it is printed in its final form and given its third and final reading. A final vote is then taken. If the bill is approved, the speaker signs the bill and it is delivered to the Senate for review and approval.

Rules for Debate in the Senate

Bills must be formally introduced by senators, who are recognized for that purpose, rather than dropping off a measure into a clerk's box. Just as in the House, however, much of the initial phase is the same: a measure is given a number starting with *S* and given a title, read twice, and referred to committee for review. It is then put on the only calendar the Senate has. In some ways, the process is much less strict than in the House. Bills in the Senate are called to the floor for consideration only at the discretion of the majority leader.

The major difference between the House and Senate procedures for passing legislation involve the debate segment of the process. As we have seen, floor debate is strictly limited in the House. In the Senate, debate has almost no restrictions. As a general rule, senators may speak on the floor as long as they please, unlike the 10-minute limit usually enforced on House members. Additionally, senators can speak about whatever they like. Senators are not limited to speaking only about the measure at hand. Senators are usually limited to speaking twice on a given question. Still, with 100 members and the ability to speak at quite some length, debate can last a very long time. The Senate is dedicated to freedom of debate to encourage the most discussion possible on a matter before it becomes law.

 ON THE RECORD

"The Senate's tradition is ruled to protect debate and guarantee that we can't be trampled upon."

—U.S. Senator Christopher Dodd (D-CT)

The Filibuster

The great latitude that senators have when debating a measure gives rise to the filibuster. A filibuster is an attempt to talk against a bill to the point where no vote is ever taken on it. This is essentially a tool to delay or prevent action on a measure that senators use to kill a bill the majority wants to vote on.

More recently, simply the threat of a filibuster will result in shelving or amending legislation. Most legislative matters or nominations now need a supermajority of 60 votes in the Senate to pass a floor vote. The era of a simple majority vote may soon become a relic of the past.

To discourage the filibuster, senators must stand upright throughout the time period that they are speaking. The last senator to stand and filibuster was Senator Rand Paul of Kentucky in May 2015 against the renewal of the USA PATRIOT Act. His 10-hour, 31-minute filibuster was ultimately not successful.

The Cloture Rule

The Senate does have a check on the filibuster; it is called the cloture rule. This rule was first adopted in 1917 after one of the most famous filibusters staged by a group of senators who opposed President Wilson's maneuvers to have the United States enter World War I. The rule basically states that if 60 senators vote to close debate on a measure, debate must end within 30 hours of debate after the cloture vote and a vote must be taken. Invoking the cloture rule is no easy task.

Many senators are hesitant to support cloture for two reasons: they're fiercely dedicated to the tradition of debate in the Senate, and they fear the value of the filibuster will be undermined for when they may want to use it.

REAL-LIFE FACTS

The longest filibuster in U.S. history was conducted by Senator Strom Thurmond from South Carolina, at the time a Democrat. He spoke for 24 hours and 18 minutes in an unsuccessful attempt to defeat a civil rights bill. The senator spoke from August 28 to August 29, 1957. (Thurmond became a Republican in 1964.)

Conference Committees

In order for a bill to be enacted by Congress, it must pass both chambers in identical form. Given all the rules and procedures, this is very difficult to accomplish in some cases. When the House and the Senate pass different versions of the same bill, the second chamber to pass the bill traditionally concurs with the version of the first chamber to have passed the bill so that the measure can be completed.

Sometimes, however, the two chambers are unwilling to accept the other's version of a bill. When this occurs, the bills are sent to a conference committee to reconcile. The conference committee is a temporary committee established with members from both chambers to work out differences and create a compromise bill. Once the conference committee produces the compromise bill, it must be considered by both chambers without the ability to make any changes. Rarely do bills that result from the conference committee's work ever get rejected.

Presidential Action

Once a bill has passed both the House and the Senate, the Constitution provides the president with the following four options:

- The president can sign the bill and it becomes law.

- The president may veto the bill, refuse to sign it, and send it back to Congress. Congress may overturn a presidential veto by a two-thirds vote in each chamber. Presidential vetoes are very difficult to overturn.

- The president may allow the bill to become law without signing it. By taking no action for 10 days, the bill automatically becomes law.

- The president can pocket veto a bill by not acting on a bill if Congress is adjourned during the 10-day period after submitting a bill for presidential action.

ON THE RECORD

"President Bush has stated that the patient's bill of rights legislation ... is dead on arrival .... If the president can't bring himself to sign a true patient's bill of rights, then he should let it become law without his signature just as he did when he was governor of Texas."

—U.S. Senator Tim Johnson (D-SD)

The Least You Need to Know

- Measures considered by the House and Senate go through a rigorous process of review and debate before they are presented for a vote.
- Although the lawmaking steps are similar for both the House and the Senate, the most significant difference involves debating procedures. In the House, debate is very limited. In the Senate, it is almost unlimited.
- Both chambers of Congress must pass bills in exactly the same language. When two different versions of a law emerge, a conference committee is created to reconcile the differences.
- Once both chambers of Congress have passed a bill, the president must take action before it can become law. The president must either sign or veto a bill or not act at all.
- Congress can only override a presidential veto with a two-thirds vote in each chamber.

The Executive Branch

The President of the United States is often referred to as "the most powerful position on Earth." In fact, the Constitution grants the president a tremendous amount of power. The legislative and judicial branches can also check these powers, which include everything from the power to use military force to pardoning federal officials. The role of the president has evolved throughout our history, with some presidents taking much more control over the federal government than others.

The federal bureaucracy is the arm of the executive branch that carries out the laws and the policies of the government. It is a vast apparatus that is a result of, and has given rise to, a powerful federal government. Sometimes the bureaucracy is referred to as the "fourth branch" of government.

CHAPTER 13

The Presidency

The president of the United States is often referred to as "the most powerful position on Earth." In fact, the Constitution grants the president a tremendous amount of power. The legislative and judicial branch can also check these powers, which include everything from the power to use military force to pardoning federal officials.

The role of the president has evolved through history, with some presidents taking much more control over the federal government than others. The vice presidency is also considered in this chapter, as he is first in line to the presidency should anything happen.

In This Chapter

- The history of the presidency
- The powers of the president
- The office of the vice president
- Problems with succession to the presidency and vice presidency

The Evolution of the Presidency

When the Constitutional Convention met, the framers debated mostly about the role of the chief executive. They feared anarchy if the chief was not powerful enough, but they also feared a monarchy if the president was too powerful.

Having just fought for their independence from England, and with the threat of foreign enemies, they knew that they needed a leader. Most of the founders believed George Washington would make a great first president. They trusted him and believed he would not overstep his role.

In early American history, the presidency was kept modest. The first five presidents established the legitimacy of the position, settled the debt acquired in the Revolutionary War and established a stable currency. Around the time of President Andrew Jackson (1829–1837), the presidency started to become a more powerful and independent office. Jackson and several presidents after him stood up to Congress and vetoed many bills. They saw their position as the voice of the people, as the only federal official elected by the entire voting citizenry.

But during the time of slavery and sectionalism, Congress regained its power. It's hard to remember the names of all the presidents during these years, and this is mainly because they were subordinate in power to Congress. During this time, President Lincoln was the only president to stand up to Congress and the partisan system that had developed. He used his executive powers to raise an army, spend money, and issue the Emancipation Proclamation, which freed the slaves in the border states. He did all of this without the approval of Congress.

After the Civil War, during Reconstruction and many years after, Congress reasserted itself and became the leading federal institution. In fact, Congress tended to ignore the suggestions of the president and would make its own agenda. It was clear, however, that in times of national emergency, such as the Great Depression, a strong leader was necessary to guide the government back in the right direction.

The presidents in office since then have had much more authority than the presidents of the past. The Congress and the president work together to propose legislation. However, as we have seen since 2010, divided government can hinder collaboration between the legislature and the executive. The government is a part of the public life and people are much more aware of the daily activities of the president and Congress. Because the president has become such a focus of media attention, the nation regards him as the head of a large federal administrative system, making him subject to increasingly more scrutiny.

The Electoral College

The founders were concerned with the election of the president. First they argued that the president should be chosen by Congress, but realized that that would place too much power in the hands of the legislature. They finally decided that the people should choose the president, but agreed that the population would not be able to make this decision on its own. Therefore, they decided to form the Electoral College.

The Electoral College is a group of electors that actually elect the president. When citizens cast their vote, they are actually participating in an indirect election, in which they are voting for electors, who will in turn vote for the president. Most of the time, these electors will vote based on the opinion of the constituents. The framers believed that this system was fair to both large and small states because small states were represented by three electors and large states would also have their say.

REAL-LIFE FACTS

Not every president and vice president has competed in an election. Gerald Ford and Nelson Rockefeller were president and vice president without ever receiving a vote in the general election or in the Electoral College.

Qualifications

The president must be a natural-born citizen, meaning he or she must be born in the United States or have parents who are American citizens. The president must also be at least 35 years old. He or she must also be a resident of the United States for at least 14 years.

Term of Office

The founders debated on how long the president's term should be, because they were afraid of creating a position as strong as the monarchy from which they had just fought for their independence. They finally settled on a four-year term. The original Constitution did not put a limit on the number of terms a president could serve. When he did not seek a third term, George Washington set a precedent that held until President Franklin D. Roosevelt ran for and won a third and then a fourth term. To prevent future presidents from following his lead, the Twenty-Second Amendment limited the president's term to two four-year terms. A president may serve for more than eight years if he succeeds another president, but no more than ten years.

Salary and Benefits

Traditionally, the president has been the highest paid public official. Congress decides the president's salary, which cannot increase or decrease during a single term. It is currently set at $400,000, along with a $50,000 expense account, a $100,000 nontaxable travel account, and $19,000 for entertainment. The president also receives health-care benefits and a pension. This current salary and benefits package was approved in 1999 and went into effect in 2001.

The president lives and works in the White House and has access to its entire staff and facilities. The president also travels on *Air Force One,* a special jet reserved solely for his use. The president can also vacation at Camp David, a resort reserved for him and his family in the mountains of Maryland.

MISINFORMATION

Despite the constitutional requirement that Congress must declare war, formal declarations of war have occurred only when the president requests them. The last declaration of war by Congress was during World War II. Since then, Congress has passed joint resolutions to authorize the president to use force on eight different occasions.

The Many Roles of the President

The Constitution outlines many different roles for the president of the United States. At any given time, the president must be ready to command the army, review legislation, and represent the United States in a global forum. Some of his roles are explicitly outlined in the Constitution, and others have been added to his job description over time.

Chief of state   The president is the formal head of the government of the United States. He represents the people of the nation. Contrary to some European countries like England, where the head of state is a queen (or king) but the prime minister rules the government, the president of the United States is both the chief of state and executive power.

Chief executive   Article II of the Constitution outlines the role of the president in the executive branch of government, of which he or she is the highest-ranking official. The vice president is also part of the executive branch. As chief executive, the president is also subject to various checks and balances by the legislative and judicial branches.

Chief administrator   As the most powerful official of the executive branch, the president must manage a staff of more than 2.7 million people and a budget of about $2.5 trillion per year. The president is the head of one of the largest governments in the world.

Chief diplomat   As chief diplomat, the president directs the nation's foreign policy. The president meets with the leaders of other countries in order to discuss global issues and negotiate treaties. His diplomacy is carefully followed in this country and abroad.

Commander-in-chief   This role is very closely connected to the president's role as chief diplomat. As commander-in-chief, the president has the constitutional power to lead the armed forces. Although Congress also has some military authority (specifically, funding it), the president has traditionally dominated this role.

Chief legislator   As chief legislator, the president can request, suggest, and even demand certain legislation be reviewed in Congress. The president has the power to veto a bill passed by both houses of Congress. This most often happens when the president and the majorities in Congress belong to different political parties.

Chief of party   The president is the highest elected official in his or her own political party. The party holding the executive branch can get its ideology put into practice through the president's many other roles.

Chief citizen   As the chief citizen, the president is seen as the representative of the people. The president is expected to work for the public interest against the many competing private interests.

 MISINFORMATION

Presidents John Quincy Adams, Rutherford B. Hayes, Benjamin Harrison, and George W. Bush won their elections without winning the majority of the popular vote. Instead, they were the candidates with the most votes from the Electoral College.

The President's Executive Powers

As chief executive, the president is in charge of enforcing the law. This is his or her power granted in the Constitution but also in the presidential oath that he or she must take on Inauguration Day: "I do solemnly swear that I will faithfully execute the office of president of the United States, and will, to the best of my ability, preserve, protect, and defend the Constitution of the United States." This statement is very meaningful in that it puts an emphasis on the president's job as chief executive and ruler of the United States.

As the executive power, the president can deliver bills into law, even bypassing the Congress in some cases. The president can also choose the staff of the executive branch, from Supreme Court justices to military offices. He can also remove these people from office if they are not fulfilling their roles in the government. These powers do come under the system of checks and balances, therefore limiting the president's powers to a certain extent.

Executing the Law

Upon taking the oath of office, the president is committed to executing all federal laws. He has the unique requirement of interpreting the usually vague wording of laws passed by Congress. The president must decide how to put these laws into action and usually delegates that responsibility to one of the many agencies of the executive branch.

A signing statement is a written comment issued by a president at the time of signing a bill. Most of the time, these statements are simple compliments that the legislation is good and meets the needs of the country. Other times, signing statements are used by the president to show disagreement with part of the bill. In these situations, the president will choose to ignore that part of the bill or implement the law in a way they deem to be constitutional.

The Ordinance Power

The president has the power to issue *executive orders*. This power arises from the Constitution and from Congress. In the Constitution, the ordinance power is implied because it grants other powers to the president that would call for him or her to mandate certain rules into law. Traditionally, Congress has delegated many issues to the president and his offices.

 **DEFINITION**

> An **executive order** is a directive, rule, or regulation that has the same effect as a law. FDR issued 3,721 executive orders, the most of any President. The number has decreased considerably. Reagan issued 381, George W. Bush issued 291, and President Obama has issued 231 as of February 2016. It is difficult to predict if this trend will continue. But one thing is certain: opponents of a sitting president will always cry foul and over-reach by the executive.

Congressional-Executive Agreements

Another method presidents have to implement policies and treaties is the Congressional-Executive Agreement. This process allows the president to negotiate a treaty, usually a trade agreement with a foreign country, and submit it to both chambers of Congress for a majority approval. This process can be less challenging than a two-thirds approval from the Senate that a typical treaty would require. President Clinton used this process to pass the North American Free Trade Agreement (NAFTA).

The Appointment Power

With Senate consent, the president has the power to appoint many government officials, such as ambassadors, Cabinet members, and their aids, the heads of various independent agencies such as NASA and the EPA, all federal judges, U.S. marshals and attorneys, and all officers in the military. The president also has the power to fill any vacancies in these positions that might occur when the Senate is not in session.

The Removal Power

The president's power to remove people from office has been contested in history. A Supreme Court decision in 1935, however, upheld that the president does have the power to remove federal officials without the consent of the Senate in the cases of the person's inefficiency, neglect of duty, or misconduct in office. Most often these officials will know (or be informed) that it's time to resign before they are removed from office.

Diplomatic and Military Powers

As commander-in-chief, the president rules in times of war and in times of peace. This role is interconnected with the president's role as chief diplomat. The President of the United States must know when to act militarily and when to use diplomacy. The president is also responsible for maintaining the many alliances the United States has created over time. He does this by making *treaties* and participating in global forums.

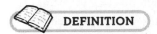 **DEFINITION**

A **treaty** is a formal agreement between two or more countries.

Many routine international obligations of the president are performed through executive agreement. These agreements differ from treaties in that they do not require the Senate's approval. The president also has the power to formally recognize another nation or government. This means that the country is legally acknowledged by the United States and is welcomed into the global family of nations. The president can use this power to aid countries revolting against their governments or claiming independence, as has occurred with Panama and Israel. Similarly, after Soviet President Mikhail Gorbachev resigned on December 25, 1991, President George H. W. Bush immediately recognized the re-emerged nation of Russia and five other countries that were part of the Soviet Union. Related closely with this role, the president can remove ambassadors from countries the Unites States chooses not to approve of. This is a very sharp diplomatic tactic that sends a very clear message to other countries.

The War Powers Resolution of 1973 was an attempt to limit the president's abilities to use military force without the approval of Congress. President Nixon vetoed the bill, but Congress over-rode it. The resolution required that the president report any actions of American troops within 48 hours; that the commitment of the troops would last no more than 60 days, unless Congress approved more days; and that Congress has the power to end the combat at any time. The constitutionality of this law is still disputed by many.

The president shares various diplomatic and military powers with Congress. In many ways, they work together to shape the United States' global image. In other respects, the president's powers are virtually unlimited.

Undeclared War Powers

In times of peace, the president, usually acting through the secretary of state, negotiates international agreements. These treaties often have to deal with trade and other foreign affairs. They must be approved by two thirds of the Senate in order to take effect. Treaties have the same status in the United States as federal laws passed by Congress. Therefore, if Congress does not agree with a treaty, it can try to pass laws that contradict the treaty's provisions. When this occurs, the case is usually brought to the Supreme Court.

Wartime Powers

The president is commander-in-chief of the armed forces. Although this title gives him an enormous amount of control over the military, the president usually delegates much of this responsibility to his subordinates. Presidents George Washington and Abraham Lincoln actually led troops to battle or directed generals in the field. Most presidents have not become as directly involved in their role as commander.

The president has authorized the use of military force without Congress's approval many times in our nation's history. These "undeclared wars" have been debated for centuries, the most recent of which include Vietnam and Iraq. Because presidents have used this power often over the years, the War Powers Resolution intended to give some of this power back to Congress.

 MISINFORMATION

The Senate does not ratify treaties—it approves them. The final formal negotiation between the president and the head of the other country is considered the official ratification of the treaty.

The Legislative and Judicial Powers of the President

The office of the president lies within the greater structure of the federal government, which includes many forms of checks and balances. In the role of chief of party, the president often has a significant amount of influence on legislation. The Constitution requires for the president to send messages to Congress. The first one of the year is the State of the Union address, in which the president outlines his agenda for the upcoming year. Soon after, the president delivers the economic report, which details the budget. The president can also send messages to particular members of Congress recommending legislation. The president can also call special sessions of Congress.

The Veto Power

Part of the president's legislative powers also includes the power to veto, or say no, to a bill passed by Congress. When a bill reaches the president's desk, he or she can do one of four things. The president can sign it and make it a law. He or she can veto it and return it to Congress, which can over-ride this veto by a two-thirds majority vote. An important check incorporated in this system is that Congress can over-ride a presidential veto.

The president can also neither sign nor veto the bill and it will become a law in 10 days (but this rarely happens). The last option is called the pocket veto, which can be used only at the end of a congressional session. If Congress sends a bill to the president less than 10 days before adjourning the session and the chief does not approve it, then the bill dies. Most of the time, the president will announce that he will veto a bill if it reaches him or her, and that is usually enough to stifle the bill's progress in Congress.

Presidents can only veto entire bills. They cannot pick and choose what parts of the bill they might want to approve. Over the years, presidents have tried to gain this power, called the line-item veto. The Supreme Court found the Line-Item Veto Act of 1996 to be unconstitutional on the grounds that Congress does not have the power to grant the president this veto. Instead, a constitutional amendment must occur in order for the line-item veto to ever be a reality.

The Power to Pardon

The judicial powers of the president include granting reprieves and pardons. Reprieves are post-ponements of sentences and pardons are the legal forgiveness of a crime. This power is absolute except in the case of impeachment, when no clemency can be granted; it cannot be contradicted by another branch of the federal government. The president also has the power to reduce the length of sentences or amount of fines enforced by the courts. These executive powers can only be used on federal officials.

Vice President

The Constitution does not provide much detail about the role of the vice president in the executive branch. It outlines two formal duties:

- To be president of the Senate
- To help decide the question of presidential disability

Although the vice president has a role in the legislative branch as president of the Senate, he is only authorized to use that vote in Senate deadlocks. In those cases, the president pro tempore of the Senate, who is permitted to cast a vote in the vice president's absence, usually fulfills this role on a day-to-day basis. Some vice presidents have tried to use this constitutional role to their advantage in the legislative branch, but the main role of the vice president is to be an adviser to the president. The vice president must also preside over the Senate in cases of an Electoral College tie and must certify the vote count.

The Constitution did not make it clear if, in the case of death of a president, the vice president would assume the role of president or as "acting" president. This issue did not come up until 1841 with the death of William Henry Harrison. The Twenty-Fifth Amendment put into law a specific set of rules regarding the succession to the presidency.

REAL-LIFE FACTS

William Henry Harrison set many presidential records in his short time in office. After giving the longest inauguration speech (105 minutes), Harrison became the first president to die in office (of pneumonia), after serving the shortest term (1 month).

Origin of Office

The office of the vice president was long considered a minor position. In fact, the natural stepping-stone to the presidency was originally considered to be secretary of state. John Adams, the first vice president, was the only vice president to regularly sit in on Cabinet meetings until 1933, when it became common practice. In fact, President Franklin D. Roosevelt kept his vice president, Harry S Truman, so uninformed of his military issues that when Truman ascended to the presidency following Roosevelt's death, he did not know about the development of the atomic bomb. This made it clear that the vice president should participate in meetings of the National Security Council.

Although the Constitution and tradition might seem to diminish the role of the vice president in government, 14 vice presidents have gone on to serve as president, either through succession or their own election victory.

Unique Duties and Responsibilities

Because the Constitution is very vague about the duties and responsibilities of the vice president, they are usually determined by the relationship between the president and vice president and the character of the vice president. For example, Al Gore was an adviser to President Clinton on issues such as foreign policy and the environment. The vice president is usually appointed chairman of the board of NASA and a member of the board of the Smithsonian Institution. The vice president also serves to represent the United States as chief of state when the president is not available to do so.

 ON THE RECORD

"I am vice president. In this I am nothing, but I may be everything."

—Vice President John Adams

Presidential Transition and the Constitution

When President William Henry Harrison died of pneumonia just one month after his inauguration, our nation's leaders were faced with the problem of presidential succession. The Constitution clearly states in Article II that the vice president can "execute" the office of the president in the event of a death or resignation. After some hesitation, Vice President John Tyler took the oath of the presidency, therefore setting a precedent for this transition.

The Presidential Succession Act of 1947 determined the current line of succession to the presidency and is outlined here. It is important to note that the qualifications for the other offices in government are different than those qualifications for president. If a person in line to succession for the presidency does not fit the qualifications of the office of the presidency, then he or she is not eligible to serve.

Presidential Succession

1. Vice President

2. Speaker of the House

3. President pro tempore of the Senate

4. Secretary of State

5. Secretary of the Treasury

6. Secretary of Defense

7. Attorney General

8. Secretary of the Interior

9. Secretary of Agriculture

10. Secretary of Commerce

11. Secretary of Labor

12. Secretary of Health and Human Services

13. Secretary of Housing and Urban Development

14. Secretary of Transportation

15. Secretary of Energy

16. Secretary of Education

17. Secretary of Veterans Affairs

18. Secretary of Homeland Security

Problems of Succession

The problem of succession arises when the president becomes ill and unable to serve in office. When should the vice president step in, and who will take his place? These problems were addressed in the Twenty-Fifth Amendment.

The Twenty-Fifth Amendment passed following the assassination of President John F. Kennedy, and permits the president to nominate a vice president in the event that that office is vacant. It also allows the vice president to serve as "acting president" in the event the president is ill or incapacitated. The new president can then nominate a new vice president, who must be confirmed by a majority vote in both houses of Congress.

 ON THE RECORD

"As of now, I am in control here, in the White House, pending return of the vice president and in close touch with him."

—President Ronald Reagan's Secretary of State Alexander Haig after the assassination attempt on President Reagan

Impeachment

The president can be removed from office in a process known as impeachment. In order for this to occur, criminal charges must be brought against the president in the House of Representatives. The Senate can convict the president (or any other federal official) with a two-thirds majority vote. Presidents Andrew Johnson and Bill Clinton are the only two presidents to have faced impeachment, but neither of them was convicted in the Senate.

The Least You Need to Know

- The office of the president is part of the executive branch. The president must be prepared to serve various roles that grant him or her many powers, but he or she is also subject to various checks and balances.

- The president's powers are outlined in Article II of the Constitution and can be divided into diplomatic, military, legislative, judicial, and executive powers. They are very extensive powers but some of them are shared with other branches of government.

- The vice presidency is also part of the executive branch. He serves as the president's adviser and as president of the Senate. He is also first in line to the presidency. The Presidential Succession Act describes the chain of command to the presidency.

- The president can serve for a maximum of two four-year terms. He can also be removed from office by impeachment from the House of Representatives and conviction in the Senate.

The Bureaucracy: A Government at Work

Everyday Americans encounter the federal bureaucracy, sometimes in very obvious ways, and also in very subtle ways. The federal bureaucracy administers and carries out a host of government tasks and responsibilities on behalf of the American people. From everyday delivery of the mail and running our national parks, to the more complex issues related to foreign policy and economic and environmental regulation, the federal bureaucracy is the government at work on our behalf.

In This Chapter

- The structure of the federal bureaucracy
- The role of the executive office of the president
- The executive departments and the president's Cabinet
- The history of the civil service
- Congressional oversight of the bureaucracy

The Federal Government Bureaucracy

When most people hear the term *bureaucracy,* they think of a large and complex administrative body. In fact, the term *bureaucracy* is a combination of a French word, *bureau,* that originally meant a desk for a government official and then came to mean a place where a government official worked, and the suffix *-cracy,* which refers to a type of government structure. Thus, bureaucracy is government by officials and specialists. These individuals are known as *bureaucrats* and each has a specific role to play.

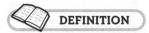

DEFINITION

A **bureaucrat** is usually a member of a bureaucracy, commonly within an institution of the government.

This form of government is based on several important principles:

- A hierarchical structure in which officials on top control and oversee those below them. Think of a pyramid structure of authority.

- Every person in the organization has defined duties and responsibilities.

- All of the bureaucracies' work is conducted by regulations and formal procedures.

The best way to think of the federal bureaucracy is to imagine all the agencies that carry out the work of the federal government, and the people who work for them. The federal bureaucracy is the way the government is able to administer, and sometimes initiate, public policy. Nearly the entire federal bureaucracy falls within the jurisdiction of the executive branch. But it has become so large that it is sometimes referred to as the fourth branch of government.

As you have read in Chapter 13, the Constitution makes the president the chief administrator because the president is charged with the power to execute the laws. The Constitution does not say how the federal bureaucracy should be organized. Yet in Article II the Constitution does give the president the power to consult with heads of executive departments, particularly with reference to the president's role as commander in chief and chief diplomat. Additionally, it was understood from the earliest days of the republic that the president would need an administration to help carry out government policies. Since then, the executive branch has grown tremendously and now includes many different groups of administrative agencies.

Departments are units of the executive branch that hold Cabinet rank. There are currently 15 Cabinet-level departments. Heads of departments hold the title of secretary, except for the attorney general, who leads the Department of Justice.

The term *agency* is generally used to identify a major unit of the executive branch that has near-Cabinet status. An agency is led by a single administrator. Examples of this unit of government are the Federal Emergency Management Agency (FEMA) and the Central Intelligence Agency (CIA).

Like an agency, an *administration* is also a unit led by one administrator of near Cabinet-level status. Several important administrations in the executive branch include the Small Business Administration, the Social Security Administration, and NASA.

 REAL-LIFE FACTS

George Washington, the first president of the United States, had a Cabinet of four: Secretary of State, Secretary of the Treasury, Secretary of War, and Attorney General.

A *commission* is a unit of the executive branch that is usually charged with regulatory or investigative bodies. Examples of commissions within the executive branch are the Securities and Exchange Commission and the Federal Election Commission.

A *corporation* is a unit of the executive branch that is run by a board and a manager. The Federal Deposit Insurance Corporation (FDIC) is an example of this type of agency. The FDIC is charged with insuring individual bank deposits up to $250,000 within its member banks.

Like a corporation, an *authority* is a unit of government that is run by a board and a manager. The Tennessee Valley Authority is currently the only agency of the executive branch that holds this designation.

Within the departments are several smaller elements or units that have distinct classifications. These include names such as *bureaus*, *service*, *branch*, *office*, or *division*. Although there is no uniform breakdown of these various units, they exist with specific areas of expertise or jurisdiction.

Staff and Line Classifications

Administrative organizations are made up of two main classifications: staff agencies or line agencies. A staff agency is a support group. The main function of a staff agency is to support the executive or the agency head by offering advice and assistance in managing the organization.

On the other hand, line agencies perform the actual tasks of the organization. Staff agencies (as you will read in the next section) exist primarily to support the president in his or her exercise of executive power. They do not actually administer a government agency. Line agencies, however, are responsible for administering and operating the federal program that they are charged with.

The Executive Office of the President

The Executive Office of the President (EOP) primarily exists to assist the president with the responsibilities of that office. The EOP is the president's immediate support network and is a complex umbrella group of separate agencies staffed by the most closely trusted assistants and advisers.

In the early days of the republic, there was no formal structure to support presidential aides and advisers. In fact, Congress did not provide any money for a presidential staff until 1857. All of the early presidents paid for their staff out of their own funds. In 1939, Congress established the EOP. This was largely due to the expansion of the federal government in light of all the New Deal legislation that was passed and the newly acquired powers of the executive branch to carry out these programs. Since that time, the EOP has grown to include thousands of employees with the creation of several important agencies and offices to assist the president.

 REAL-LIFE FACTS

The first president to receive a paid staff was James Buchanan in 1857. Congress authorized $2,500 for one clerk for the president.

The White House Office

The White House Office is composed of the key personal and political aides of the president. It is often called the nerve center of the EOP. The White House Office is located in the East and West Wings of the White House. The staff has grown so large (more than 400) that some are now located in an adjacent building.

The president's chief of staff is in charge of the White House Office and wields considerable political power. He or she is generally the most influential of all the presidential aides. The White House Office is responsible for assisting the president in all vital areas of government, as well as contacts with the public and the media.

The National Security Council

The National Security Council (NSC) is responsible for all major foreign-policy initiatives and was established by an act of Congress in 1947. The NSC advises the president on all matters that affect the nation's security. The NSC is comprised of the National Security Advisor, the NSC staff members, the president (who serves as the chair), the vice president, the Secretary of State, the Secretary of Defense, the Director of the CIA, and the Chairman of the Joint Chiefs of Staff.

The chief of staff to the president, counsel to the president, and the assistant to the president for economic policy are invited to attend any NSC meeting. The Attorney General and the Director of the Office of Management and Budget (OMB) are invited to attend meetings pertaining to their responsibilities. The heads of other executive departments and agencies, as well as other senior officials, are invited to attend meetings of the NSC when appropriate.

The Office of Management and Budget

After the White House Office, the OMB is the largest and most influential unit of the executive branch. The OMB's predominant mission is to assist the president in overseeing the preparation of the federal budget and to supervise its administration in executive-branch agencies. The budget proposal represents the public-policy initiatives of the president in terms of dollars.

In helping to formulate the president's spending plans, the OMB evaluates the effectiveness of agency programs, policies, and procedures; assesses competing funding demands among agencies; and sets funding priorities. The OMB ensures that agency reports, rules, testimony, and proposed legislation are consistent with the president's budget and with administration policies. The OMB is also responsible for monitoring the spending of funds that Congress ultimately must allocate. In this sense, it is responsible for executing the federal budget.

The Office of National Drug Control Policy

The Office of National Drug Control Policy (ONDCP) was established by the Anti-Drug Abuse Act of 1988. The principal purpose of ONDCP is to establish policies, priorities, and objectives for the nation's drug control program. The goals of the program are to reduce illicit drug use, manufacturing, and trafficking; drug-related crime and violence; and drug-related health consequences.

By law, the director of the ONDCP also evaluates, coordinates, and oversees both the international and domestic antidrug efforts of executive branch agencies and ensures that such efforts sustain and complement state and local antidrug activities (ondcp.gov).

The Council of Economic Advisers

The Employment Act of 1946 established the Council of Economic Advisers (CEA). It stated:

> "There is hereby created in the Executive Office of the president a Council of Economic Advisers (hereinafter called the 'Council'). The Council shall be composed of three members who shall be appointed by the president, by and with the advice and consent of the Senate, and each of whom shall be a person who, as a result of his training, experience, and attainments, is exceptionally qualified to analyze and interpret

economic developments, to appraise programs and activities of the Government ...,
and to formulate and recommend national economic policy to promote employment,
production, and purchasing power under free competitive enterprise. The president shall
designate one of the members of the Council as Chairman."

The Council on Environmental Quality

The Council on Environmental Quality (CEQ) coordinates federal environmental efforts and
works closely with agencies and other White House offices in the development of environmental
policies and initiatives. The council's chair serves as the principal environmental policy adviser
to the president. In addition, CEQ reports annually to the president on the state of the environment; oversees federal agency implementation of the environmental impact assessment process;
and acts as a referee when agencies disagree over the adequacy of such assessments (whitehouse
.gov).

The Office of the United States Trade Representative

The Office of the United States Trade Representative (USTR) is an agency of more than 200
people who have specialized experience in trade issues and regions of the world. They negotiate
directly with foreign governments to create trade agreements, resolve disputes, and participate in
global trade policy organizations. They also meet with governments, business groups, legislators,
and public interest groups to gather input on trade issues and explain the president's trade policy
positions.

The agency was founded in 1962 and has offices in Washington, Geneva, and Brussels. The
USTR holds the title of ambassador. The USTR is a member of the president's Cabinet and
serves as the president's principal trade advisor, negotiator, and spokesperson on trade issues
(ustr.gov).

The Office of Science and Technology Policy

The Office of Science and Technology Policy (OSTP) advises the president on the effects of
science and technology on domestic and international affairs. The office serves as a source of scientific and technological analysis and judgment for the president with respect to major policies,
plans, and programs of the federal government.

OSTP leads an interagency effort to develop and implement sound science and technology policies and budgets. The office works with the private sector to ensure federal investments in science
and technology contribute to economic prosperity, environmental quality, and national security
(ostp.gov).

The Office of Administration

The Office of Administration was established by executive order on December 12, 1977. The organization's mission is to provide administrative services to all entities of the Executive Office of the President (EOP), including direct support services to the president of the United States.

The services include financial management and information technology support, human resources management, library and research assistance, facilities management, procurement, printing and graphics support, security, and mail and messenger operations. The director of the organization oversees the submission of the annual EOP budget request and represents the organization before congressional funding panels (whitehouse.gov).

Domestic Policy Council

The Domestic Policy Council (DPC) coordinates the domestic policy-making process in the White House and offers policy advice to the president. The DPC also works to ensure that domestic policy initiatives are coordinated and consistent throughout federal agencies. Finally, the DPC monitors the implementation of domestic policy, and represents the president's priorities to other branches of government (whitehouse.gov).

Office of Faith-Based and Neighborhood Partnerships

Established by executive order by President George W. Bush in 2001, as the White House Office of Faith-Based and Community Initiatives (FBCO) and renamed in 2009 by President Barack Obama, the Office of Faith-Based and Neighborhood Partnerships (OFBNP) is charged with strengthening and expanding services to Americans in need. The OFBNP forms partnerships between government and nonprofit organizations, both religious and secular.

Additionally, by making information about federal grants more accessible and the application process less burdensome, the initiative has empowered faith-based organizations and neighborhood partnerships to compete more effectively for federal funds.

 ON THE RECORD

"The particular faith that motivates each of us can promote a greater good for all of us. Instead of driving us apart, our varied beliefs can bring us together to feed the hungry and comfort the afflicted; to make peace where there is strife and rebuild what has broken; to lift up those who have fallen on hard times."

—President Barack Obama

Office of Global Communications

The Office of Global Communications (OGC) was formed in 2002 to coordinate strategic communications overseas that integrate the president's themes and truthfully depicts America and administration policies. The OGC advises the president and his key representatives on the strategic direction and themes that the U.S. government uses to reach foreign audiences.

The office assists in the development of communications that disseminate truthful, accurate, and effective messages about the American people and their government (whitehouse.gov).

Office of National AIDS Policy

The Office of National AIDS Policy will focus on coordinating our continuing domestic efforts to reduce the number of new infections in the United States, in particular in segments of the population that are experiencing new or renewed increases in the rate of infection.

In addition, the office will be working to coordinate an increasingly integrated approach to the prevention, care, and treatment of HIV/AIDS. The office will also emphasize the integration of domestic and international efforts to combat HIV/AIDS (whitehouse.gov).

President's Foreign Intelligence Advisory Board

The President's Intelligence Advisory Board and Intelligence Oversight Board (PIAB) provide advice to the president concerning the quality and adequacy of intelligence collection, of analysis and estimates, of counterintelligence, and of other intelligence activities.

The PIAB, through its Intelligence Oversight Board, also advises the president on the legality of foreign intelligence activities (dni.gov).

USA Freedom Corps Volunteer Network

President George W. Bush created USA Freedom Corps (USAFC) in 2002 to build on the acts of service, sacrifice, and generosity that followed September 11. The USAFC is charged with building a culture of service, citizenship, and responsibility in America. USAFC promotes and expands volunteer service in America by partnering with national service programs, working to strengthen the nonprofit sector, recognizing volunteers, and helping to connect individuals with volunteer opportunities (policevolunteers.org).

White House Military Office

The director of the White House Military Office (WHMO) serves as the principal advisor to the White House for all military support. The WHMO director oversees the policies that affect the WHMO-wide issues or involve department of defense assets. He or she ensures that White House requirements are clearly communicated and meet the highest standards of presidential quality. The WHMO director oversees all military operations aboard *Air Force One* on presidential missions worldwide (whitehouse.gov).

MISINFORMATION

Air Force One is the proper designation only if the aircraft that the United States president is in is a USAF craft. If it is operated by the army, then it is called *Army One*, if by the marines, *Marine One*, and so on. If it is a private or commercial aircraft, it is *Executive One*. And the aircraft's designation becomes *X One* as soon as the president is aboard.

The Executive Departments

The Constitution authorizes the appointment of executive departments in Article II, Section 2 where it states that the president may "require the Opinion, in writing, of the principal Officer in each of the executive Departments, upon any Subject relating to the Duties of their respective Offices." Since the founding of the republic, executive departments have existed as an extension of the president. The first departments to be created were the departments of State, War, and the Treasury. In addition to the leadership role of their respective departments, department secretaries also form a line of succession to succeed the president and vice president after the House Speaker and president pro tempore of the Senate.

The president nominates each department head and the Senate must confirm the nominee. Each department head is the chief officer of his or her own department. Department heads are the primary link between the president's policies and his or her own department. The department head must also work to promote and protect the department with the executive branch, congressional committees, and the public. Each department has several undersecretaries, a number of subunits, and support staff to carry out the responsibilities and services the department is charged with.

The largest department in the executive branch is the Defense Department with more than 3 million employees. Many departments have regional offices to help conduct activities. For example, the Internal Revenue Service, a division of the Treasury Department, is headquartered in Washington, D.C. Yet the IRS has many regional offices in the country to carry out the tax-collection process and assist taxpayers with IRS audits and issues that may arise.

The following table lists the makeup of the president's Cabinet and the year the post was created, as applicable.

The President's Cabinet

Cabinet Post	Year Created (If Applicable)
Secretary of State	1789
Secretary of the Treasury	1789
Secretary of Defense	1947
Attorney General	1789
Secretary of the Interior	1849
Secretary of Agriculture	1889
Secretary of Commerce	1903
Secretary of Labor	1913
Secretary of Health and Human Services	1953
Secretary of Housing and Urban Development	1965
Secretary of Transportation	1967
Secretary of Energy	1977
Secretary of Education	1979
Secretary of Veterans Affairs	1989
Secretary of Homeland Security	2002
Cabinet Rank Members	
The Vice President	1789
The White House Chief of Staff	1939
The Office of Management and Budget	1970
The United States Trade Representative	1962
The Environmental Protection Agency	1970
Office of National Drug Control Policy	1989

The Independent Agencies

The independent executive agencies are organized much the same way as the Cabinet departments. They are headed by a single administrator and generally have many subunits. The most significant difference between the independent executive agencies and the Cabinet departments is that the agencies do not have Cabinet status. The independent agencies serve primarily to regulate and provide services to businesses and citizens. The Environmental Protection Agency—which is responsible for protecting the environment—and the Library of Congress are two examples of independent agencies.

Congress has structured the independent regulatory commissions in large measure to be independent of the White House because of their responsibility to regulate important aspects of public policy. The regulatory commissions are made up of members appointed by the president and approved by the Senate. However, their terms are of such lengths that it is unlikely for any one president to gain control of these agencies through the appointment process. The rules and regulations of these commissions have the weight of law. In this way, these executive-branch agencies have both quasi-legislative and quasi-judicial powers.

Congress has also created government-owned corporations to operate commercially on behalf of the government. These entities are legally structured like any other business corporation in the United States. Although these corporations, such as Amtrak and the U.S. Post Office, are required to carry out their mission, they do not have to worry about profits. The "shareholders" they report to are the members of Congress who represent the American people.

The Civil Service

Today, more than 3 million people work for the federal government. Of these, nearly 3,000 hold high-ranking positions appointed by the president. The rest are career employees, or bureaucrats, who have jobs in Washington and regional offices throughout the United States and the world. These career employees are part of the civil-service system. The Constitution says very little about the federal bureaucracy, other than that the president shall have the power to appoint people to carry out the laws. Over time, the civil service system developed as the means to staff the growing federal bureaucracy.

In the early days of the republic, presidents appointed members of their own party to positions of government. When Thomas Jefferson became president, he found that all posts in government were filled by Federalists who had been appointed by Washington and Adams. Jefferson dismissed most of the employees and replaced them with members of his own party. By the 1820s, government employees totaled more than 20,000. When Andrew Jackson became president, he put in place the *spoils system.* Jackson rationalized this practice because he believed the president was entitled to have people from his political party in government positions to carry out his policies.

Unfortunately, this practice favors political loyalty (and financial support) over expertise and often breeds inefficiency, incompetence, and corruption.

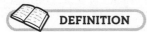 **DEFINITION**

> The **spoils system** is the practice of giving jobs and favors of government to political supporters and friends.

After the assassination of President Garfield by a disgruntled man who sought a government job, Congress passed the Pendleton Act of 1883. This law established the foundation for the present civil-service system. The act established merit criteria for hiring government employees. Additionally, it banned federal employees from participating in partisan politics. As the Pendleton Act was enforced, the spoils system essentially became a thing of the past.

In 1978, Congress passed the Civil Service Reform Act, which made major changes to the civil-service system. First, it created the Office of Personnel Management. This office examines, recruits, and trains all federal government employees. Secondly, it created the Merit Systems Protection Board to police and to protect the merit principle in the federal bureaucracy. In 1993, Congress passed the National Performance Review, which requires federal agencies to set goals, measure performance, and report on results.

Federal employees may join unions, but they are banned from conducting strikes under the Taft-Hartley Act of 1947. Additionally, federal employees may participate in elections but they are banned from serving as party activists. They can belong to a party, make political contributions, and of course, vote. But they may not lead or organize political rallies, become an officer of a political organization, or serve as a delegate to a political party convention. Some have argued that these bans infringe on the civil and political rights of federal employees.

Congressional Oversight of the Bureaucracy

Congress supervises the federal bureaucracy in several important ways:

- Most federal agencies cannot exist without congressional approval.
- Congress is the only branch of government that can authorize funds for the federal agencies.
- After Congress has authorized funds, it must appropriate money annually to the agency.
- Congress can hold hearings and investigate any federal agency.

- Congress can order audits of the federal programs through the Government Accountability Office.

- The U.S. Senate can wield considerable review of an agency when it must confirm political appointments by the President.

These powers give Congress considerable influence over the policies and practices of the federal agencies. This is another example of the system of checks and balances.

Judicial Oversight of the Bureaucracy

The federal courts play an important role in checking and limiting the power of the bureaucracy. Cases that come before the federal courts generally involve complaints that a federal agency has exceed its authority or acted in an unreasonable or unconstitutional manner in carrying out its duties and functions. Since Americans are allowed to sue the federal government for specific violations of the Constitution, the threat of being challenged in court has proven to be an effective means of controlling the bureaucracy.

The courts play a role in shaping the role of the branches of government, particularly when the dispute is between the executive and legislative branches over control of an agency. The states can also seek recourse against the bureaucracy through the courts. In February 2016, 29 states asked the Supreme Court to order a stay of a new EPA regulation limiting greenhouse-gas emissions called the Clean Power Plan. The Supreme Court sided with the states and has ordered a full review before the regulation can go into effect.

Other Restraints on the Bureaucracy

The myriad agencies in the federal bureaucracy create competition for resources and influence and are another source of limits. Many agencies in the Defense and Homeland Security branches compete with one another for a bigger slice of the defense budget dollars. A strong sense of patriotism and professionalism also serves to check the power and possible inappropriate behavior of the bureaucracy.

Individuals who come forward and expose bad and/or illegal behavior are called *whistle-blowers*. These individuals are offered some protection under federal laws and some agencies have a special office to which inappropriate activity can be reported. Lastly, the Freedom of Information Act gives citizens and the media access to government records that can uncover illegal or unconstitutional behavior.

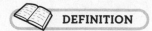 DEFINITION

Whistle-blowers are employees who risk their careers by reporting corruption or waste in government agencies.

The Least You Need to Know

- The federal government is a bureaucracy. It is an organization that includes hierarchical authority, job specialization, and formal rules.
- The bureaucracy consists of many agencies that are all in the executive branch of government. They are the Executive Office of the President, the 15 Cabinet departments, and numerous independent agencies.
- The civil-service system established by the Pendleton Act of 1883 replaced the spoils system. The civil service is now a meritocracy. Federal government employees are banned from conducting work strikes.
- Many congressional actions have sought to strengthen the civil service. Additionally, Congress has powerful tools at its disposal to oversee the federal bureaucracy. Congress must authorize the federal departments and agencies and fund their operations.

The Judicial Branch

The American judiciary has historically been viewed as yielding extraordinary power. Alexis de Tocqueville wrote: "… Scarcely any political question arises in the United States that is not resolved, sooner or later, into a judicial question." Judges play a central role in our political life and have a large role in making public policy. Often times, judges not only settle legal disputes, but also devise remedies to deal with injustices and inequities.

Civil liberties can generally be defined as freedoms that protect individuals from the government. Civil rights are those rights that guarantee us equality. Although many liberties and rights are outlined in the first 10 amendments to the Constitution, many other amendments and laws have been passed to include everyone in the spirit of the ideals written in the Declaration of Independence and the Constitution.

The Federal Court System

The American judiciary has historically been viewed as wielding extraordinary power. Alexis de Tocqueville wrote: "If I were asked where I place the American aristocracy, I should reply without hesitation ... that it occupies the judicial bench and bar .... Scarcely any political question arises in the United States that is not resolved, sooner or later, into a judicial question."

Judges play a central role in our political life and have a large role in making public policy. The main reason for this prominence is the power of judicial review. Since the early days of the republic, the Supreme Court has declared many federal laws and executive acts to be unconstitutional. Today, Supreme Court justices and federal judges resolve disputes involving large financial settlements, decide conflicts between competing parties and groups, and render decisions that affect the lives of all Americans. Often times, judges not only settle legal disputes, but also devise remedies to deal with injustices and inequities. Still, the Constitution limits the scope and nature of judicial power in America.

In This Chapter

- Traditions in the American judiciary
- History of American courts
- The scope of the judiciary
- Judicial power in American democracy

Judicial Review

Judicial review is the tool of the federal courts in our American system of checks and balances on which the U.S. government is based. Although judicial power is largely passive in that judges cannot instigate a case, most Americans accept the right of the courts to decide whether a law or act is constitutional.

There are two competing views of how judges should decide the constitutionality of a law or act. The *strict-constructionist approach* maintains that judges should adhere to the language clearly written or implied in the Constitution. The *activist approach* suggests that judges should interpret the Constitution to reflect current social, economic, and political conditions and values.

 ON THE RECORD

"It is emphatically the province and duty of the judicial department to say what the law is."

—Chief Justice John Marshall, 1803

It would be simplistic to assume that there is no difference between judicial philosophy and political ideology. Judges can be political liberals and still believe that they are bound by the limitations set forth in the Constitution. Today, many politically conservative judges favor judicial activism in order to reverse many court rulings of the last half-century.

The United States has two separate court systems. Each state has its own system of courts. These courts number in the thousands and hear most of the cases in the country. We also have a national judiciary system that covers the entire country with more than 100 courts. The national judiciary is also known as the federal courts.

The Development of the Federal Courts

The Constitution created the Supreme Court and leaves to Congress the power to create lower courts. Congress has created two types of lower courts. The *constitutional courts* are federal courts that exercise the power of the U.S. government. The *special courts* hear cases arising out of powers given to Congress.

The present level of influence of the federal courts has been shaped by ideological, economic, and political forces over several important historical periods.

1787 to 1865: The First Historical Period

From the founding of the republic to the Civil War (1787–1865), the main focus of the courts was to build a unified nation, establish the legitimacy of the government in Washington, and address the divisive issue of slavery.

Under the leadership of Chief Justice John Marshall (1801–1835), the Supreme Court established the dominance of national law and the right of the Supreme Court to interpret the Constitution. The two important cases that laid the groundwork for these principles are *Marbury* v. *Madison* (1803) and *McCulloch* v. *Maryland* (1819).

The *Marbury* case arose when President Adams tried to pack the court with party members after his defeat by Thomas Jefferson in 1800. In *Marbury*, the ruling established that the Supreme Court could declare an act of Congress unconstitutional. In the *McCulloch* case, the State of Maryland took a strict-constructivist approach and argued that the federal government did not have the power to create a national bank, and, therefore, the state could tax the bank. The Supreme Court set forth the doctrine of implied powers and the doctrine of national supremacy. The *doctrine of implied powers* gives the national government the authority to carry out the duties assigned to it in the Constitution. The *doctrine of national supremacy* maintains that in cases of conflict between the national and state governments, the national government is supreme.

During this early period, the Supreme Court also established the power of the federal government to regulate interstate commerce and to acknowledge the supremacy of the U.S. Constitution over the constitutions of the individual states.

However, the divisive issue of slavery is an example of the pendulum swinging back to the prerogative of states' rights. Dred Scott, a slave, made a claim for freedom since he had been transported to free states by his master, Dr. John Emerson. In the now infamous 1857 *Dred Scott* v. *Sandford* case, the Supreme Court held that slaves were not citizens of the United States and were not entitled to the rights and privileges of citizenship.

Furthermore, the court ruled that laws prohibiting slavery in Northern territories were unconstitutional. In addition, this decision declared that the Missouri Compromise was unconstitutional and that Congress did not have the authority to prohibit slavery in the territories. The *Dred Scott* decision was overturned by the Thirteenth and Fourteenth amendments to the Constitution. This ruling was a significant factor leading to the Civil War.

 REAL-LIFE FACTS

The Missouri Compromise was an agreement passed in 1820 between the proslavery and antislavery factions in the U.S. Congress, involving primarily the regulation of slavery in the Western territories. It prohibited slavery in what are now the Great Plains states and permitted it in Missouri and what is now Arkansas and Oklahoma.

1865 to 1932: The Second Historical Period

The second historical period that significantly influenced the development of the federal courts was the nineteenth- and twentieth-century periods of industrialization and economic growth. During this period, the Supreme Court addressed when and how it was appropriate for the federal government to regulate the economy, or when it was constitutional for the states to do so. The United States has a long tradition of revering the right to and protection of private property.

The Fourteenth Amendment, adopted in 1868 primarily to protect the citizenship of African Americans, also came to be viewed as a means of protecting private property and corporations from hostile government action by the federal courts. Once the federal courts included corporations within the definition of "person," businesses challenged various forms of national and state regulation of their industries. Notable during this period were rulings that prevented labor strikes, struck down income tax laws, and prevented child labor laws from being enacted.

 REAL-LIFE FACTS

In *Pollock v. Farmers' Loan and Trust Co.* (1895), the Supreme Court declared the federal income tax unconstitutional. The decision was essentially overturned with the ratification of the Sixteenth Amendment (1913).

The Supreme Court did uphold many regulations involving the Fourteenth Amendment with regards to corporations, particularly laws that regulated wages and hours. However, when it came to the rights of African Americans, the court upheld segregation and permitted their exclusion from voting in many states.

1932 to 1976: The Third Historical Period

Since the Great Depression and up until the late 1970s, the court has focused considerably on personal rights and liberties. This new direction started when the Supreme Court reversed itself and started to approve many of the New Deal initiatives proposed by FDR and passed by Congress. Subsequently, the court voided as unconstitutional many laws that restricted free speech, and by the 1950s entered its most active period yet in the area of civil liberties and civil rights.

The court assumed a new role; not only was it the arbiter of constitutional protections and laws, but now was charged with protecting citizens from *encroachment* and arbitrary government. This role was previously embraced by conservative ideologues in defense of their business constituents. During this period, however, it was liberals who preferred the activist court.

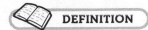

DEFINITION

Encroachment by the government is the gradual loss of rights and possessions of citizens.

1980s to 2005

Starting in the 1980s, there has been a revival of state sovereignty on the Supreme Court. States have been given the right to challenge federal power and we may be in a new era that places real limits on the supremacy of the federal government over the states. In the *United States* v. *Lopez* (1995), the court invalidated a federal law banning anyone from carrying a gun near schools. Alfonso Lopez Jr. was charged with violating the Gun-Free School Zones Act of 1990 when he carried a handgun and cartridges into his high school. Lopez argued that Congress acted beyond its power to legislate over our public schools.

In 1997, the court also struck down the Brady Law. This federal law required the states to do background checks on individuals buying guns.

ON THE RECORD

"The [Gun-Free School Zones] Act neither regulates a commercial activity nor contains a requirement that the possession be connected in any way to interstate commerce. We hold that the Act exceeds the authority of Congress 'to regulate Commerce ... among the several States ....'"

—Chief Justice William H. Rehnquist, 1995

The Roberts Court Since 2005

The first five years of the Roberts Court seemed to shift the direction of the court in a more conservative manner. Justice O'Connor, the first woman to serve as a Supreme Court Justice, retired and was replaced by Samuel Alito. Justice Alito has been a more consistently conservative justice than Justice O'Connor. For example, in 2000 the Supreme Court struck down a law that banned an abortion procedure. In 2007, the Supreme Court upheld a federal law banning a similar procedure commonly known as partial-birth abortion. On issues related to campaign finance, gun control, race, voting rights, and abortion, the Roberts Court has been largely conservative to date.

Interestingly, the Roberts Court has ruled in favor of liberal positions on such issues as national health care, same-sex marriage, and the environment. The current Supreme Court appears to maintain a "liberal" majority voting bloc on issues of liberties but a "conservative" majority voting bloc on issues relating to federal supremacy. However, with Justice Scalia's death, the balance of the Supreme Court may be tipped in favor of one political ideology with his replacement by the president.

The Jurisdiction of the Federal Courts

The U.S. Constitution limits the *jurisdiction* of the federal courts in Article III and the Eleventh Amendment. Federal courts can hear all cases that are federal-question cases and diversity of citizenship cases. A federal-question case is a civil case brought by a plaintiff who alleges a violation of the Constitution, a law, or a treaty of the United States. A diversity of citizenship case is when the parties to a case reside in two different states.

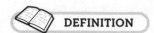 **DEFINITION**

Jurisdiction is the right and power to interpret and apply the law.

The federal court system is a three-tiered model consisting of district courts and various specialized courts of jurisdiction, the courts of appeals, and lastly the United States Supreme Court.

The district courts were created by Congress in the Judiciary Act of 1789. The courts of appeals were created by Congress in 1891. They were established primarily to relieve the Supreme Court of the burden of hearing appeals from the district courts. Congress created the thirteenth court of appeals in 1982 to have nationwide jurisdiction over special civil cases. The Court of International Trade, so renamed in 1980, was originally created in 1890, and deals with cases arising out of tariff and trade-related laws. The Supreme Court is the only court specifically created in the Constitution.

U.S. District Courts

The U.S. district courts are essentially trial courts. These courts have general jurisdiction, which means they hear cases involved in a broad number of issues. During these trials, testimony is taken and decisions are rendered. There is at least one district court in every state and the number of districts can vary over time due to population changes.

Currently, there are 94 federal districts. The courts are divided into 89 judicial districts in the 50 states, as well as 5 others that cover the District of Columbia, Puerto Rico, Guam, Virgin Islands, and the Northern Mariana Islands. Congress is solely responsible for establishing the number of these courts. The more populous states are divided into two or more districts. Each of these district courts falls within the boundary of an appellate court.

U.S. Courts of Appeals

Appellate courts do not conduct trials. Instead, a panel of judges reviews the details of the district trial and determines whether an error was made. Appellate courts have a prominent role in the policy-making process because less than 1 percent of their decisions are appealed to the U.S. Supreme Court.

There are 13 U.S. Courts of Appeals. Eleven of these hear appeals from the federal district courts within their geographic area made up of several states. A twelfth is located in the District of Columbia and hears the largest number of cases challenging federal statutes, regulations, and administrative decisions. The Court of Appeals for the Thirteenth Circuit, located in Washington, D.C., has national appellate jurisdiction over certain types of cases. These include patent cases and cases in which the U.S. government is a defendant.

The U.S. Supreme Court

The U.S. Supreme Court is the highest level in the three-tier federal court system. Originally, the Supreme Court had five justices; since 1869, there have been nine. The Supreme Court is the only court mentioned in the Constitution. All the other federal courts we have discussed have been created by Congress. Congress can create other inferior courts as it deems necessary.

The original jurisdiction of the Supreme Court involved cases involving two or more states, the United States and a state, foreign ambassadors and diplomats, and a state and a citizen of a different state. Today, the Supreme Court hears appeals from the federal appellate courts and from the highest courts at the state level that involve a federal or constitutional matter.

Selecting Federal Judges

The selection of federal judges has always been highly political. Because the judges serve for life and have the power of judicial review, the attitudes they bring to the court are very important. All judges are nominated by the president and must be confirmed by the Senate. The president almost always nominates a member of his own political party, or one that shares his own political ideology. Many figures are involved in the nominating process. Besides the president and the Senate, the Department of Justice, individual senators, the American Bar Association, the White House staff, and various interest groups all play a significant role in the selection process.

The Department of Justice and the White House staff review proposed candidates and are in charge of background checks. They are also responsible for determining the judicial philosophy of the candidate based on the record. Before the White House submits a candidate for the district and appeals courts, it observes the practice of senatorial courtesy—the practice of submitting the names of possible appointees to the senators from the states in which the appointee will work.

Normally, the Senate will not confirm a judge if the senior senator from that state exercises a veto called the *blue slip*. This custom does not apply to Supreme Court nominees because they have national jurisdiction and would be very impractical and time consuming. Interest groups monitor potential nominees, provide valuable information on the candidates, and make their views known to the White House and the senators before the names are sent for approval. The American Bar Association provides a professional evaluation of the candidate before the nomination is sent to the Senate Judiciary Committee. The rating is either "qualified" or "not qualified." Candidates who receive an unfavorable rating from the ABA are not likely to be considered.

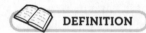 **DEFINITION**

The **blue slip** refers to the piece of paper that the chairman of the committee sends to a senator informing him or her that the president has made a nomination to a position in the senator's home state and inviting him or her to object or offer support.

Terms and Pay of Judges

Most federal judges are appointed for life unless they resign or retire. Congress may also remove them by the impeachment process. Only seven judges have ever been removed from office by Congress. Life tenure is intended to ensure the independence of the judicial branch of government. Some federal judges to special courts are appointed for fixed terms. Congress sets the salaries of all federal judges. Most judges receive a full salary for the rest of their lives after retirement.

The Court's Docket

The Supreme Court meets from early October to the end of June. During this time, the court decides between 75 and 100 cases—only a small fraction of those it receives. The *solicitor general* decides what cases the government should ask the Supreme Court to review.

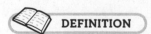 **DEFINITION**

The **solicitor general** is the federal government's chief lawyer. The president nominates a candidate and the Senate confirms the position. As the fourth-ranking officer in the Department of Justice, the solicitor general is part of the executive branch.

The review jurisdiction of the Supreme Court is almost entirely discretionary: the court can choose which cases it will decide to hear. Several important factors influence the decision to hear a case:

- If a legal question has been decided differently by various lower courts, the Supreme Court is likely to step in and resolve the matter.

- If a lower court's ruling conflicts with a prior Supreme Court ruling, that's another factor.

- A third factor is whether the issue can have significance beyond the parties involved in the case.

 REAL-LIFE FACTS

In 2009, Elena Kagan became the first woman to serve as Solicitor General of the United States. In 2010, President Obama nominated Kagan to the Supreme Court. Justice Kagan became the fourth woman to serve on the nation's highest court.

Writ of Certiorari

If the court decides to grant a petition for review, it must issue a *writ of certiorari*, an order to a lower court to send up the record of a case for review. The term writ of certiorari is a fifteenth century Middle English term, from the Latin, literally, to be informed. More than 90 percent of the petitions for writs of certiorari are denied. In order for the court to order a writ, it must be approved by four justices. This is known as the rule of four. This rule has been established since the Judiciary Act of 1925 to prevent a majority of the Supreme Court from controlling the cases it agrees to hear.

Decisions and Opinions

Once certiorari is granted, the justices do extensive research on the legal issues and facts of the case. Each side in the case submits a *brief* to the court. The court then hears oral arguments from the attorneys representing the parties to the case. When the court reaches a decision, an opinion is written. The opinion contains the court's ruling. The decision of the lower court is either affirmed, reversed, or the case is remanded back for a new trial or other proceeding.

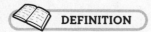

DEFINITION

A **brief** is a document that states the facts of the case, summarizes the lower-court decision, gives the argument of the lawyer, and discusses prior cases that bear on the issue.

When all justices don't come to a unanimous decision, the court issues a majority opinion and a dissenting opinion. Concurring opinions are written by justices who side with the majority or minority but do not agree with the specific opinion. Dissenting opinions are sometimes used in the future to overturn previous decisions and establish new precedent.

If the chief justice is in the majority on a case, he or she decides who will write the court's opinion. When the chief justice is in the minority, the most senior justice on the majority side decides who will write the case.

The Powers of the Court

Federal courts make public policy when they rule on and interpret laws and regulations. Constitutional interpretations can extend the reach of existing laws and regulations, or be determined to be unconstitutional, and therefore null and void. Ideology plays a significant factor in the rulings of the court. During the period of the 1950s and 1960s, the court was seen as activist and liberal. Since the 1990s, the Supreme Court has been viewed as activist and conservative.

One frequent principle employed by the court is the use of precedent. *Stare decisis*, sometimes referred to as the rule of precedent, is an informal rule of judicial decision-making that is held in high regard by both liberals and conservatives on the court. This principle is important for two main reasons. First, it is a practical matter. The law cannot continuously change without causing instability and chaos. Secondly, it supports the principle of equal justice in cases of a similar manner.

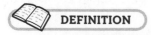

DEFINITION

Stare decisis, Latin for "to stand by that which is decided," is the principle to abide or adhere to decided cases.

However, times do change, and the court has made mistakes. The Supreme Court has overruled its own precedents many times. Furthermore, in the absence of congressional action, the court has ordered remedies in matters that have traditionally been left to the legislature. Some of these political questions include congressional district boundaries and many school system issues. One example of this is the court's decision in *Brown* v. *The Board of Education of Topeka* (1954) when the Supreme Court overturned rulings going back to *Plessy* v. *Ferguson* in 1896.

Checks on Judicial Power

The judicial system in the United States is arguably the most independent in the entire world. But the fact remains that the judiciary is part of the political process; therefore, courts do not have absolute independence. Several important checks limit judicial review and judicial activism.

Executive Checks

The executive branch has the important task of enforcing judicial decisions. It is commonly thought that President Andrew Jackson once said, "John Marshall made his decision; now let him enforce it." Whether or not Jackson actually said it is not the real point. The point is that the Supreme Court does not have any enforcement powers, and whether a decision will be implemented or voided depends on the cooperation of the other two branches of government. But rarely does the president refuse to enforce a Supreme Court decision. Instead, the president is more likely to interpret the way to enforce the Supreme Court's decision.

Presidents largely exercise influence over the judiciary by their power of appointment when a judicial seat becomes vacant.

Legislative Checks

Congress has significant ways that it can check the judicial branch of government. The Senate must confirm judicial appointments. The Senate can change the composition or ideology of the courts by the kind of nominee it is willing to confirm.

Congress can impeach judges whose positions it does not agree with, and simply the threat of impeachment can greatly influence other members of the bench. The House drafts the impeachment charges and the Senate conducts the trial to remove the judge from office.

Congress has the constitutional authority to change the number of judges. Over the last several decades, Congress has increased the number of federal judgeships, which has given the sitting presidents unusually large numbers of judges to appoint.

Congress can pass an amendment to the Constitution to overturn a Supreme Court decision.

Congress has power over the budget and, therefore, maintains the prerogative whether to allocate funds to carry out court decisions and rulings.

Congress can decide the jurisdiction of the lower courts and, thereby, could prevent matters from ever coming before the courts, or from review by the Supreme Court.

REAL-LIFE FACTS

In 1937, President Roosevelt, frustrated because the Supreme Court declared much of the New Deal unconstitutional, proposed to increase the number of justices to 15. This initiative became known as the "packing the court" plan. The proposal failed, but the court soon began to uphold many parts of the New Deal.

Public Opinion

Judges are human and sensitive to certain bodies of opinion, especially from among the ideological group to which they belong. Judges are also aware that, if they completely ignore public opinion, they run the risk of harming the legitimacy of the judiciary itself. Public opinion can serve to restrain or energize the courts. Their attitudes are often influenced by social trends. In 1992, *Planned Parenthood* v. *Casey*, the Supreme Court upheld restrictions on women seeking abortions, but declared that there exists a right to an abortion as determined in *Roe* v. *Wade*. Similarly, the Supreme Court's decision to uphold a constitutional right to marriage by same-sex couples in 2015 reflects the opinion of a majority of Americans.

Judicial Traditions and Doctrines

The Supreme Court rarely makes broad, sweeping decisions on issues. Instead the courts follow established precedent when deciding cases. The doctrine of *stare decisis* implies that courts will rarely overrule a precedent.

The court generally does not engage in political questions that should be decided by the elected branches of government. The Supreme Court has, for example, deferred to the executive branch on the matter of gays in the military. Yet the Supreme Court did actively engage in one of the most hotly contested presidential elections when it ruled in *Bush* v. *Gore* (2000). By a 5–4 vote, the court held that no alternative method of recounting the ballots could be established within the time limits set by Florida. Three of the concurring justices also asserted that the Florida Supreme Court had violated Article II, Section 1, Clause 2 of the Constitution, by misinterpreting Florida election law enacted by the Florida Legislature. The decision allowed Florida Secretary of State Katherine Harris's previous certification of George W. Bush as the winner of Florida's electoral votes to stand. Florida's 25 electoral votes gave Bush, the Republican candidate, 271 electoral votes. A majority (270) of the electoral votes are needed to win the presidency or vice presidency in the electoral college.

The Least You Need to Know

- The independent judicial branch is a powerful force in American political life because of the power of judicial review.
- Congress determines the jurisdiction of federal courts, except for the Supreme Court, which has complete control over the cases it chooses to review.
- Federal judges are nominated by the president and confirmed by the Senate.
- The manner in which judges interpret the laws makes them policymakers. The two main philosophies of judicial interpretation are strict constructivism and judicial activism.
- There are significant executive and legislative checks on the powers of the federal courts.

Civil Liberties

Civil liberties can generally be defined as individual freedoms that are protected from the government. These are outlined in the Bill of Rights and include freedom of religion; freedom of assembly; freedom of speech; freedom of association; the right to a fair trial, to privacy, to due process, and to own property.

Essentially, civil liberties limit the government's power and prevent the government from intervening in the lives of its citizens. Civil liberties are distinct from civil rights, which are inherent freedoms upheld, not granted, by the government.

In This Chapter

- What are civil liberties?
- First Amendment rights
- Due process of law
- The rights of the accused

The Inalienable Rights

The notion of the rights of citizens against the government was a tradition founded in the English roots of the United States. The English had a history of struggling with the government for more protection under the law. The American colonists who declared their independence from England fought for these *inalienable* rights—those which cannot be taken away.

ON THE RECORD

"We hold these truths to be self-evident, that all men are created equal, that they are endowed by their Creator with certain unalienable rights, that among these are Life, Liberty and the pursuit of Happiness."

—The Declaration of Independence

When the Constitution was ratified, many states were not pleased that there was no list of these freedoms included in the document, as there had been in many of the state constitutions. Therefore, the business of the first new Congress was to amend the Constitution to include these protections. On December 15, 1791, Congress passed the Bill of Rights. The Bill of Rights includes the first 10 amendments to the Constitution. Later, Congress would pass the Thirteenth and Fourteenth amendments, both of which ensure important freedoms for all Americans.

REAL-LIFE FACTS

Most constitutional rights are granted to all people, including aliens (people who are not citizens but live in the United States) most of the time. However, the right to unrestricted travel around the country can be regulated with aliens.

Government in the United States is limited. Individuals have certain rights that are guaranteed by the Constitution that the government cannot take away. Compared to a dictatorship, a democratic government has very little authority over its citizens. This does not mean that people can do whatever they want. Rights are relative in that they are only rights if they do not violate other freedoms. Essentially, people are free to do what they like as long as they do not impose on other people's rights.

Federalism and Individual Rights

Federalism is a very complex system of government that the founders developed to balance the power between the three branches of the federal government and the state governments. The Bill of Rights was aimed at protecting citizens from the federal government and does not actually include any freedoms from the state governments. The Supreme Court first upheld this in

Barron v. *Baltimore* (1833) and has followed this precedent ever since. Most states have their own Bill of Rights very similar to the Constitution's, and the states cannot infringe upon any rights guaranteed by the Constitution.

The rights of the individual against the state government are thus not the same as the civil liberties guaranteed by the Constitution. In fact, the Fifth Amendment claims that a person can only be charged with a capital crime by a grand jury. This is not the case with the state governments: they are free to use other means, as only about half the states have grand juries that participate in this process.

The Fourteenth Amendment contains a very important clause known as the due process clause. This clause has been interpreted by the Supreme Court to mean that no state can violate the basic and essential American liberties. The Supreme Court has upheld that most of the Bill of Rights falls under the jurisdiction of the due process clause and, therefore, also applies to state governments.

 ON THE RECORD

"Whatever disagreement there may be as to the scope of the phrase 'due process of law' there can be no doubt that it embraces the fundamental conception of a fair trial, with opportunity to be heard."

—Oliver Wendell Holmes Jr.

The Ninth Amendment is special in that it does not list any specific rights, but guarantees rights "retained by the people." The Supreme Court has set the precedent on which rights are protected under this amendment. Some examples include the right of an accused person to be tried only on evidence obtained legally and a woman's right to have an abortion without government interference.

The Establishment Clause: Religion and Education

The United States is deeply rooted in a religious, particularly Christian, tradition. The early colonists fled their European countries because of religious persecution, and incorporated their values and customs into their new society. Government in the United States has a history of including religion as part of its daily operations. For example, Congress begins with an opening prayer at its daily sessions and public officials take an oath in the name of God. Even the U.S. currency makes reference to God. Although these traditions have stood the test of time, Supreme Court cases have established the barrier between the state and religions in the public sphere.

Freedom of religion is guaranteed in the First and Fourteenth amendments. The so-called establishment clause prohibits the government from establishing religion, and the free exercise clause bans interferences by the government in the free exercise of religion.

REAL-LIFE FACTS

In 1952, Congress passed, and President Truman signed, a law designating the first Thursday of every May National Day of Prayer. This law is a product of the anticommunist fear during the Cold War era.

The establishment clause is the basis of the concept of separation of church and state. Interestingly, the Supreme Court did not hear its first case on this issue until 1947. The case is commonly called the New Jersey School Bus Case, in which the court upheld a state law that provided public transportation to all students to and from school, even if the school was a parochial (religious) school. The court felt that this law provided for safety of children and was not in support of religion at all. Since that case, the Supreme Court has continued to make rulings pertaining to religious involvement in public schools and the role government should play in parochial schools.

The Supreme Court uses guidelines to determine if a law regarding government involvement in religious activities is constitutional:

- The law must have a secular purpose.

- Its primary effect can neither endorse nor oppose a religion.

- It does not endorse an excessive government involvement with religion.

A 1952 case, *Zorach* v. *Clauson,* upheld New York City's "released time" program. Released time programs provide public schools with the opportunity to release some students early for religious instruction elsewhere. This case mandated that these religious classes be held on private property (like the church), not the public school itself.

The Supreme Court deems student religious groups free to organize in public schools. The Equal Access Act of 1984 states that all high schools receiving federal funds must allow student religious groups to meet and organize like other student organizations.

Prayers and the Bible in Schools

The Supreme Court has ruled in many major cases regarding the practice of prayer and reading of the Bible in schools. In *Engel* v. *Vitale* (1962), the court outlawed reciting prayers in public schools, even if it is voluntary. In *Abington School District* v. *Schempp* (1963), the court overruled the

Pennsylvania law requiring that each school day begin with a reading from the Bible and organized prayer. A similar law in Baltimore was also struck down. The Supreme Court defended its rulings by stating that the First Amendment requires the government to be religiously neutral and that it can neither endorse nor oppose any one religion.

Since these cases, the Supreme Court has also overturned a Kentucky law that mandated the display of the Ten Commandments in every classroom and the "moment of silence" law in Alabama, which allowed for meditation and silent prayer at the beginning of the school day. It has also ruled against offering prayer as part of graduation ceremonies and student-led prayers at high school football games.

The court has made it clear that it is unconstitutional for public schools to endorse religious activity. However, students are free to pray in school. Teachers are also free to teach the Bible in a literary and historical context. Despite the opinion of the Supreme Court, voluntary prayer and Bible readings still occur in many classrooms across the United States.

Teaching Evolution and Creationism in Schools

Evolution and *creationism* have been very controversial subjects taught in schools. The Supreme Court has decided that it is unconstitutional for school districts to ban the teaching of evolution or to mandate that both get equal consideration in the curriculum. The Supreme Court argues that these types of laws are religiously inspired and therefore unconstitutional. According to the courts, creationism can be seen as a religion and not science.

The courts have ruled that creationism cannot be taught as science, so creationists constructed the idea of "intelligent design" as a way of avoiding the prior references to God as the creator of the universe. By omitting any reference to God and instead arguing for the notion of an "intelligent" force, the opponents of evolution hoped to circumvent the legal hurdles and precedent that did not favor their view. Today, the leading supporters of "intelligent design" are conservative and orthodox believers in the God of Abraham—Jews, Christians, and Muslims.

 **DEFINITION**

The theory of **evolution** is based on Charles Darwin's studies and involves the process of a gradual change in life forms over generations. It claims that humans are a part of this process and that they evolved from lower life forms. **Creationism** is a belief based on the Bible that God created all life, including the Earth, universe, and human beings in their original form and they have not undergone any change or evolution.

Public Aid to Parochial Schools

Many states give aid to parochial schools and to parents who send their children to these schools. The laws provide tax deductions for tuition payments to parochial schools, tax-exempt status to parochial schools, textbooks to parochial schools, and construction aid for new buildings. Government cannot pay salaries of parochial school teachers, reimburse parents for the tuition they pay, supply parochial schools with services such as counseling, and provide money for instructional materials.

In the 1980s, the Reagan administration endorsed vouchers. President George H. W. Bush also endorsed them, and presidents since have tried to navigate the waters of this controversial issue. Americans are united in their view that education must be improved, but they are divided on shifting public funds to charter schools to achieve improvement in educational outcomes. In 2015 and 2016, more than 6,800 public charter schools operate in 42 states and the District of Columbia. These schools service approximately 3 million students—a six-fold increase in enrollment since 2000. Most voucher programs have been offered to students in low-income families, low-performing schools, or special education programs. These programs have received a great deal of attention by the courts.

A program launched in Cleveland, Ohio, in 1995 was found by the local federal district court to violate both the principle of church and state and the guarantee of religious liberty in the Ohio Constitution. This decision was made based on the fact that almost all of the families receiving the vouchers were sending their children to Catholic schools. The case was brought to the Supreme Court in 2002. In a 5–4 decision, the justices ruled the Ohio program constitutional. They argued that the private choice made by the parents had the ultimate goal of improving elementary education, which is a secular idea.

 ON THE RECORD

"Eighty percent of the American people want Bible readings and Prayer in the schools. ... Why should the majority be so severely penalized by the protests of a handful?"

—Reverend Billy Graham, evangelist

Still, political support for school vouchers is mixed. Statewide programs in Utah have been struck down while privately operated programs in Pittsburgh, Pennsylvania, have produced very positive results in low-income communities. As of 2006, the federal government operates the largest voucher program for evacuees of the areas affected by Hurricane Katrina. The Supreme Court's guidelines for determining if a law regarding government involvement in religious activities has been used to decide that public funds can be used to provide interpreters for deaf students in parochial schools and the government can hand out vouchers (grants for tuition) to parents for use in private schools.

Separation of Church and State

The Supreme Court has interpreted the establishment clause in many cases involving public and private education. But there have also been many cases involving seasonal displays in government offices, chaplains in legislative offices, and the public display of the Ten Commandments.

In *Lynch* v. *Donnelly* (1984) the Supreme Court held that a Rhode Island city could include a nativity scene in its Christmas decorations, as long as it included other nonreligious symbols such as Santa Claus, reindeer, and candy canes. A similar court case, *County of Allegheny* v. *ACLU* (1989), provided that displays containing only religious symbols are not allowed in or on government buildings because they violate the First and Fourteenth amendments.

The Supreme Court has also decided that, unlike prayer in public schools, prayer in Congress and state legislatures is permitted. The distinction is based on the tradition that prayer and religion have in American governmental history. Also, the Supreme Court believes that, unlike schoolchildren, lawmakers are not subject to religious indoctrination or peer pressure.

The public display of the Ten Commandments has been controversial in the Supreme Court. In *Van Orden* v. *Perry* (2005), the court considered a monument in the Texas state capitol to be secular and, therefore, acceptable, because it was a historical monument constructed by a private organization. On the other hand, the court also ruled against a public display of the Ten Commandments in *McCreary County* v. *ACLU of Kentucky* (2005) because framed copies of the Ten Commandments were placed around the courthouse and were deemed to be promoting religious doctrine.

The Free Exercise Clause

The free exercise clause protects a person's individual right to believe whatever he or she would like to believe in terms of religion. This is an absolute right guaranteed by the First and Fourteenth amendments. The courts have made a distinction between the right to believe and the right to act on those beliefs.

The most famous case regarding the free exercise clause is *Reynolds* v. *United States* (1878). Reynolds was a Mormon man who practiced polygamy, meaning he had two wives. The Supreme Court upheld Reynolds' conviction and established that the free exercise clause does not give anyone the right to violate criminal laws or public values, or otherwise impinge on the safety of the community by exercising his or her religion.

The court has imposed limits on free exercise on the basis of those guidelines. The court has upheld the mandatory vaccination of schoolchildren, even if it is against a person's religion, on the grounds that it is a public health issue. The court has also upheld laws that forbid the use of poisonous snakes in religious practices and laws that require businesses to be closed on Sundays. A state can require that a religious group have a permit to hold a parade, just as any other organization. Groups that recruit young children to sell religious literature must obey the child labor laws.

The court has also held that the government can draft those who have religious objections to military service. Conscientious objectors are individuals who refuse to participate in combat based on their religious, moral, or ethical grounds. During World War I, the conscientious objectors were permitted to serve in noncombatant roles. About 2,000 men refused to participate in any way in the military and were imprisoned. During World War II, all registrants of the draft were sent questionnaires regarding their stance on serving in the military. Nearly 12,000 men provided alternative services during the period from 1941 to 1947 in a program known as Civilian Public Service (CPS). These men served without wages and minimal support from the federal government. They also served for longer amounts of time than regular draftees. They were supported by the local congregations and families. Initially skeptical about the program, the federal government grew to appreciate the services provided by these men, such as forest fire prevention, erosion and flood control, and advances in the state-run mental health institutions. CPS was replaced by 1-W service in the early 1950s. It eliminated the base camps of the CPS and provided wages for the men.

The U.S. Forest Service can allow private companies to use land that American Indians have used for religious purposes. A state cannot forbid ministers from holding elected public offices. States must also give worker's compensation benefits to workers who quit their jobs because of religious conflicts.

The Religious Freedom Restoration Act of 1993 (RFRA) was passed in response to a Supreme Court decision that ruled the use of peyote in American Indian religious ceremonies unlawful. This law permitted the use of peyote and other drugs during a genuinely religious ceremony. The Supreme Court has also upheld many religious rights to free exercise in some historic cases.

In *Cantwell* v. *Connecticut* (1940) the Supreme Court deemed a law unconstitutional that required a person to get a license before soliciting money for a religious cause.

The Supreme Court has decided that Amish schoolchildren cannot be forced to attend school beyond the eighth grade, which is against their belief. The Amish people may be exempt from paying Social Security taxes if they waive their rights to any benefits.

The Jehovah's Witnesses are a religious group that has brought many controversial cases to the Supreme Court. The most important of these cases pertained to saluting the flag. The Jehovah's Witnesses believe that saluting the flag is against the Bible's commandment against idol worship.

The Supreme Court in one case in 1940 claimed that mandatory flag saluting is constitutional because it promotes patriotism. Three years later, in *West Virginia Board of Education* v. *Barnette*, the court reversed its decision and held that a mandatory flag salute law is unconstitutional.

 ON THE RECORD

"To believe that patriotism will not flourish if patriotic ceremonies are voluntary and spontaneous, instead of a compulsory routine, is to make an unflattering estimate of the appeal of our institutions to free minds."

—Justice Robert H. Jackson in *West Virginia Board of Education* v. *Barnette* (1943)

Several recent Supreme Court cases have addressed and clarified the constitutional protections on the matter of religious freedoms protected by the First Amendment. In *Burwell* v. *Hobby Lobby Stores, Inc.* (2014) the Supreme Court ruled in a 5–4 decision that a portion of the Affordable Healthcare Act violated the RFRA of 1993. Justice Alito, writing for the majority said, "As applied to closely held corporations, the HHS regulations imposing the contraceptive mandate violate RFRA. Religious employers, such as churches, are exempt from this contraceptive mandate."

In a major victory for freedom to practice religion, the Supreme Court ruled in a unanimous decision in 2015 that the government cannot forbid Muslim inmates from growing beards in prison. The opinion in the case, *Holt* v. *Hobbs*, was also written by Justice Alito. He said the prison's "interest in eliminating contraband cannot sustain its refusal to allow petitioner to grow a half-inch beard." The court unanimously stated that the prison's policy violated Holt's religious rights under a 2000 law called the Religious Land Use and Institutionalized Persons Act.

Freedom of Expression: Speech and Press

The right to free speech and press is guaranteed in the First and Fourteenth amendments. These rights guarantee each person the right to free expression and guarantee to everyone the right to hear what others have to say. These freedoms are intended to protect unpopular or minority viewpoints, but, like most of the other rights described in the Constitution, freedom of expression also has its limits.

For example, *libel* and *slander* are unlawful and not protected under the First or Fourteenth amendments. A person is also prohibited from yelling "Fire!" in a crowded theater. The use of false advertising and printing obscenities is also against the law.

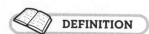 **DEFINITION**

Libel is the crime of publishing a false statement that is damaging to a person's reputation. **Slander** is a false spoken statement that is damaging to a person's reputation.

Seditious Speech

Seditious speech is not protected by the First Amendment. Sedition is conduct or speech inciting people to rebel against the government. In 1798, Congress passed the Alien and Sedition Acts, which gave the president the power to deport any rebel against the government. This law was intended to stifle the adversaries of the Federalist Party. About 10 people were convicted under this law but were pardoned later by Thomas Jefferson.

The Sedition Act of 1917 made it illegal to encourage governmental disloyalty, interfere with the draft, prevent the sale of government bonds, and publish anything detrimental about the U.S. government. The constitutionality of this law was upheld many times in court and about 2,000 people were convicted for violating this law. The Alien and Sedition Acts were not appealed to the Supreme Court for review, so it was never officially ruled unconstitutional. However, later mentions of the Alien and Sedition Acts in Supreme Court opinions have implied that it would be ruled unconstitutional if ever tested in court.

The Smith Act of 1940 makes it illegal for a person to endorse the overthrow of the American government, to distribute any materials regarding the overthrow of the American government, or to belong to a group that intends to overthrow the government. Many Communists were taken to court because of this law. The court has made the distinction between encouraging people to believe something, which they consider legal and encouraging people to do something, which is considered illegal.

Obscenity

Common law rule in the United States banned material that could influence people whose minds were open to "immoral" tendencies. Under this notion, works by authors such as Balzac, James Joyce, and D. H. Lawrence were banned based on specific passages thought to possibly affect young children. This prevailed up until 1957, when *Roth* v. *United States* repudiated this idea and defined obscenity more strictly as "material whose dominant theme taken as a whole appeals to the prurient interest" to the "average person, applying contemporary community standards." The court also reaffirmed that obscenity was not protected by the First Amendment and thus upheld the conviction of Samuel Roth for sending obscene materials through the mail as advertising for his literary business.

The court ruled in a 6–3 decision and other cases further demonstrated the plurality of the court on this issue. The justices were put in the position of having to come to an agreement and proceeded to review almost every obscenity prosecution in the United States. As a result of the sexual revolution of the 1960s, the court felt pressure to allow leeway for state and local governments to crack down on obscenity. Justices were attacked vigorously by conservatives in Congress because of the liberalized protection of pornography during that time.

Finally in *Miller* v. *California* (1973), the court came to an agreement and developed the Miller test. This test defines a work as obscene if it appeals to the prurient interest based on contemporary community standards, it depicts or describes in an obviously offensive way, sexual conduct or excretory functions specifically defined by a state law to be obscene, and if the work lacks literary, artistic, political, or scientific value. The work is considered obscene only if all three criteria are met. The court has upheld laws prohibiting the mailing of such materials, the establishment of adult stores within 1,000 feet of churches and schools, and the banning of taverns and nude dancing clubs in cities that choose to do so. The law also prohibits the use of pornographic websites in public libraries.

In *Pope* v. *Illinois* (1987), the Supreme Court ruled that a local community standard to determine "value" established in Miller was unconstitutional. The majority opinion in the case stated:

> "The proper inquiry is not whether an ordinary member of any given community would find serious literary, artistic, political, or scientific value in allegedly obscene material, but whether a reasonable person would find such value in the material, taken as a whole."

Prior Restraint

The government can punish people for acts of slander and libel after they are done, but it cannot attempt to restrict ideas before they are expressed, except in times of war or if the ideas are obscene or have the potential to incite violence. The court has given school officials the right to censor school papers and publications with a much closer eye.

The Media

Reporters and other people in the media are often protected by shield laws, which in about 30 states protect them from having to reveal their sources or other confidential information. The government extensively regulates the radio and television industries because they use the public's property (the public airwaves) to distribute their information.

The Federal Communications Commission (FCC) can prohibit the use of indecent language but cannot censor programs before they air. Congress has given increasingly more freedom to cable channels as opposed to public channels, which are still strictly regulated.

 ON THE RECORD

"Words can be weapons .... The question in every case is whether the words used are used in such circumstances and are of such nature as to create a clear and present danger that they will bring about the substantive evils that Congress has the right to prevent."

—Justice Oliver Wendell Holmes Jr. in *Schenck* v. *United States* (1919)

Symbolic Speech

Symbolic speech, if peaceful, is protected by the First and Fourteenth amendments. For example, picketing around a business where workers are on strike is considered constitutional. However, picketing that is conducted for an illegal purpose is not protected under the Constitution.

The court has held that certain acts of symbolic speech can be punished if the goal of the protest is within the constitutional powers of the government to prevent, the government's interest is not solely in stifling the dissent, and the restrictions placed on expression are no greater than necessary. The acts that have been questioned include the burning of draft cards and crosses, and wearing black armbands at school in protest of war. The Supreme Court, in two divided decisions, has upheld burning of the American flag, on the grounds that the government may not prohibit an act of expression solely because society finds the idea offensive.

 ON THE RECORD

"If I were king, I would not allow people to go about burning the American flag. However, we have a First Amendment, which says that the right of free speech shall not be abridged."

—Justice Antonin Scalia

Freedom of Assembly and Petition

The First and Fourteenth amendments protect the people's right to peaceful assembly. The court has differentiated between peaceful assembly and civil disobedience, which they have held as unconstitutional. Civil disobedience refers to behavior that is peaceful but is in violation of the law for the purpose of making a political statement.

The government can make and enforce laws regarding the time, place, and manner of assemblies. Government's rules must be content-neutral, meaning that they must apply to any form of assembly and not change based on what the assembly represents. However, the government can use other means to ban certain forms of protest. They can use the excuse of crowd and traffic control to prevent certain groups from organizing a rally or protest.

The rights to assembly and petition do not give people the right to trespass on private property. The Supreme Court cases have dealt with shopping centers and have concluded that the owners of shopping centers are required to allow the reasonable exercise of the right of petition on their property.

Most protests occur on public property, because it is generally legal, and demonstrators usually want to appeal to the general public. The court has often upheld laws that require advance notice or permits in order to organize a demonstration and laws that create certain "buffer zones" around abortion clinics where it is unlawful to protest or block entrance to the building.

The right of assembly and petition incorporates the freedom of association, which is the right to affiliate with others to promote a political, economic, or social agenda. The court has ruled in *Boy Scouts of America* v. *Dale* in 2000 that the government cannot force the Boy Scouts to admit members when those members would not represent what the organization stands for. Therefore, the Boy Scouts have refused leadership positions to homosexuals. The Boy Scouts also exclude atheists and agnostics as leaders.

Due Process

The Constitution contains two due process clauses in the Fifth and Fourteenth amendments. The Supreme Court has been purposefully vague in defining this term and has opted to deal with it on a case-by-case basis. In general, due process has come to mean that, in whatever it does, the government must act justly and uphold established rules. The court has determined that laws must be fair and must be enforced in a just manner.

In *Pierce* v. *Society of Sisters* (1925), the Supreme Court ruled that a law requiring all children ages 8 to 16 to attend public school was unconstitutional. This law was intended to destroy the private and parochial school systems. The court found that the contents of this law were unfair and went against parents' liberty to control the education of their children.

Rochin v. *California* (1952) condemned the police for obtaining evidence from Rochin by forcing him to the hospital to pump his stomach in order to retrieve the capsules of morphine he had swallowed when the police stormed his residence without a search warrant. The Supreme Court sided with Rochin and found him protected under the Fourteenth Amendment's guarantee of procedural due process.

The Police Power

The police power is the reserved power of the state to protect the public's health, safety, morals, and general welfare. This is controversial because in some cases, the police power has been thought to infringe upon individual's rights.

The courts have most often sided with the police power. For example, to promote health, states can limit the sale of alcohol and tobacco, make laws to prevent pollution, and require vaccination of all children. To promote safety, states can utilize breathalyzer and other tests in order to arrest drunk drivers, control the carrying of concealed weapons, and mandate the use of seatbelts. To promote morality, states can outlaw gambling and prostitution. To advocate for the general welfare, the government can make education mandatory and provide aid to the medically compromised. In doing so, the government must not violate the due process clause of the Fourteenth Amendment.

The Right to Privacy

The first case to address the right to privacy, which is not explicitly named or guaranteed in the Constitution, was *Griswold* v. *Connecticut* in 1965. In that case, the Supreme Court deemed a law prohibiting the use of birth control a violation of the Fourteenth Amendment.

The most controversial of the right to privacy cases have dealt with abortion issues, the most famous being *Roe* v. *Wade* (1973). In this case, the Supreme Court overruled a Texas law that criminalized abortion unless the mother's life was in danger. The court agreed that the Fourteenth Amendment includes a woman's right to choose whether or not to end her pregnancy.

Rulings on abortion are influenced heavily by the composition of the Supreme Court itself. A more conservative court is likely to place more restrictions on abortion than a more liberal court. The court has set many guidelines in terms of abortion. In the first trimester, the state cannot interfere with a woman's right to an abortion. In the second trimester, a state can make reasonable rules regarding how, when, and where abortions can be performed, but cannot outlaw the procedure. In the final trimester of pregnancy, states can opt to outlaw abortion except in the instances of danger to the mother's life.

In 1990, two cases addressed abortion and minors. The court ruled that a state could require a minor to inform at least one parent before she can obtain an abortion. A state could also require that she tell both parents unless a judge granted her permission to obtain an abortion without parental consent.

 REAL-LIFE FACTS

Roe v. *Wade* was decided on January 22, 1973. By then the plaintiff, whose name was actually Norma McCorvey, had already given birth.

After *Roe* v. *Wade*, the next most important abortion case was *Planned Parenthood of Southeastern Pennsylvania* v. *Casey* in 1992. There the court declared that the government can impose restrictions on abortion as long as they do not create an "undue burden" on the woman's choice. In Pennsylvania and many other states, a woman must be given professional counseling intended to persuade her to change her mind. A woman must wait 24 hours between that counseling and when she can actually have her abortion. Doctors and clinics must keep records of all abortions they perform.

The court has also upheld a law stating that married women are not required to tell their husbands about their plans for abortion. In 2007, the court agreed that the Partial Birth Abortion Ban Act of 2003 is constitutional. This law incriminates doctors who perform this procedure even when they believe the health of the woman involved is at risk.

The battle over abortion rights is currently being waged in state legislatures, and some of these laws will ultimately be reviewed by the Supreme Court. Many states already have some restrictions that are constitutional; some include having a licensed doctor perform the abortion. (This is the case in 38 states.) Recently, some states have tested how far they can go when imposing restrictions. Texas and Mississippi, for example, have passed laws that require doctors who perform abortions to have admitting rights at a hospital. This added requirement limits the number of doctors available to perform abortions. If this requirement is upheld by the Supreme Court, Mississippi might have to shut down the only abortion clinic in the state. In March 2016, Indiana passed an even-more restrictive law. In addition to the admitting requirement for doctors, Indiana now holds doctors liable if a woman has an abortion solely because she objects to the sex, race, or disability of the fetus. Whether or not these new laws are unconstitutional will certainly be an issue in the 2016 presidential election and will ultimately be decided by the Supreme Court.

Freedom and Security of the Person

The Thirteenth Amendment was added to the Constitution in 1865, thereby ending more than 200 years of slavery in the United States. The Thirteenth Amendment protects individuals against slavery and involuntary servitude. It also calls for Congress to enforce this freedom through legislation. The Thirteenth Amendment does not forbid all forms of involuntary servitude, or forced labor. This issue has been addressed in terms of the military draft.

Congress passed the first Civil Rights Act in 1866. This was the most important measure passed by Congress to protect the rights of the freed slaves during Reconstruction. This law included the right to make contracts, sue, bear witness in court, and own private property. President Andrew Jackson vetoed the bill because he felt that because blacks were not qualified to be citizens, the bill would be operating "in favor of the colored and against the white race." The Republican Congress overturned his veto. Furthermore, any person found to deny these rights to the slaves faced a fine and imprisonment. The Supreme Court essentially upheld racial discrimination for many years on the grounds that it did not infringe on the Thirteenth Amendment. It was not until 1968 in *Jones* v. *Mayer* that the Supreme Court began to enforce the Civil Rights Act.

Mayer refused to sell Jones his house because Jones was African American. The court upheld this law and continued to extend the law to any group subject to discrimination primarily because of their ethnicity and ancestry.

The Right to Keep and Bear Arms

The Second Amendment deals with the right to keep and bear arms. It was intended to protect the rights of each state to keep a militia. The court has only heard one important case on this issue. In *United States* v. *Miller* (1939), the court upheld a section of the National Firearms Act of 1934, which prohibited shipping guns across state lines without registering them with the Treasury Department and paying a tax.

In 2008, in a 5–4 ruling, the Supreme Court upheld the right of citizens to bear arms in the landmark case *District of Columbia v. Heller.* This is the first time that the court ruled directly on the constitutional merits of this civil liberty. Since the District of Columbia is not a state, the due process clause of the Fourteenth Amendment did not apply in this case and was not incorporated. However, the question of whether the Second Amendment applies to states was resolved in the landmark case *McDonald* v. *City of Chicago* (2010). In a 5–4 decision, the Supreme Court held that the Fourteenth Amendment makes the Second Amendment right for the purpose of self-defense applicable to the states.

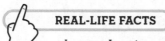 **REAL-LIFE FACTS**

In 2015, Americans owned approximately 300 million guns. There are approximately 100,000 gun injuries and deaths annually in the United States.

The Exclusionary Rule

The exclusionary rule declares that any evidence gained unlawfully by the police cannot be used in the trial of the person from who the evidence was taken. The first case in 1914 dealt with the exclusionary rule at the federal level. This rule was extended to the states in *Mapp* v. *Ohio* in 1961. The exclusionary rule's purpose is to make sure officers obey the law when they enforce the law.

The Supreme Court has found some exceptions to the rule in four important cases. In *Nix* v. *Williams* (1984), the court claimed that evidence that would have inevitably been discovered can be used in court. The use of this type of evidence is determined by the judge of the case. In *United States* v. *Leon* (1984), the court found a "good faith" exception to the rule when police thought they were using a valid search warrant, but it was later found to be void.

The court has also allowed for officers' "honest mistakes," when in *Maryland* v. *Garrison* (1987) police accidentally searched the wrong apartment and found drugs there. In 2006, the Supreme Court ruled that evidence acquired in violation of the knock-and-announce requirement, which requires officers to announce their presence and provide residents with the opportunity to open the door prior to a valid Fourth Amendment search, is not subject to the exclusionary rule.

The "good faith" exception established in 1984 was questioned in the case *Davis* v. *United States* (2011). The court was asked to address whether the "good faith" exception applies to a search in compliance with binding precedent but is later overturned. In a 7–2 decision, the majority opinion, written by Justice Alito, concluded that the "good faith" exception does not apply. This retroactive application was criticized in the dissent by Justice Breyer.

Security of Home and Person

The Third and Fourth Amendments protect the individual against the government's intrusion into private homes. The Third Amendment prevents soldiers from housing in people's homes without their consent. This amendment was based on the practice of British soldiers in colonial times and has had little significance since its inception in 1791.

Similarly, the Fourth Amendment is derived from the colonial practice of broad search warrants called writs of assistance. The Fourth Amendment protects individuals against these writs of assistance and invasion of their private homes without probable cause. Police must have reasonable suspicion to obtain a warrant to search a private home. The court has decided that police do not need warrants if the evidence they obtain is in plain view.

Police are not required to have a warrant to arrest someone in a public place as long as they have probable cause. The court has established that the Fourth Amendment does protect individuals when the police restrain the individual's right to freedom by the "physical force or show of authority" in *Terry* v. *Ohio* (1968). The court has dealt with many issues regarding what is considered protected under the Fourth Amendment.

The court has decided that officers do not need a warrant to search a car, boat, airplane, or other vehicle on the grounds that these are "movable crime scenes" that will likely disappear in the time it takes to acquire a warrant.

Police also do not need a warrant to use a specially trained dog to sniff around the outside of a car for narcotics at a routine traffic checkpoint. Ultimately, police do not need a warrant to search any part of a car if they have reasonable suspicion there is evidence of a crime.

The court has upheld random drug testing of student athletes, drug enforcement officers who carry firearms, and railroad workers after a train accident. The court has generally agreed that drug testing can be performed without warrants or even any indication of drug use.

Wiretapping

In *Katz* v. *United States* (1967), the court declared that evidence obtained from a wiretapping device on a public phone could not be used against Katz in court. Under the Fourth Amendment, Katz had the right to make a private call from a public phone booth. In its decision, the court did say had the police obtained a warrant to tap the phone booth, the evidence would have been valid.

As part of President George W. Bush's "War on Terror," the National Security Agency (NSA) is authorized by executive order to monitor, without seeking court approved warrants, phone calls, emails, internet activity, text messages, and other communication involving any party believed to be outside the United States. On December 16, 2005, Attorney General Alberto Gonzales confirmed the existence of this program, which aroused concern among elected officials, civil rights activists, and the general public about the constitutionality and legality of the program and the potential for its abuse. Since then, the criticism has extended to include the press's role in exposing a classified program, the role and responsibility of Congress in the program's oversight, and the extent of presidential powers under Article II of the Constitution.

Rights of the Accused

In the United States, persons accused of a crime are innocent until proven guilty by fair and lawful means. They are entitled to rights including habeas corpus, a legal action through which a person can seek relief from unlawful detention. Officers are required to explain to the court why a person should be held in custody of the police. The Constitution allows for this right to be suspended in "cases of rebellion or invasion." Habeas corpus has been suspended during the Civil War, Reconstruction, and the war on terror. On June 12, 2008, the Supreme Court ruled 5–4 in *Boumediene* v. *Bush* that terror suspects detained in Guantanamo Bay detainment camp have the right to seek a writ of habeas corpus in U.S. federal court.

A bill of attainder is a law that declares a person or group guilty of a crime and punishes them without a trial. This practice is prohibited by the Constitution at both the federal and state levels.

Ex post facto laws are criminal laws that retroactively change the legal consequences of actions committed. These laws may criminalize actions that were legal when they were committed, worsen the punishment of a crime, or change the level of evidence needed for conviction. These cases do not come up very often in the Supreme Court, but in the most recent one, the court overturned a man's sexual abuse conviction because of a change in a Texas state law that had made it easier for the prosecution to prove its case than it was when the abuse was committed.

Grand juries determine whether or not there is enough evidence for a trial. Under the Fifth Amendment, anyone charged with "capital or infamous" crimes under federal jurisdiction must be presented to a grand jury. The Supreme Court has ruled that this requirement does not pertain to the states under the Fourteenth Amendment and therefore states may elect whether or not to use grand juries.

The Constitution guarantees a speedy trial. The Supreme Court has listed the criteria for determining if this right has been violated by assessing the length of the delay, the reasons for it, whether the delay has harmed the defendant and whether the defendant asked for a speedy trial. Congress passed the Speedy Trial Act of 1974, which states that the time between a person's arrest and the beginning of his or her trial cannot exceed 100 days.

The Sixth Amendment states that a trial must be public. However, a judge can limit both the number and kinds of people who may be present at trial. The court has also ruled that televising a trial is not prohibited as long as measures are taken to avoid too much publicity and to protect the defendant's rights of privacy.

The Sixth Amendment also guarantees a trial by an impartial jury. The defendant has the right to ask to be tried in another place if he or she feels that the jury might be too prejudiced. The judge makes the decision to move the trial if necessary. A defendant can also waive the right to a jury trial and instead have a bench trial, where the judge alone hears the case. Juries must consist of a balanced cross section of the U.S. population, and no person can be denied a position on a jury based on race, sex, or religion.

Every person accused of a crime has the right to a proper defense. If this is not provided, the accused person can appeal the court's decision. If an accused person cannot afford a lawyer, the state must provide one, called the public defender.

Once a person has been tried for a crime, he or she cannot be put on trial for the same crime ever again. However, if a person violates both federal and state laws in one single act, he or she can be tried in federal court for the federal crime and in state court for the state crime.

Self-Incrimination: Miranda Rights

The Fifth Amendment states that no person can be forced to be a witness against himself or herself. This protection is honored in both federal and state court, and in criminal and civil cases. It is a personal right that can only be claimed for oneself. A person cannot be forced to confess to a crime by intimidation, torture, or psychological pressures.

The most famous case regarding self-incrimination was *Miranda* v. *Arizona* (1966), in which a mentally retarded man confessed to rape and kidnapping without ever being told of his constitutional rights. This case put forth the Miranda Rule, which requires the police to:

- Inform the suspect of his or her right to remain silent.

- Warn the suspect that anything he or she says can be used against him or her in court.

- Inform the suspect of the right to have an attorney present during questioning.

- Inform the suspect that if he or she cannot afford an attorney, one will be provided by the state.

- Inform the suspect that he or she can end questioning at any time.

MISINFORMATION

A person cannot always "take the Fifth." The court decides when the right can properly be used. If an individual does not comply, then he or she can be held in contempt of court.

The Eighth Amendment

The Eighth Amendment claims that bail or fines must be reasonable in relation to the seriousness of the crime involved. Bail is an amount of money that is deposited to the court as a guarantee that the accused person will appear in court at the proper time.

The practice of bail is justified on the grounds that a person should not be jailed until they are proven guilty and a defendant can better prepare for trial outside of jail. The Constitution does not guarantee the right of bail in all crimes. A defendant has the right to appeal if bail is denied in his or her case. People who cannot afford bail are sometimes released on their honor, because failure to appear to trial is a crime in and of itself.

The Supreme Court has upheld the practice of preventative detention, which is holding the defendant without bail because there is reason to believe he or she might be a flight risk or commit another crime before his or her trial begins.

The Eighth Amendment also prohibits "cruel and unusual punishment." In *Wilkerson* v. *Utah* in 1879, a convicted murderer was sentenced to death by a firing squad. The Supreme Court ruled this constitutional, as they claimed the Eighth Amendment intended to protect the convicted from punishments such as burning at the stake, crucifixion, and other "barbaric tortures."

More often than not, the court has rejected the argument of cruel and unusual punishment. Most of the Eighth Amendment cases that have been heard pertain to capital punishment, or punishment by death. Capital punishment was carried over to the United States by the colonists. The methods and crimes subject to the penalty have varied throughout history. Some states and jurisdictions have banned it or suspended its use while other areas have tried to expand it.

From 1972 to 1976, capital punishment was suspended in the United States as a result of the Supreme Court's decision in *Furman* v. *Georgia* (1972). After this decision, 37 states enacted new death penalty laws that attempted to address the inconsistent use of the death penalty, but the

Supreme Court found mandatory death penalty laws unconstitutional (for example, mandatory death penalty for conviction of killing a police officer). When executions resumed in 1977, many prisoners delayed their execution dates by filing for repeated writs of habeas corpus. Therefore, between the 1970s and 1980s, hundreds of individuals were sentenced to death but only 10 were executed before 1984.

With the passage of the Antiterrorism and Effective Death Penalty Act of 1996, federal judges could not remedy unjust convictions as easily, and it seems like the speed of executions has picked up, with more than 1,100 since 1990. The Supreme Court has also utilized IQ test results when determining a criminal's sentence and has upheld that executions of mentally retarded criminals are "cruel and unusual punishments" prohibited by the Eighth Amendment. The Supreme Court has also raised the minimum age a criminal can be sentenced to death to 18 years old in the case *Roper* v. *Simmons* (2005). In *Kennedy* v. *Louisiana* (2008), the Supreme Court ruled that states may not impose the death penalty when the victim's life was not taken in the crime.

The method of execution has been controversial, but the use of lethal injection has become somewhat standard in the United States. Due to several botched executions and a shortage of the drug used to induce death, some states have turned to alternative methods rather than rely exclusively on lethal injections. In 2014, Tennessee reinstated the use of the electric chair. That same year, Wyoming and Utah reinstated firing squads.

Interestingly, the death penalty is sought and applied more often in some states and even within some states. Approximately 2.5 percent of murderers are sentenced to death nationwide. In Nevada, 6 percent are sentenced to death, while in Texas it is 2 percent. Texas, however, executed 40 percent of those sentenced, which is about four times higher than the national average. Researchers have also implicated death penalty biases, in that only 1.4 percent of those executed since 1976 have been women and African Americans make up about 40 percent of death row inmates but only about 12 percent of the general population. Studies have shown that the best predictor of a death sentence is not the race of the murderer, but the race of the victim, with more than 80 percent of death sentences involving white victims.

Treason against the U.S. government is the only crime that is defined in the Constitution. Treason refers to imposing war on the United States or aligning oneself with the enemies of the United States. A person can commit treason only in wartime, but Congress has made it illegal to commit espionage or sabotage during times of peace as well. The maximum punishment for treason is death, but no one has ever been executed for this crime.

The Least You Need to Know

- Civil liberties protect individuals from the government. These are outlined in the Bill of Rights and include freedom of religion; freedom of assembly; freedom of speech; freedom of association; the right to a fair trial, to privacy, to due process, and to own property.

- The Supreme Court plays the role of interpreter of the vague wording of the Constitution and is often given the task of deciding the extent to which individual's civil liberties are protected under the Constitution.

- Separation of church and state, a woman's right to an abortion, the rights of the accused, and due process have all been controversial issues in American history. The Supreme Court has sometimes changed what is considered constitutional.

- The Fourteenth Amendment is important because it extends the rights outlined in the Bill of Rights beyond Congress to include the states. However, the Supreme Court has ruled so that it does not incorporate the Second, Third, or Seventh amendments; the right to indictment by a grand jury (Fifth Amendment); or the protection against excessive bail and fines (Eighth Amendment).

Civil Rights

Equality is at the heart of the concept of civil rights. Civil rights are the rights of individuals to receive equal treatment and to be free from unfair treatment or discrimination in a number of settings, including education, employment, housing, and more, and based on certain legally protected properties.

What Are Civil Rights?

Civil rights have historically been associated with the struggle among African Americans for social and legal equality. Presently, the term is used to encompass the struggle to eradicate discrimination on the basis of any inherent individual characteristic such as race, sex, sexual orientation, age, or disability. Most of the laws passed to ensure civil rights have originated with court decisions or federal laws and executive orders.

Civil rights differ primarily from civil liberties in that civil rights aim to guarantee equal treatment while civil liberties are those rights and freedoms that the government may not impede upon and are protected by the U.S. Constitution. The struggle for civil rights in American history is a testament to the ideals embodied in our Declaration of Independence "that all men are created equal."

Slavery and Civil Rights

When the founders met in Philadelphia to write the Constitution, they apportioned congressional representatives among the states according to population counts. In addition to the total number of "free" persons, they included in the count "three fifths of all other persons." This clause was added to include slaves, though not as actual people, in order to increase the number of representatives in the Southern states and thus guarantee their support for the new framework of government. Thus, from the founding of the republic, slavery was protected by virtue of the language in the Constitution found in Article I, Section 2.

The institution of slavery was found to be constitutional in the 1857 case *Dred Scott* v. *Sanford*. The ruling in this case is considered one of the important factors that led directly to the Civil War. In the *Dred Scott* case, the Supreme Court ruled that slaves were not citizens of the United States and, therefore, not entitled to the rights and privileges of citizenship. Furthermore, the court ruled that the ban on slavery in Northern territories of the United States—part of the Missouri Compromise—was unconstitutional.

President Lincoln issued the Emancipation Proclamation of January 1, 1863. This presidential order declared that the over 3 million slaves in the Confederate states were free and set the nation on the path to end slavery:

> "Now, therefore I, Abraham Lincoln, President of the United States, by virtue of the power in me vested as Commander in Chief, of the Army and Navy of the United States in time of actual armed rebellion against authority and government of the United States, and as a fit and necessary war measure for suppressing said rebellion, do, on this first day of January, in the year of our Lord one thousand eight hundred and sixty three, and in accordance with my purpose so to do publicly proclaimed for the full period of one hundred days, from the day first above mentioned … order and declare that all persons

held as slaves within said designated States, and parts of States, are, and henceforward shall be free; and that the Executive government of the United States, including the military and naval authorities thereof, will recognize and maintain the freedom of said persons."

The language of the Proclamation, and the legal basis that President Lincoln used in issuing it, stem from the president's role as commander-in-chief. Additionally, amendments to the Constitution and congressional acts contributed significantly to ending the institution of slavery and extending civil rights to African Americans.

The Emancipation Proclamation did not abolish slavery. That was done by the Thirteenth Amendment in 1865 after the North won the Civil War. This amendment to the Constitution banned slavery and involuntary servitude in the United States.

ON THE RECORD

President Lincoln wrote that the Emancipation Proclamation would prove to be "the central act of my administration, and the great event of the nineteenth century."

The Fourteenth Amendment, passed in 1868, states that all persons born in the United States or become naturalized in the United States are citizens of the United States and entitled to all the privileges and immunities of citizenship. The due process clause, in the Fourteenth Amendment, extends to all persons (not just citizens) equal protection under the law.

Passed in 1870, the Fifteenth Amendment extends the right to vote to men regardless of "race, color, or previous condition of servitude." This amendment *enfranchised* former male slaves.

DEFINITION

To **enfranchise** is to endow with the right to vote.

Early Civil Rights Laws

After the Civil War ended, several civil rights acts were passed to extend certain rights to the emancipated slaves. The Civil Rights Act of 1866 extended citizenship to anyone born in the United States and gave African Americans full equality before the law. It also gave the president the power to enforce the law with the armed forces if necessary. This was highly controversial and was vetoed by President Johnson, but Congress overwhelmingly overturned the veto. The passage of the Fourteenth Amendment put this issue to rest.

The Enforcement Act of 1870 established criminal sanctions for interfering with the right to vote as protected by the Fifteenth Amendment and the Civil Rights Act of 1866.

The Civil Rights Act of 1872 made it a federal crime to use laws or customs to deprive anyone of their rights and privileges guaranteed by the Constitution and federal laws. This act, also known as the Anti–Ku Klux Klan Act, specified specific penalties or damages for violations of the act.

The Civil Rights Act of 1875, also known as the Second Civil Rights Act, declared that everyone is entitled to full and equal enjoyment of public accommodations, theaters, and other places of public amusement. This act also imposed specific penalties for violators of the law.

How Effective Were Early Civil Rights Laws?

The civil rights acts of the post–Civil War era demonstrated congressional power over the states and individuals. These laws were directed at individuals who were violating the constitutional rights of others when the states failed to protect those rights. In essence, Congress assumed the power to act to protect individual rights in the absence of individual state action. This is an example of power shifting to the federal government from the states.

In theory, these acts served to protect the newly acquired rights of African Americans. In practice, the laws and protections would not be fully implemented for another 100 years, until the 1960s. This *Reconstruction* legislation ultimately did very little to secure the civil rights of African Americans. Several important court cases dealing with this legislation, and the case of *Plessy* v. *Ferguson* (1896), effectively nullified the legislation. Additionally, stringent voting barriers were created by the states to prevent African Americans from voting.

In 1883, the Supreme Court invalidated the 1875 Civil Rights Act when it ruled that the enforcement clause of the Fourteenth Amendment was limited to correcting actions by states acting in an official capacity. Therefore, the court's decision established that acts of discrimination by private citizens were not unconstitutional. The court stated, "Individual invasion of individual rights is not the subject matter of the Amendment."

The court decision was met with widespread approval throughout the United States. Less than 20 years after the Civil War, the country was all too willing to forget the injustice that nearly destroyed the republic. Many of the laws that were not overturned directly by the court simply became moot and not enforced. As white Southern Democrats regained political power, the enactment of Jim Crow laws established racial segregation, with separate restrooms, drinking fountains, separate seats in public venues such as restaurants and theaters, and separate waiting rooms at train stations and bus depots.

Plessy v. Ferguson

A key decision during the post-Reconstruction period involved Homer Plessy. Mr. Plessy was one-eighth African American and was ordered to sit in a car for nonwhites while on a train heading to New Orleans in 1892. Louisiana had a law that provided for separate railcars for whites and nonwhites.

Plessy went to court, claiming that the law violated the equal protection clause of the Fourteenth Amendment. In 1896, the Supreme Court rejected Plessy's argument. The court said that the Fourteenth Amendment "could not have been intended to abolish distinctions based upon color, or to enforce social equality." The court concluded that segregation did not violate the Constitution, and thereby established the separate-but-equal doctrine.

 ON THE RECORD

"Laws permitting, and even requiring, their separation in places where they are liable to be brought into contact do not necessarily imply the inferiority of either race to the other."

—From the Supreme Court ruling in *Plessy v. Ferguson*

Barriers to Voting

The voting privileges of African American males essentially came to an end in 1877 when federal troops withdrew from the South. As Southern politicians reclaimed political power, they enacted several measures that effectively deprived African Americans of their right to vote.

- The White Primary was a method to exclude African Americans by claiming that political party primaries were private.

- The Grandfather Clause was a law that required proof that one's grandfather had voted prior to 1867.

- Poll taxes were instituted that required a fee in order to vote.

- Literacy tests were used to exclude people who could not read or write to the satisfaction of local authorities.

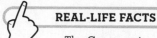

Overturning the "Separate but Equal" Doctrine

The process of overturning the separate-but-equal doctrine was started in the 1930s and culminated in the 1954 Supreme Court ruling in *Brown* v. *Board of Education of Topeka*. The first assaults on the doctrine were lawsuits that successfully admitted African Americans to state professional schools. By 1950, the court had ruled that students admitted into state universities could not be segregated by classroom, in the library, or in the cafeterias and dining halls.

In 1951, Oliver Brown brought a suit against the Board of Education of Topeka claiming that his daughter should not have to attend an all nonwhite elementary school one mile away when a white school was much closer to their home. The case was taken up by the NAACP and the Supreme Court heard arguments in 1953. The 1954 unanimous ruling in *Brown* v. *Board of Education of Topeka* established that the segregation of races violates the equal protection clause of the Fourteenth Amendment. The court concluded that separate schools are inherently unequal and that separation implied inferiority.

The following year the Supreme Court ordered the lower courts to ensure that African American students be admitted to schools in a nondiscriminatory manner. The courts essentially were ordered to take an activist role in implementing the desegregation of schools in the United States using all means possible and as quickly as possible. In some school districts, administrators and local officials purposely slowed the process down. In other places, white families moved to other districts or sent their children to private schools.

In a flagrant rebuke to federal authority, Governor Orval Faubus of Arkansas ordered the state's National Guard to block the integration of Central High School in Little Rock. This matter was resolved when President Eisenhower took control of the Arkansas National Guard and sent them to Little Rock to enforce the integration of Central High. Several years later, Alabama Governor George Wallace stood on the steps of the University of Alabama in Tuscaloosa and promised "to stand in the schoolhouse door" to prevent African Americans from entering the University of Alabama. Wallace ultimately backed down when President Kennedy threatened to federalize the Alabama National Guard as President Eisenhower had done in Arkansas.

ON THE RECORD

"… to separate [African Americans] from others of similar age and qualifications solely because of their race generates a feeling of inferiority as to the status in the community that may affect their hearts and minds in a way unlikely ever to be undone."

—Chief Justice Earl Warren, from the unanimous ruling in *Brown* v. *Board of Education of Topeka*

The Modern Civil Rights Movement

Since the Brown decision applied only to public schools, not much else of structural segregation was affected. However, that would soon change. In 1955, Rosa Parks boarded a public bus in Montgomery, Alabama, and took a seat in the white section of the bus. As more people boarded the bus, Rosa Parks was asked to surrender her seat and move to the rear of the bus in the colored section. She refused and was arrested and fined.

As a result of Parks's action, African Americans boycotted the Montgomery bus system for one entire year. The protest was led by Rev. Dr. Martin Luther King Jr. During this protest year, Dr. King was arrested, his home was firebombed, and he received numerous threats to his life. In 1956, a federal court ordered the desegregation of the bus system in Montgomery and the modern Civil Rights Era, characterized by civil protests, had begun.

Dr. King's philosophy of nonviolent protests was largely influenced by the teachings and life of Mahatma Gandhi. Dr. King successfully used such tactics as marches and public disobedience. In Greensboro, North Carolina, he organized a sit-in at a local Woolworth lunch counter to protest the policy of not serving African Americans at the counter. Within six months, the Woolworth Company changed its policy and started to serve African Americans at all their lunch counters.

In 1963, King organized a protest in Birmingham, Alabama, that resulted in a violent reaction by local police. This scene, televised on national television horrified many Americans. Dr. King was imprisoned by the local authorities and this set the stage for the passage of the historic Civil Rights Act of 1964. In August 1963, King organized the famous March on Washington, where he delivered his "I Have a Dream" speech.

Twentieth-Century Civil Rights Legislation

Congress passed many laws to address the injustices faced by African Americans. This period is often referred to as the second Reconstruction era. In 1957, Congress established a Civil Rights Commission within the Department of Justice. With the passage of the Civil Rights Act of 1960, the Justice Department could bring a case to court for any practice or pattern of discrimination by any entity, including the States. The law set penalties for anyone interfering with a court order that addressed discrimination. However, the law had little impact. Subsequently, Congress took a more active approach and passed the Civil Rights Acts of 1964 and 1968, as well as the Voting Rights Act of 1965.

In 1964, Congress passed the most far-reaching law to address civil rights. This law forbade discrimination on the basis of race, color, religion, gender, and national origin. The major points of the Civil Rights Act of 1964 are:

- It outlawed discrimination in voter registration.

- It outlawed discrimination in public accommodations.

- It empowered the federal government with the right to desegregate schools.

- It expanded the powers of the Civil Rights Commission.

- It allowed the federal government to withhold funds from programs that practiced discrimination.

- It established equal opportunity in the work place and established the Equal Employment Opportunity Commission.

 REAL-LIFE FACTS

The provision of the Civil Rights Act of 1964 that is the cornerstone of equal opportunity in employment is referred to as Title VII.

In 1960, less than 30 percent of African Americans were registered to vote in the Southern states. To address this voting rights problem, Congress passed the Voting Rights Act of 1965. The law had two major provisions:

- It outlawed voter registration tests.

- It empowered the federal government to administer voting procedures where discrimination existed.

The Voting Rights Act of 1965 (VRA) has been challenged in the courts for several years recently. In a controversial and historic 5–4 decision in 2013, the Supreme Court struck down Section 4 of the VRA, which applied to states that had a voting test in place as of November 1964 and less than 50 percent turnout in the 1964 presidential election. Chief Justice Roberts, writing for the majority, stated: "Our country has changed, and while any racial discrimination in voting is too much, Congress must ensure that the legislation it passes to remedy that problem speaks to current conditions."

The Civil Rights Act of 1968 prohibited discrimination in most housing and provided penalties for anyone interfering with individual civil rights. It also banned discrimination in lending practices for mortgages based on race, gender, and income levels.

Affirmative Action

Government action to remedy discrimination is referred to as affirmative action. In the 1960s and 1970s, the federal government took many actions to reduce the disadvantages created by past discrimination, particularly in the areas of higher education, employment, and the process of awarding government contracts.

These remedies were challenged in the courts as unconstitutional. In 1978, the Supreme Court issued its first major decision on the constitutionality of affirmative action. In the case *University of California Regents v. Bakke* (1978), the Supreme Court ruled that affirmative action programs are not necessarily unconstitutional if they consider race as one factor in admissions. However, *quota systems* were ruled to be unconstitutional.

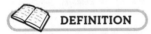 **DEFINITION**

A **quota system** is a hiring system that gives preference to protected group members.

Since the Bakke case, the Supreme Court has consistently ruled that race may be a factor when considering admission but race alone cannot be the deciding preference. In 2003 in *Gratz v. Bollinger,* the Supreme Court ruled 6–3 that the University of Michigan's undergraduate affirmative-action admissions policy, which automatically awarded points to underrepresented ethnic groups, was unconstitutional. In that case, the Supreme Court felt that the university was acting too mechanistically. That same year, in *Grutter v. Bollinger,* the Supreme Court ruled that Michigan's Law School admissions policy was constitutional, thereby upholding the previous decision in the Bakke case. Some opponents of affirmative action believe that affirmative action programs are discriminatory and that they promote underqualified people over higher-qualified individuals on the basis of race, ethnicity, or gender. They also believe that affirmative action should take into account one's current socioeconomic status, not that of one's ancestors.

The future of affirmative action programs has been thrown into doubt with recent rulings and the death of Justice Scalia in February 2016. In 2007, the court invalidated school programs that used race as a criterion in school admissions and placement. In the 2013 Supreme Court case, *Fisher v. University of Texas,* the court was asked to consider whether the Equal Protection Clause applied to the admissions policy of UT. It ruled 7–1 in favor of Fisher. In December 2015, the Supreme Court heard arguments on the question of whether the University of Texas' use of race as a consideration in the admissions process violates the Equal Protection Clause of the

Fourteenth Amendment. It was largely thought that the court would rule 5–4 in favor of Fisher. However, the unexpected death of Justice Scalia leaves the outcome in doubt.

Immigration and Civil Rights

The United States is a nation of immigrants and of their descendants. Yet nearly all immigrant groups have faced the challenges involved with living in a new political and cultural environment. Most have faced discrimination in one form or another, whether it is because of their color, ethnicity, customs, or their fluency in English. Many immigrants have been considered suspect by those who have arrived earlier. Formal barriers of law and informal barriers of custom have frequently denied immigrant groups equal rights.

However, as immigrant groups establish themselves, first economically and then politically, most of these barriers have been swept away and their constitutional rights have been asserted. Much of the civil rights legislation passed since the 1960s has been instrumental in this process.

Since the late 1970s, four out of every five immigrants to this country have come from Central America, South America, or Asia. If current trends continue, it is estimated that by 2045 non-whites collectively will constitute the majority of Americans. Today, immigration is one of the most hotly debated issues in American politics. The outcome of this debate will surely be defined by the demographic realities that have been set in motion.

Hispanics

Hispanics have suffered similar kinds of discrimination as African Americans in employment, education, and public accommodations. While they collectively make up one of the largest minority groups in the United States, they are underrepresented in higher education and in the ranks of professionals and corporate executives.

The Hispanic "Civil Rights Movement" has a long and varied history. In 1903, Mexican and Japanese farm workers formed the Japanese-Mexican Labor Association—the first farm workers' union. In 1904, the Supreme Court ruled that Puerto Ricans were U.S. citizens in the case *Gonzalez v. Williams.* In 1917, Congress passed and President Wilson signed, the Jones Act that bestowed U.S. citizenship on all Puerto Ricans. In *Mendez v. Westminster* (1947), the Supreme Court ruled that Mexican Americans could not be banned from all white public schools. This case helped set the precedent for Brown. In 1954, *Hernandez* v. *Texas,* the Supreme Court ruled that the Fourteenth Amendment protects those beyond just White and Black racial classifications. In 1988, President Ronald Reagan appointed the first Hispanic to serve on the President's cabinet—Dr. Lauro-Cavazos as Secretary of Education. In 2009, Sonia Maria Sotomayor became the first Latina appointed to the Supreme Court.

Due to the internal political differences within their community, Hispanics have a history of diminished political clout. Furthermore, a substantial number of Hispanics living in the United States are undocumented and, therefore, unable to participate in the political process. However, the number of undocumented Hispanics applying for citizenship has increased substantially since 1994. In the two states with the largest Hispanic population, California and Texas, Hispanics have registered to vote in large numbers and have dramatically changed the political landscape. In both these states, where more than 50 percent of Hispanics live, nonwhites are already in the majority.

REAL-LIFE FACTS

The first Hispanic U.S. Senator was Octaviano Larrazolo. He was elected in 1928 to finish the term of New Mexico Senator Andieus Jones, who had died in office. Larrazolo served for six months before falling ill and stepping down; he died in 1930. The first Hispanic Senator to serve an entire term was Dennis Chávez of New Mexico, who served from 1935 through 1962.

Asian Americans

The term Asian American refers to nearly 5 percent of the U.S. population from many different countries and many ethnic backgrounds. These individuals live mainly in the West Coast states, New York, and Texas. Although Asian Americans have encountered success in education and business, they still face widespread prejudice, discrimination, and barriers to equal opportunity.

The Chinese were the first Asian group to arrive in the United States in the mid-nineteenth century. They were confronted with many laws that forbade them from the privileges enjoyed by other Americans, including the right to vote, own property, and access to quality education. The Chinese Exclusion Act of 1882 restricted skilled and unskilled laborers and miners from entering the United States for 10 years under penalty of imprisonment and deportation.

The Japanese started to arrive in the late nineteenth century and faced many of the same hardships that Chinese immigrants faced before them. During World War II, more than 110,000 Japanese Americans were sent to internment camps as a result of the hysteria provoked by the Japanese attack on Pearl Harbor. The overwhelming majority of these American citizens had committed no crime.

Subsequent immigrants from Asia, including those from Korea, the Philippines, Vietnam, Laos, and Cambodia, have faced overt discrimination in jobs and housing. Today, the top five countries of origin from Asia are India, China, the Philippines, Vietnam, and Korea. As Asian Americans have established themselves economically, they have started to enjoy political influence. There are currently 11 Asian American members of the House and one in the Senate.

REAL-LIFE FACTS

In 1988, President Reagan signed a law that provided $20,000 in restitution to the nearly 60,000 surviving Japanese Americans incarcerated during World War II.

Bilingual Education

The continuous arrival of immigrants has always confronted policymakers with the challenge of how best to educate children who do not speak, or are not sufficiently fluent in, English. All of the restrictive laws that were passed that required English-only instruction have been struck down by the courts. Starting in the 1960s, and as a result of the civil rights movement, bilingual education programs began to be implemented as a solution to the language problems facing immigrants.

Bilingual education programs teach children in their native language while also teaching them English. In 1968, Congress passed the Bilingual Education Act, which was intended primarily to help Hispanic children learn English. In 1974, the Supreme Court ruled that special programs must be implemented for students with language difficulties if there are a substantial number of these children within a school district.

MISINFORMATION

In the nineteenth century, many school districts provided instruction in a language other than English. In the Midwest, many classes were conducted in German, the second most common language at the time.

Women and the Struggle for Equal Rights

Women, like African Americans and other minorities, have had to struggle for equality and their civil rights. A significant difference between these struggles is that while minorities have had to fight against laws that explicitly denied them their rights, women had to struggle against a culture and tradition that barred them by claiming to protect them.

As early as the colonial period, women have argued to be included in the political process. In 1776, Abigail Adams wrote to her husband John Adams, a founding father and later the second president of the United States, "I desire you would remember the ladies .... If particular care and attention is not paid to the ladies, we are determined to foment a rebellion and will not hold ourselves bound by any laws in which we have no voice or representation."

The founders did not heed her advice. No provisions were made in the Constitution to guarantee women the right to vote. However, it was not denied either.

The first political struggle that women were engaged in was the slavery abolition movement. After the World Antislavery Convention in London in 1840, Lucretia Mott and Elizabeth Cady Stanton returned to the United States and organized the first women's right convention in Seneca Falls, New York, in 1848. At this convention, the women's movement was launched. More than 300 people attended the convention and approved the Declaration of Sentiments. It stated, "We hold these truths to be self-evident: that all men *and* women are created equal."

With the outbreak of the Civil War, advocates of women's suffrage put their efforts on the sideline to support the war effort and the abolition of slavery.

Suffrage and the Fifteenth Amendment

The campaign for the passage of the Fifteenth Amendment in 1870 divided the women's suffrage movement. The Fifteenth Amendment states, "The right of citizens of the United States to vote shall not be denied or abridged by the United States or by any of the States on account of race, color, or previous condition of servitude." Many women wanted to add "sex" to "race, color, or previous condition of servitude." Others wanted to separate the two so that the amendment would pass. Although many African Americans supported women's right to vote, most wanted to keep the movement for racial equality separate from the women's movement.

Passage of the Nineteenth Amendment

At the start of the twentieth century, a vigorous campaign was already underway for women's suffrage. By the end of World War I, nearly half the states already had passed laws that granted women the right to vote. However, this state-by-state approach was slow and the future of national suffrage was uncertain.

In 1919, Congress proposed the Nineteenth Amendment that would give women the right to vote and empower the federal government to enforce this right. Many Southern states opposed the amendment. In the end, the amendment was ratified in 1920.

 REAL-LIFE FACTS

The first state to be admitted into the Union where women already had the right to vote was Wyoming, which granted this right to women when it was still a territory. Wyoming stated that it would not enter the Union without women's suffrage.

The Modern Women's Movement

After obtaining the right to vote, the women's movement, as an active political movement, remained largely dormant. However, in the 1960s, the Civil Rights movement resulted in a growing awareness of rights for all groups, including women. In 1963, Betty Friedan published *The Feminine Mystique* (1963), which focused national attention on the unequal status of women in the United States.

In response to what she believed to be a lack of action on the part of existing women's groups against discrimination, Friedan helped form the National Organization of Women (NOW). The mission of NOW was "to bring women into full participation in the mainstream of American society now, exercising all the privileges and responsibilities thereof in truly equal partnership with men."

Thus was born the feminist movement. The focus of this movement was to abolish gender inequality through a constitutional amendment.

The Equal Rights Amendment

The Equal Rights Amendment (ERA) was first proposed in 1923. It states, "Equality of rights under the law shall not be denied or abridged by the United States or by any State on account of sex." However, Congress never gave the amendment a hearing. It was finally passed by both chambers of Congress in 1972 and sent to the state legislatures for ratification.

Although the measure was supported by both chambers of Congress, the platforms of the political parties, and the president, the measure failed to obtain the necessary 38 states to ratify it in order to pass. To date, all efforts to reintroduce the amendment have failed.

Gender Discrimination

With the failure of the ERA, women took their battle to challenge discrimination to the courts. Armed with the Fourteenth Amendment's equal protection clause, women's organizations filed suits to overturn laws and policies that rendered them unequal to men. Some of the institutional policies affected by the courts' actions include police and fire department requirements for employment and acceptance into military academies.

Although women have made great strides in employment opportunities, women continue to earn less on average than men for equal work. During World War II, the federal government established the War Labor Board. The board was to evaluate jobs and ensure that equal pay was rendered for comparable work. However, the board's authority expired with the end of the war.

In 1963, Congress passed the Equal Pay Act. This law requires employers to pay equal salaries for substantially equal work. However, this did not address the matter that is mostly responsible for unequal earning power: women usually held lower paying jobs than men. In 1963, women earned 56¢ for every dollar a man made. Today, that figure is 80¢ for every dollar.

Title VII of the Civil Rights Act of 1964 prohibits gender discrimination in employment. In 1978, Congress amended Title VII to ban discrimination based on pregnancy. Since the early 1990s, the Supreme Court has ruled that Title VII's prohibition of gender discrimination also extends to sexual harassment in the workplace. Employers as well as individuals are liable for sexually harassing behavior, whether it is opposite-sex or same-sex harassment.

In *Ledbetter* v. *Goodyear Tire & Rubber Co.* (2007), the Supreme Court held in a 5–4 decision that employers are protected from lawsuits over race or gender pay discrimination if the claims are based on decisions made by the employer 180 days ago or more. Reaction to the court's decision spilled over into the 2008 elections. When Democrats regained the House in 2009, they moved quickly to pass legislation to amend the ruling and allow lawsuits with fewer restrictions. On January 29, 2009, President Obama signed into law the Lilly Ledbetter Fair Pay Act of 2009. It was the first piece of legislation he signed as president.

The "glass ceiling" refers to the subtle barriers faced by women in the workplace on the road to advancing their careers, particularly among the highest paying jobs. Although women make up more than 50 percent of the workforce, they hold less than 15 percent of executive positions in large corporations. Many have stated that a glass ceiling exists in American politics as well. This ceiling will be tested in the race for the Democratic nomination in 2016. Hillary Rodham Clinton is running for the second time and is positioned to be the first woman candidate of a major party for President of the United States.

 ON THE RECORD

"Although we weren't able to shatter that highest, hardest glass ceiling this time, thanks to you, it's got about 18 million cracks in it. ... And the light is shining through like never before, filling us all with the hope and the sure knowledge that the path will be a little easier next time."

—Senator Hillary Clinton, referring to the more than 18 million votes she received in her first bid for the Democratic presidential nomination in 2008

Homosexuals and Civil Rights

In 1969, in New York City, a police raid at a local gay bar—the Stonewall Inn—resulted in riots that lasted two days. As a result the Gay Liberation Front and the Gay Activist Alliance were formed and the modern gay rights movement was born. Since then, many organizations have been formed to exert pressure on political and social institutions to recognize the right of homosexuals to equal treatment.

Prior to the Stonewall riots, 49 states had sodomy laws. During the 1970s and 1980s, many of these laws were repealed by state legislatures or struck down by the courts. However, in 1986, the Supreme Court ruled in *Bowers* v. *Hardwick* that a Georgia law that made homosexual conduct between two adults a crime was constitutional. Many states reacted by invalidating existing state sodomy laws on the basis of the rights guaranteed in their constitutions to all citizens.

In 1996, the Supreme Court moved away from its decision in Bowers. In *Romer* v. *Evans,* the Supreme Court ruled that a state constitutional amendment passed in Colorado invalidating laws that protect homosexuals to be in violation of the equal protection clause. The court ruled that Colorado cannot permit homosexuals to be unequal to everyone else.

Lawrence v. *Texas*

In 2003, the Supreme Court overturned *Bowers* v. *Hardwick* (1986) in its landmark 6–3 decision in the case *Lawrence* v. *Texas* (2003). Justice Kennedy, writing for the majority, said, "When sexuality finds overt expression in intimate conduct with another person, the conduct can be but one element in a personal bond that is more enduring. The liberty protected by the Constitution allows homosexual persons the right to make this choice." With this ruling, all laws in the United States criminalizing sodomy between consenting adults were overturned.

Homosexuals and the Military

The position of the U.S. Department of Defense traditionally has been that homosexuality is incompatible with military service. In 1993, President Clinton modified the policy to be characterized as "don't ask, don't tell" (DADT). Individuals wishing to enlist in the military would not be asked about their sexual orientation, and gay men and lesbians would be allowed to serve as long as they did not declare their preference or engage in homosexual acts while in the armed services.

Many cases challenged this policy and the courts rendered conflicting decisions. In 2010, Congress voted to repeal DADT. The repeal went into effect in September 2011.

Same-Sex Marriage

Perhaps the most sensitive political issue of the gay rights movement is whether same-sex couples should be allowed to marry. In 1996, the Hawaii Supreme Court ruled that a ban on same-sex marriage violated the state constitution. Many states began to worry that their courts would follow the lead of the Hawaii court and many pushed for state laws banning same-sex marriage. In 1996, Congress passed, and President Clinton signed, the Defense of Marriage Act. This act bans federal recognition of same-sex marriage and allows states not to recognize marriages performed in other states.

In 1998, the citizens of Hawaii passed a constitutional amendment banning same-sex marriage. In 2000, Vermont passed a law permitting same-sex couples to enter into civil unions. These unions allow same-sex couples to receive many of the same benefits as heterosexual married couples.

Soon after, three states have legalized same-sex marriage: Massachusetts, California, and Connecticut. Several others have followed Vermont's lead and passed civil-union laws. Proposition 8 was a California ballot proposition in the 2008 election. It changed the state's constitution, which had previously allowed same-sex marriage, to restrict the definition of marriage to opposite-sex couples only. In 2015, in the landmark case *Obergefell v. Hodges,* the court ruled in a 5–4 decision that the fundamental right to marry is guaranteed by the Fourteenth Amendment of the U.S. Constitution.

Protecting Americans with Disabilities

The protective umbrella of the Civil Rights Act of 1964 did not cover Americans with disabilities. Starting in the 1970s, Congress started to pass legislation to protect Americans with disabilities:

- The Rehabilitation Act of 1973 prohibited discrimination against persons with disabilities in programs receiving federal funding.

- In 1978, Congress amended the Rehabilitation Act to mandate that ramps, elevators, and similar modes of access were installed in all federal buildings.

- The Education for All Handicapped Children Act of 1975 mandated that all children with disabilities receive an education.

- The Americans with Disabilities Act of 1990 is the most significant federal legislation with respect to disabled Americans. It requires all public facilities and services be accessible to disabled individuals. Furthermore, it requires employers to reasonably accommodate the needs of disabled workers.

The Least You Need to Know

- The Civil Rights movement started with the struggle by African Americans for equality. The Civil War, the Emancipation Proclamation, and the Thirteenth, Fourteenth, and Fifteenth amendments legally and constitutionally ended slavery.

- Legal segregation was declared unconstitutional in *Brown* v. *Board of Education of Topeka*. Boycotts and civil unrest led to the modern civil rights movement.

- The United States is a nation of immigrants, yet all immigrant groups have confronted injustice as they adapt to their new country. The civil rights legislation of the 1960s has helped immigrant groups overcome the legal and cultural discrimination and prejudice they have faced.

- Women were given the right to vote in 1920 with the passage of the Nineteenth Amendment. Women have been able to apply much of the Civil Rights legislation of the 1960s to secure equal standing in society and protect themselves against sexual harassment.

- Gay and lesbian Americans have secured some of their constitutional rights through the legislative, executive, and judicial process. The Supreme Court ruled all state sodomy laws unconstitutional in the landmark case *Lawrence* v. *Texas*. In 2015, the Supreme Court ruled that a constitutional right to same-sex marriage exists.

- Federal legislation requires that federal facilities have access venues for persons with disabilities. All children with disabilities are entitled to an education. Employers must reasonably accommodate the needs of disabled employees.

PART 6

The Politics of Public Policy

The First Amendment to the U.S. Constitution guarantees Americans the freedom of speech and "... the right of the people ... to petition the Government for a redress of grievances." Interest groups, or lobbies, are constitutionally protected in the United States. The media is also protected by our Constitution and also serves an important role in our democratic process. Ultimately, special interest groups play an important role in formulating public policy.

Public policy reflects the goals and ideas of a democratic nation. The economic, foreign, defense, social, and environmental policies adopted by a government often reflect the complex relationships among the major players, including the three branches of government, interest groups, and the media. How the agenda is determined and which ideas become laws and policies are the focus of this concluding part of the book.

Interest Groups

The First Amendment to the U.S. Constitution guarantees Americans the freedom of speech and "… the right of the people … to petition the Government for a redress of grievances."

Interest groups, or lobbies, are constitutionally protected in the United States, representing not only people with money, power, and influence, but also groups that care deeply about a cause or policy. They represent the diversity that is the United States of America.

President George H. W. Bush said, "We are a nation of communities, of tens and tens of thousands of ethnic, religious, social, business, labor union, neighborhood, regional, and other organizations, all of them varied, voluntary, and unique …."

In This Chapter

- How interest groups originated in the United States
- The organization and structure of various interest groups
- How interest groups promote their agenda
- Financial influence of interest groups
- Government attempts to regulate interest groups

The Birth of Interest Groups

James Madison, in *The Federalist*, No. 10, warned the nascent nation against the dangers of interest groups, what he called "factions." He defined a faction as "… a number of citizens, whether amounting to a majority or minority of the whole, who are united and actuated by some common impulse of passion, or of interest, adverse to the rights of other citizens, or the permanent and aggregate interests of the community." Madison also recognized that in order to eliminate factions, you would need to eliminate the freedom of people to assemble and the freedom of speech.

Interest groups have been present in the United States since its beginning for many reasons. First, there are many political cleavages in America's diverse society; the greater the variety of views, the greater the number of interests that will exist. Think of all the different socioeconomic groups and religious organizations, and you can imagine all the different interest groups that exist. Secondly, our Constitution and federal system of government gives people many points of access to influence officials and the policy-making process.

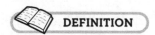 **DEFINITION**

An **interest group** is a private organization that tries to persuade public officials to respond to the shared views of the group. An interest group tries to influence public policy.

Lastly, as political parties have lost some of their influence, this vacuum has been filled by the number and strength of interest groups. People who do not identify with either major party are very likely to be a member of one or more interest groups. In fact, if you think about it, you are probably a member of at least one interest group already.

Interest groups have expanded in numbers since the beginning of the republic, but particularly since the 1960s. According to the *Journal of Politics* (1983), 70 percent of interest groups based in Washington, D.C., have formed since then. Interest groups are born more rapidly in certain periods than others, arising in response to political, social, and/or economic developments. As government becomes larger and takes on a more prominent role, the more interest groups will continue to grow.

Economic conditions create new interest groups and redefine old ones. Farmers are among the oldest group to be organized. As the nation industrialized, union interest groups arose in response to the interest of large companies. Additionally, the new global economy has seen the rise of interest groups that seek to protect American-made goods and services.

Government policy creates interest groups. Any government action causes people to organize. War creates veterans. Energy policy creates groups to emerge to promote their form of energy. Every social welfare program—or move to cut or eliminate them—from student loans to family assistance, causes people to organize.

From the divisive issue of slavery to the Civil Rights movement to the environmental movement, interest groups have formed to promote their position and influence public policy. The more involved government becomes in the lives of Americans, the more likely it is that these groups will continue to emerge.

 ON THE RECORD

"In no country in the world has the principle of association been more successfully used, or more unsparingly applied to a multitude of different objects, than in America."

—Alexis de Tocqueville

Types of Interest Groups

Interest groups seek to influence public policy, so there are many different types of interest groups. They vary widely in structure and organization. Some are very formal and tightly organized, like the National Rifle Association. Others are more informal and have very little organization, if any. These groups tend to be more local and usually have a vague unifying theme. Still, it is possible to categorize interest groups into five broad categories:

1. Economic, including both labor and business

2. Ideological

3. Public interest

4. Foreign policy

5. Government

These categories are not mutually exclusive. In fact, they often vary and overlap. Most Americans are represented by a number of different interest groups, some of which they are aware of and some of which they are not. The U.S. Chamber of Commerce represents thousands of businesses and lobbies for the whole business industry, as opposed to only those businesses that join.

Some interest groups only lobby in the interest of their members and are usually issue oriented. The Sierra Club, for example, is made up of members who are deeply passionate about preserving the environment. For example, when an environmental group lobbies for fewer fuel emissions, the cleaner air they lobby for benefits everyone.

From the earliest days of the republic, business has looked to government to protect and promote its interests. Protective tariffs, foreign trade agreements, less regulation, and industry subsidies are some of the interests that businesses lobby for. Still, business interests often conflict. The oil industry, for example, seeks the lowest tax on gasoline possible, while other energy businesses seek higher gas taxes to promote the use of their energy source. Competition among businesses fosters a proliferation of business interest groups.

Labor unions lobby the government for policies that will benefit their members. They tend to focus on such social welfare and job-related matters such as Social Security, the minimum wage, unemployment benefits, and safety regulations. The diversity of the American economy, however, sometimes divides labor groups along industrial and economic lines.

Today, fewer than 2 percent of Americans live on farms, yet the farm industry is very powerful because the agricultural sector has been largely taken over by large corporations. Together, the small farmer and these large agricultural corporations lobby the government to promote agricultural policies and subsidies. Federal aid to farmers is among the largest federal aid programs, as farms and agricultural businesses are found in nearly every state. However, regional competition among growers often pits one group against the other. For example, California citrus growers are often at odds with their counterparts in Florida.

Professional groups are made up of members with extensive and specialized training who seek to protect and promote their interests. They include engineers, journalists, social workers, doctors, lawyers, and teachers. Most professional interest groups are not large or well financed. However, there are three exceptions: the American Medical Association, the American Bar Association, and the National Education Association. The NEA, for example, has nearly 3 million members.

Ideological interest groups are usually driven by a single issue or family of issues and are made up of highly motivated people who seek to influence the public policy agenda. These people are very adamant about their position and usually unwilling to negotiate. The two sides on the abortion issue are a good example of this category. NARAL (formerly, the National Association for the Repeal of Abortion Laws and now the National Abortion Rights Action League) is an example of an ideological group that strongly supports reproductive rights for women.

 MISINFORMATION

Although women did not yet have the right to vote, the Women's Christian Temperance Movement, a group dedicated to the prohibition of drinking liquor, succeeded in forcing the passage of the Eighteenth Amendment, which outlawed the manufacture and sale of alcoholic beverages. Women received the right to vote with the passage of the Nineteenth Amendment. Prohibition was repealed by the Twenty-First Amendment.

Public interest research groups, often called PIRGs, were founded by Ralph Nader in the 1960s and 1970s and are the best known of these ideological groups. They believe they are working selflessly to implement public policy for the common good on issues of public safety, campaign reform, the environment, and consumer protection, among other things. The League of Women Voters is another such group.

Many interest groups focus on U.S. foreign policy. These groups try to influence the president and Congress to enact specific policies. The most prestigious of these groups is the Council on Foreign Relations in New York City. Other foreign policy interest groups focus specifically on U.S. relations with a specific country or region of the world. An example of this is the American-Israel Political Action Committee.

Many state and local governments have interest groups that lobby the national government. Cities also have interest groups that lobby state governments. Some of these interest groups include the National Governors Association, the National League of Cities, and the National Association of Counties.

Hundreds of groups in the United States are formed around ethnic similarities, religious beliefs and preferences, and groups of people who might simply share a common experience. War veterans, for example, have several interest groups including the American Legion and the Veterans of Foreign Wars. Most recently, the Iraq War Veterans Group has formed to advocate for better health care for injured war veterans returning from Iraq.

Why People Join Interest Groups

People join interest groups to get incentives, or something of value that they cannot get on their own. Three kinds of incentives drive membership to interest groups. Solidary incentives are a sense of pleasure, status, or companionship. Usually large national organizations have local chapters that people can join and participate in, which support the national organization. PTAs and Rotary Clubs are examples of these.

The second incentive is material, that is, money or services that can be translated into a monetary value. Farm groups and the AARP are examples of this.

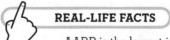 **REAL-LIFE FACTS**

AARP is the largest interest group in the United States.

The third type of incentive is goal-oriented and driven by the purpose of the organization. These organizations tend to draw more ideological and passionate people about a particular issue.

The Activities and Strategies of Interest Groups

The extent to which an interest group is influential cannot be measured only by its size or the depth of its pockets. Rather it is more important to note whether the interest group is able to get the attention of the public, the media, and government officials. Interest groups can do this in many ways:

- Generate headlines in the news

- Mobilize their members to contact elected officials and vote

- Stage public protests and rallies

- File lawsuits and grievances

- Supply information to government officials

Of all these tactics, perhaps the most significant one is providing information. Interest groups must provide credible information to elected officials and government administrators, because the officials are usually too busy or overwhelmed to do the amount of research they would have to conduct in order to formulate policies. Interest groups offer a level of expertise and perspective that most legislators and bureaucrats do not possess.

All interest groups obviously present their argument in the most favorable light in order to achieve their goals, but they cannot risk misrepresenting facts or misleading government officials without suffering consequences. The worst consequence, of course, would be for an interest group to lose the confidence of government officials—and their access to the corridors of power.

Government officials look to interest groups not only for expert advice but also for political signals. Interest groups identify the players around an issue. This helps government officials articulate and fit the particular issue into his or her political beliefs, as well as the interests of other constituents. Ultimately, elected officials are interested in how their own position on an issue will play out with their voting constituents.

Another important political signal that interest groups render is ratings. Ratings are compiled by interest groups on legislators based on their voting record. Interest groups monitor the votes in the House and Senate and then publish their ratings to garner support, or opposition, to an elected official. For example, NARAL has given President Obama a 10, its highest rating, while it has given Senator McCain a 0. These are often biased, but they can be very helpful resources both to the government official and the voting public.

Public Opinion

Interest groups try to influence public opinion as a way to influence public policy as well. They supply the public with information through advertisements and mass mailings. They try to portray their group and issue in a positive light in order to promote public policy.

Interest groups create public attitudes by using propaganda, a technique of persuasion aimed at influencing behavior. Propaganda begins with a conclusion and gathers evidence to support that conclusion and always disregards evidence that does not support it. It is an effective tool, but a deceptive and sometimes dishonest one.

Parties and Elections

Interest groups and political parties exist in the same environment, but they are very different. Parties are interested in winning elections. Interest groups want to influence public policy. Interest groups try to influence the behavior of political parties in a number of ways:

- They keep close ties with both parties.

- They urge their members to become active in party affairs.

- They donate money to candidates and to the parties through political action committees (PACs).

The following table lists the top 10 PACs that gave the most to candidates in 2015 and 2016.

PAC Name	Contribution
Honeywell International	$1.63 million
AT&T	$1.55 million
Lockheed Martin	$1.51 million
National Beer Wholesalers Association	$1.38 million
International Brotherhood of Electrical Workers	$1.29 million
Northrop Grumman	$1.28 million
Blue Cross/Blue Shield	$1.25 million
Credit Union National Association	$1.25 million
National Association of Realtors	$1.24 million
American Bankers Association	$1.14 million

Money, PACs, and Lobbying

Money is arguably the least effective way for interest groups to promote their causes. Since the passage of the first campaign finance reform laws in 1973, Congress has severely limited the amount of money any interest group can give to a candidate. However, it did allow for the formation of political action committees (PACs), which can make political contributions.

Because so many PACs have formed (nearly anyone or any group can form one), it makes it more difficult for one group to financially influence a candidate. Most candidates and elected officials take money from all sorts of PACs. This diminishes the influence any one PAC may have.

Most PACs are sponsored by corporations, labor unions, and ideological interest groups, but ideological PACs tend to give less money directly to candidates than do corporate or labor union PACs, because they prefer to spend the money on direct mail and advertisements.

Another important point to keep in mind is that, because incumbents are overwhelmingly reelected, corporate and labor union PACs gave most of their money to incumbents seeking reelection. As a general rule, corporate PACs give more to Republican candidates and labor union PACs give more to Democratic candidates.

Super PACs

In January 2010, with a Supreme Court ruling now referred to simply as Citizens United, super PACs were born. The Supreme Court overturned any limits on the amount of money an individual could give to a PAC. Furthermore, it concluded that corporations and unions also could make unlimited contributions.

That same year, in the case *SpeechNow.org* v. *Federal Election Commission,* the Supreme Court ruled that "independent expenditure only" groups were legal. So long as these super PACs did not coordinate their activities with political campaigns, they were now allowed to spend as much money to promote the candidate or issue they support.

So far in 2016, 2,255 super PACs have raised a total of more than $612 million. Right to Rise USA, a super PAC that supported Jeb Bush for president, raised more than $118 million.

 ON THE RECORD

"Few developments in campaigning have been as vilified and misunderstood as independent expenditure PACs, or, as they are colloquially known, super PACs."

—Bradley A. Smith, author

Lobbyists at Work

Besides using PAC donations, interest groups lobby legislators very hard to make their issues part of public policy. They will seek to influence legislation with all the legal means available to them. This is often referred to as polite persuasion. They know how to maneuver the corridors of Congress and have close contacts with elected officials.

Many lobbyists are lawyers, former journalists, or come from the field related to the policy issue at hand. Lobbyists are also professionals who testify before congressional committees when bills are being considered. But perhaps the most effective tool of the interest group lobbyist is to bring grass-roots pressures on elected officials. Grass-roots means of, or from the people: the average voter.

REAL-LIFE FACTS

The "lobby" is actually an outer room of a capitol building to which the general public is admitted. The term *lobby-agent* was used to identify favor-seekers at sessions of the New York State legislature in Albany by the late 1820s. By the 1830s, the term was shortened to *lobbyist* and was in wide use in Washington and other state capitals.

The Revolving Door

Every year and after every election cycle, hundreds of people leave important jobs in the government to take much more lucrative jobs with private corporations. Some of these former government officials go on to work as lobbyists or consultants. This process has come to be called the revolving door. In some cases, public officials act in certain ways in exchange for a private position after they leave office. Still others use their personal contacts from when they were in office on behalf of their new private employer.

This process clearly undermines the public good. There have been many examples of this kind of behavior but it is difficult to say exactly how systemic it is. Congress has passed laws that put a time limit on when people who leave government can go work for private industry and lobby the government, but the language is quite vague.

Regulating Interest Groups

Interest group activity is a form of free speech protected by the First Amendment to the Constitution; therefore, it cannot be lawfully abolished, and curtailing it is quite difficult. In 1946, Congress passed the Federal Regulation of Lobbying Act that required lobbyists in Washington who collected and spent money for the "principal purpose" of influencing legislation to register with the clerks of the House and the Senate. The law had little or no practical effect. Most lobbyists refused to register, and the government had no way to enforce the law.

In 1995, Congress passed a law to tighten up the registration and financial disclosure requirements. It eliminated the principal purpose language and now required all individual and organizational lobbyists to register and disclose basic information about their activities. The states have also passed similar laws. However, beyond making bribery or obviously corrupt behavior illegal, there is very little Congress can do to regulate interest groups because of the constitutional protection of free speech.

As we have seen in Chapter 7, even though Congress has passed campaign finance laws that limit how much PACs and individuals can contribute during one election cycle, individuals can still contribute to as many PACs as they like and there is no limit to the number of PACs that can be created. In many ways it might be what the founders wanted: factions born to counter other factions, to create balance and sustain a system that gives everyone the possibility to be heard.

The Least You Need to Know

- Interest groups are constitutionally protected by the First Amendment right to free speech. Interest groups are private organizations that try to persuade public officials to respond to their attitudes.

- Interest groups provide many positive benefits to society, including stimulating interest in public affairs and informing elected officials and the public on important issues.

- Interest groups lobby elected and government officials to influence public policy. PACs are political action committees, the financial arm with which interest groups help candidates, give money to the major parties, and legally spend an unlimited amount of money to promote their candidate or issue.

- Congress has placed some limits on what lobbyists can do and what PACs can spend. Still, interest groups are very difficult to regulate, except for obvious illegal activities, given the constitutional protection they have.

CHAPTER 19

The Media

The media has changed over time and these changes have influenced American politics. As political parties have declined in power and influence, candidates and public officials have looked to the media to communicate directly with the American public, while at the same time decrying the media for fact-checking them and highlighting their missteps. Journalists and news organizations play a pivotal role in a free democracy, and in the United States a free press is constitutionally protected by the First Amendment. Although the influence of the media on politics has grown, government rules limit some aspects and behaviors of the media.

In this chapter, you will read more about how people get their information and how news information needs to be processed for bias and motive.

In This Chapter

- The history and development of journalism in American politics
- The structure of the media
- How the media is governed
- The roles and influence of the media
- Is the media biased?

Journalism in American Political History

The relationship between the media and the government in the United States is governed by rules, laws, and constitutional protections, as well as by ever-evolving social and cultural norms. The media has a great deal of freedom due to the First Amendment right of free speech and a free press. The media in the United States has fewer restrictions than the press in any other country in the world.

Almost all radio and television stations in the United States are privately owned but are granted licenses by the government to operate. These licenses are granted for five and seven years and come with very few strings attached. Censorship of content is nearly unheard of in the United States, although the governing agency, the Federal Communications Commission (FCC) does impose certain rules on broadcasters.

Freedom from government control has positively affected the media in this country. In some ways it can be argued that for a free people to be informed and able to govern themselves wisely, it is necessary to have a press free of government control. The press has been referred to as the "fourth estate" or the "fourth branch of government." Information is power, or, better yet, information can be a powerful tool!

Still, some news organizations have been known to distort stories in order to reach larger audiences, garner higher ratings, sell advertising, or serve the broader political agenda of their corporate ownership. The strength of media outlets has changed over time, often simultaneously with changes in American politics. There are five important periods in journalistic history to consider: the eras of the party press, the popular press, opinion magazines, electronic journalism, and the internet.

The Party Press

In the early years of the republic, newspapers were created and controlled by political parties to further their political interests. Literacy and, therefore, readership was not yet widespread, and these newspapers circulated among an elite group of individuals and never presented both sides of an issue.

The Popular Press

As the nation moved into an industrial phase, improvements in education and technology brought about mass readership of newspapers. The invention of the telegraph in 1848 also changed the speed at which news traveled from region to region. This period saw the rise of the newswire service, which presented a balanced view of news events.

However, it also saw the rise of highly partisan news empires, which often influenced and even created news events. Joseph Pulitzer and William Randolph Hearst are among two of the best-known founders of *yellow journalism* newspapers during this time. The Spanish-American War of 1898 is considered by historians to be the first U.S. war ignited by yellow journalism. Proponents of American expansionism found an ally in the newspapers of William Randolph Hearst. Prior to the sinking of the USS *Maine* in the harbor in Havana, Cuba, Hearst's newspapers loudly opposed the political aspirations of the liberal anti-Spanish revolutionaries in Cuba, which were led by the writer Jose Marti and other Cuban exiles. This was largely due to the threat any revolution would pose to American business interests in Cuba. Instead, many political conservatives and the business sector called for Cuban "annexation."

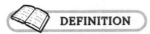 **DEFINITION**

Yellow journalism refers to the use of sensationalized and exaggerated reporting by newspapers or magazines to attract readers.

When the USS *Maine* was destroyed—an event whose causes many historians now debate—Hearst's newspapers insisted on Spain's culpability. This swayed American sentiment against the Spanish colonial government. Within three months, the United States was at war with Spain. Before the year's end, the United States had defeated the Spanish, Spain recognized Cuba's independence, and the United States took control of Spanish territories in the Caribbean and the Pacific, including Puerto Rico, the Philippines, and Guam.

 REAL-LIFE FACTS

During George Washington's administration, Alexander Hamilton and the Federalists started the *Gazette of the United States* and Thomas Jefferson and his supporters started the *National Gazette* to promote their opposing political views.

Opinion Magazines

The end of the nineteenth century saw the development of a larger middle and consumer class. To satisfy this market, magazines started to appear that discussed issues of public policy and investigative reporting. During this time, a professional class of journalists emerged, who were more independent of publishers such as Pulitzer and Hearst. These journalists, commonly referred to as *muckrakers,* were reform-minded and focused on investigative journalism. They helped usher in the Progressive Movement in response to corporate and political abuses. Teddy Roosevelt rode this momentum all the way to the White House.

Electronic Journalism

Radio and television transformed the news and politics in ways that few understood at the time. Starting in the 1920s with radio and then in the 1940s with television, politicians were able to speak directly to the people. Unfiltered speeches permitted public officials and candidates to be heard first hand.

Still, radio and television broadcasts are more expensive than newspapers to produce, and the news coverage through radio and television is more limited than in a newspaper. Today, politicians and elected officials try to gain access to news shows by doing something newsworthy. Starting in the late 1980s, cable television introduced the phenomenon of 24-hour news. Ted Turner's CNN was the first all-news, 24-hour, 7-day cable channel.

Many modern cable news organizations openly acknowledge their political bias and attract consumers of similar political leanings. Fox News is unabashedly conservative in its coverage of political events, just as MSNBC is liberal in its coverage. Ask people where they get their political news from, and you can infer with a high degree of accuracy what their political leanings are.

In the last two decades, with the explosion of digital technology and the use of the internet to publish and access news, the role and status of the mass media has undergone profound changes. As consumers demand more compact coverage, traditional news organizations have been challenged to shift their attention away from print and television channels to ereaders, smartphones, and other electronic devices.

The Internet

The internet has transformed the way Americans get and share news and it is still transforming politics today. More Americans go online to get their news today than through any other media outlet.

The web is not only an effective way to get news, it is also an inexpensive way to communicate. Interest groups can easily communicate their ideas and positions on issues, elected officials, and candidates. Many websites now share video, pictures, and commentary on all news events with the public. Candidates have also used the web effectively to raise money. The internet also has given rise to the "citizen journalist." Using smartphones equipped with video cameras, active citizens now record events as they occur and stream the coverage to millions of people via YouTube or Facebook, for example.

According to the Pew Research Center, 60 percent of American adults use social networking sites like Facebook or Twitter. Of those social media users, 66 percent—or 39 percent of all American adults—have done at least one of eight civic or political activities with social media. The 2016 presidential primary race has seen all the candidates using social media to post and tweet on a daily basis to their followers to share the message of the day. Republican candidate Donald Trump, for example, has 7.4 million followers on Twitter and has posted more than 37,000 messages to date.

The Structure of the National Media

Politics and journalism need each other: public officials, candidates, and interest groups try their best to use the media as a means of communication with the public. The media needs politics, and especially politicians, to keep their audiences both informed and entertained. Although the media serves an important role in the democratic process, it is still big business, and that means profits.

All media is biased to some degree. While some media outlets bill themselves as impartial and balanced, all media outlets go through a process of selecting the stories and personalities they will cover in order to serve, keep, and expand their audience. In the media, the larger the audience, the more you can charge for advertising time.

The degree of competition in the media has changed the number and type of players that deliver news. Despite competition from radio and television, Americans continue to read newspapers. The internet, however, seems to be diminishing print readership, as people can now read the news online. But newspapers have declined substantially in numbers since the beginning of the twentieth century, and the national press is now dominated by just a few sources. Radio and television, however, remain intensely competitive, and tend to be focused on local markets. The internet, it can be argued, is even more competitive, given the ease with which one can place and access information on it.

It is generally accepted in the United States that certain media outlets constitute what is referred to as a national press, or media outlets that have a national following, even though some are locally published. The news magazines *Time* and *Newsweek,* the network evening newscasts (ABC, CBS, and NBC), the cable networks (such as CNN, MSNBC, and FOX), and five newspapers (*The Wall Street Journal, USA Today, Christian Science Monitor, The New York Times,* and *The Washington Post*) all have acquired a following and national government officials pay a great deal of attention to what they have to say. The national media plays several important roles in American politics. It serves as a gatekeeper, scorekeeper, and watchdog of the government.

 ON THE RECORD

"I think it is absolutely essential in a democracy to have competition in the media, a lot of competition, and we seem to be moving away from that."

—Walter Cronkite, CBS News anchor

The Gatekeeper Role

In its role as gatekeeper, the national press can influence what issues will become news, discussed and debated in national politics. The national media can also control the length of time they are willing to cover a particular topic or subject. In a sense, they can create a reality or an importance around an issue that might not exist without the coverage.

The Scorekeeper Role

One of the most important roles the national media plays is to make or break reputations of political leaders. The coverage a candidate receives during an election campaign can help catapult him or her to victory, or render them marginal. What the general public knows about candidates is based largely on what is reported in the media. The media is also the means by which Americans receive the results of elections.

 MISINFORMATION

In 1948, the *Chicago Tribune* famously published an incorrect banner headline on its front page regarding the presidential election results. The headline read "Dewey Defeats Truman," when in fact Harry Truman had won the election.

The Watchdog Role

In this capacity, the media investigates and exposes legal and personal wrongdoings by public officials. Today, the public and the media seem to be fascinated by titillating news about public officials. How relevant that type of news is to an official's capacity to serve is questionable.

Illegal behavior is quite another story. In the early 1970s, two *Washington Post* journalists, Carl Bernstein and Bob Woodward, exposed the Watergate burglary and how it was tied directly to the White House. This media coverage led to congressional impeachment hearings that brought about the resignation of President Nixon.

Rules and Governance of the Media

Newspapers are almost entirely free of government regulation and interference, while radio and television must have government-issued licenses in order to operate and must follow government regulations. Newspapers, for example, are free to publish whatever they like and are restricted in only the rarest of circumstances. This is largely due to judicial rulings that have upheld the First Amendment right to freedom of the press.

Once a newspaper or magazine publishes a story, it can be sued or prosecuted only for the following reasons:

- It is libelous.

- It is obscene.

- It incites people to commit an illegal act.

However, the courts have ruled that libel suits against the media can only be successful if it is proven that the information was damaging and that the media outlet knew it was false. This, of course, is very difficult to prove.

Obscenity is a whole other matter. What the courts have ruled to be obscene has changed over time, usually along with changes in social mores. What would have been considered obscene in the late nineteenth century would probably not even raise an eyebrow today, even among the most conservative Americans.

Also, it is illegal for printed publications to incite people to act illegally. Newspapers, for example, cannot call for the violent overthrow of the government. But they can publish "Vote the Crooks Out!"

Journalists generally have the right to maintain the confidentiality of their sources for news stories. In most cases, the media is protected. However, the courts have ruled that if criminal conduct is being investigated, the press must divulge their source or risk fines and/or imprisonment. The courts have also ruled that the police need subpoenas in order to search the offices of media outlets.

Unlike the print media, broadcasting is regulated by the government. This is justified because broadcasting is sent over airwaves that belong to the people. In a sense, the government leases the airwaves to the broadcasters. All broadcasters must receive a government license in order to operate. License renewals are almost never rejected.

The governing agency of broadcasting, the FCC, can influence the types of shows that are broadcast and administer fines if regulations are broken. In the area of politics and elections, the FCC has established important rules of conduct for broadcasters:

- **Equal time rule**   If a broadcaster sells advertising time to one candidate, it must be willing to sell time to opposing candidates.

- **Right-of-reply rule**   If a candidate is attacked on a station, he or she must have the right to reply on that station.

- **Editorializing rule**   If a broadcast endorses a candidate for office, the opposing candidate must have the right to reply.

The Effect of the Media on Politics

Media coverage affects how politics are conducted, how candidates are perceived, which public policies are discussed, and how public policy is formulated. Historically, radio and television have played an important role. Today, the internet plays an equally important role.

Radio broadcast the first election results starting in 1920. By the 1930s, radio reached millions of Americans directly in their homes. The first American president to effectively use radio as a medium of communication with the American public was President Franklin D. Roosevelt. Before Roosevelt, most Americans never saw or heard their president. Roosevelt spoke directly to the American people with his fireside chats—presidential radio addresses that were broadcast live into American homes.

Overnight, radio became a major source of news and political information. Elected officials could now speak directly to the American people unfiltered. Today, talk radio is still an important source of political commentary. Some of the most prominent broadcasters are aired nationally to millions of listeners.

 ON THE RECORD

"He [Roosevelt] was the first great American radio voice ... that voice strong, confident, totally at ease .... It was literally and figuratively electrifying."

—David Halberstam, in his book on political journalism, *The Powers That Be*

By the 1950s, television started to make its mark on the American political scene replacing news-papers as the main source of political information. Some estimate that for more than 80 percent of Americans, television is the main source of political news and information. Television added a visual component that was generally left to the imagination with radio. Suddenly, appearance mattered nearly as much, if not more than, the message.

In the first televised presidential debates between the Democratic nominee, John F. Kennedy, and Republican nominee, Richard M. Nixon, Kennedy's youthful good looks contrasted dramat-ically with Nixon's perspiring performance. Kennedy went on to win the election and was the first president to master the use of the televised press conference. Additionally, many members of Congress have used televised hearings to propel themselves to national fame. Still, the media plays a significant role in many other ways beyond personalizing politics.

The Public Agenda

Media coverage of societal problems and concerns influences political leaders and focuses public attention. As they report on events and issues, the media to a large extent determine what the public and public officials talk about and become concerned about. This is very evident today with the media's relative focus on the wars in Syria and Iraq, the campaign to destroy ISIS, and the state of the U.S. economy.

Electoral Politics

Television has made candidates much less dependent on political parties because they can now appeal directly to the American people. Candidates can hire professional media consultants to form their public image and try to manipulate media coverage. And because most Americans get their political news from television, candidates focus on *sound bites* that television news sources can use on their programs. Also, as previously mentioned, the digital age and social media are transforming electoral politics. Since the 2008 Obama campaign, political sound bites are immediately delivered to millions via social media and often go viral within hours. How this will ultimately affect our democracy is still debated and will be played out in the next few election cycles.

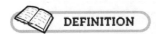 **DEFINITION**

A **sound bite** is a carefully orchestrated event that news organizations can use in a minute or less on their program.

Choice of Candidates

The media influences which candidates have a chance to win elections by deciding who to cover and the type of coverage they offer. In the 1930s, for example, the media never showed President Roosevelt in his wheelchair or using braces to walk. Today, the public's perception of candidates and public officials is influenced directly by the coverage an individual receives. In the 1992 presidential election, candidate George H. W. Bush was caught on camera seemingly puzzled by the check-out scanner at a grocery store. He was immediately labeled as out of touch with ordinary Americans.

More recently, a video of Mitt Romney speaking to supporters at a fundraiser in 2012, where he stated that "47 percent of Americans who pay no taxes" went viral and portrayed him as an elitist out of touch with nearly half the electorate. In the 2016 presidential primary race, the populist candidacies of Bernie Sanders and Donald Trump have portrayed them as antiestablishment and as candidates willing to take on the entrenched interests in Washington.

Campaign and Political Events

Candidates and elected officials schedule events that get media coverage to reinforce their image and message. These events are usually elaborately staged in settings that work well on television. A candidate might wear safety goggles while touring a factory or a president might land on an aircraft carrier to announce a military victory, in order to get their message and their preferred visuals across.

REAL-LIFE FACTS

The first televised political party convention was the Republican Party National Convention in Chicago in 1952. The Democratic Party Convention was also held in Chicago that year and televised later that summer.

The News and the Government

To some extent, all government officials try to shape public opinion. The media is the most direct means of reaching millions of Americans. Framing an issue is a key component of this function. For example, candidates, elected officials, and interest groups that support abortion rights tend to frame the argument in the context of choice and personal freedom. Opponents on the other hand try to frame the issue in terms of rights for the unborn fetus.

Coverage of important public policy issues, however, is almost never carried to its conclusion by the media. The tendency is to get the attention of the public and public officials, and then have the political process form a policy and propose an implementation plan.

In the end, however, the media's most influential role might be at the local level. Because there are fewer sources reporting on local news, those organizations have greater influence over what the public hears, sees, and reads than in the national media, where competition is more widespread.

Coverage of the President

The president is the most prominent political figure in the United States. The president and the vice president are the only political leaders selected by all the people. As such, coverage of the president has a prominent position in media coverage. In fact, the president has a *bully pulpit* unlike any other public official. The president can use speeches to put things on the national agenda or to get Congress to act.

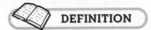 **DEFINITION**

A **bully pulpit** is a public office of sufficiently high rank that it provides the holder with an opportunity to speak out and be listened to on any matter. This term was coined by President Theodore Roosevelt, who referred to the American presidency as a "bully pulpit," by which he meant a terrific platform from which to advocate an agenda.

President Ronald Reagan, for example, would conclude important policy addresses to the nation by asking the public to contact their officials in Congress to voice their opinions. The first president to perfect the use of the bully pulpit was President Theodore Roosevelt in the early twentieth century. The media not only covers presidential press conferences, it is fully organized to cover every presidential action from formal trips abroad to vacations to the president's health.

In 2003, President George W. Bush delivered a speech to the American public on a Navy aircraft carrier announcing that our military objectives had been accomplished in Iraq with a huge banner in the background pronouncing "Mission Accomplished." Nearly 15 years later, we are still entrenched in efforts to maintain stability in Iraq, and the United States is still engaged in fighting radical Islamic terrorists unleashed by our war efforts in the Middle East.

Coverage of Congress

As you can imagine, members of Congress tend to watch media coverage of the president with a sense of envy. After all, the founders intended for Congress to be the preeminent branch of government. Yet it is strategically difficult for news organizations to cover 435 House members and 100 members of the Senate. Unlike the executive branch, Congress does not have one person who can speak for the entire institution.

Furthermore, television cameras were banned from Congress until 1978, except for a few ceremonial occasions. Congressional sessions have been covered by C-SPAN since 1979, and the media does cover important congressional hearings. The first such hearings to get live television national media coverage were the impeachment proceedings in the House against President Nixon.

Coverage of the Judiciary

Of the three branches of government, the independent nature of the federal judiciary makes it the least dependent on the press. The Supreme Court, for example, does not communicate with or through the media or allow cameras during arguments. The judiciary tries to maintain its independent role in order to avoid being perceived as manipulated by the media. Of course, it would be naïve to deny that the courts look to public opinion when rendering decisions.

How to Interpret Political News

Americans blame the media for many things. Conservatives complain that the media is too liberal. Liberals complain that Republicans have a stranglehold on corporate media (and vice versa). Both claim that television networks are owned by big business conglomerates who are largely concerned with profits and boosting ratings rather than providing fair and impartial coverage of events. Most national news organizations do try to insulate their reporters from the business division to check media bias. Still, reporters, journalists, and editors are human and their personal politics inevitably influence their perspectives.

The important question is not whether the media is biased, but whether that bias finds its way into news coverage. In order to determine if this is so, it is important to distinguish among the types of news events that are covered. The three types of news stories are routine stories, feature stories, and investigative stories.

Routine stories are public events usually carried by all media outlets. They are almost always carried the same way by the various news outlets. Routine stories can occasionally be misreported, particularly if something out of the ordinary occurs.

Feature stories and investigative stories must be selected, and, therefore, are more likely to reflect bias. In these cases, the reporter or the editor must make a decision about what he or she thinks ought to be covered and be given public attention. The political ideologies of the journalist and editor are more likely to be prominent in these types of stories. For example, a liberal news organization might choose to cover improprieties among business people, or give extra coverage to environmental stories. Conservative news organizations might elect to cover urban crime and the decline of family values.

It is important to understand that there are motives for the news stories that are covered and for information that is leaked to the media within those stories. The media, the public, and public officials have a complex relationship in American politics.

 ON THE RECORD

"The media is too concentrated, too few people own too much. There's really five companies that control 90 percent of what we read, see, and hear. It's not healthy."

—Ted Turner, founder of CNN

The Least You Need to Know

- The news media includes newspapers, radio, television, and the internet. The rise of new media at different stages has changed the way elected officials, policy makers, and candidates communicate with the public.

- Broadcast journalism, and more recently the internet, has increased the effect of the mass media on public opinion. The media plays three significant roles in American politics: gatekeeper, scorekeeper, and watchdog.

- Several important rules and regulations govern media behavior. Broadcast journalism is the most restricted and print media is the least restricted. The Constitution protects freedom of the press under the First Amendment.

- Media coverage of the government varies greatly. The President receives the most coverage, largely at the expense of the other two branches of government. Members of Congress vie for media coverage through newsworthy events like committee hearings and staged political appearances.

- Most media stories are selected by journalists and editors who have their own political ideologies. Therefore, it is important to read, hear, and see the news knowing that bias exists and to what extent it has permeated the story.

The Policy-Making Process

Now that you have read how Congress, the presidency, the bureaucracy, the courts, the media, and interest groups work, it is time to explain how public policies get made and are implemented. One way to explain how this process works is to look at the outcomes of public policy and to understand the political influence at work. For example, when regulations are removed on a particular industry, or new ones applied to other industries, it quickly becomes clear which group or institution is wielding political power.

Americans take for granted that the federal government is involved in almost all aspects of life. The government levies taxes, regulates business and the environment, oversees many entitlement programs, gives assistance to the states and cities, and protects our civil rights. Yet this was not always the case.

In This Chapter

- The main policy-makers
- Cost-benefit analysis of policy issues
- The politics of public policy
- How the policy-making process works

Who Sets the Agenda?

The expansive role of the federal government was born during the Great Depression and grew rapidly after the 1960s. Therefore, the first step in the policy process is to get one's item on the government's agenda of things to address. In order for this to occur, there must be a consensus that what the government is about to undertake is necessary, within its legitimate authority, and appropriate for its role. There are four important factors that determine legitimacy:

- Shared political values

- Custom and tradition

- Impact of major events or crises

- Attitudes of political elites

The scope of legitimate government action is always increasing because people believe that the government ought to be doing what it's doing and should continue to do so. Also, in response to major events, such as war, natural disasters, or economic crises, the people demand government action. Sometimes the government will expand its policy agenda in response to a crisis, sometimes without any demand from the people, and sometimes when it would seem to many that no government action is necessary at all.

 MISINFORMATION

Although it took congressional action and presidential approval to pass the Great Society legislation of the 1960s, including the War on Poverty, most people do not know that the programs were developed, designed, and advocated by bureaucrats and their political allies.

In order to understand why government adds new issues to the policy agenda, we need to look at the behavior of interest groups, large institutions, and the opinions of political elites. The demands made by interest groups can only result in public policy if there is, or they are able to foster, a parallel set of values or beliefs among the general public on the matter. For example, unions have favored tough government regulation of the work environment to ensure employees safety. The public generally believes that workers should be safe when performing their jobs.

Among the most important government institutions to influence the policy agenda of the government are the courts and the federal bureaucracy. Courts can make decisions that require government to act. The bureaucracy, largely due to its sheer size and because it is a venue for policy experts, has become a source of new ideas and changes.

Political elites, largely through the national media, can either place matters on the agenda or publicize those matters important to them. Media attention can help propel ideas into policy by bringing public attention to certain matters and raising political support for those policy ideas—or it can ignore them and leave them to wither away unnoticed.

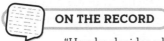 **ON THE RECORD**

"He who decides what politics is about runs the country."

—E. E. Schattschneider, *The Semisovereign People* (1960)

How Are Decisions Made?

The political scientist, James Q. Wilson, has written extensively on the subject of how decisions are made in the area of public policy. Wilson argues that in order to understand the politics of arriving at public policy once an idea has been placed on the policy agenda, one must analyze the cost and benefit of the proposed policy. Some issues ignite intense conflict among interest groups. Still others pass relatively unchallenged, or with general approval. The nature of the issue will determine the kinds of groups that become politically active and to what degree temperatures will rise in the body politic.

One way to understand how an issue will affect the distribution of power among various groups is to examine the cost and benefit of the policy. Once this analysis has taken place, and once it is understood how the cost and benefits will be distributed, then we can begin to understand the various political coalitions that form in support, or in opposition to, proposed policies. You will read about cost-benefit analysis and then examine the politics of four types of public policies: majoritarian politics, interest group politics, client politics, and entrepreneurial politics.

Cost and Benefit Analysis

A cost is any burden, monetary or otherwise, that some people must or perceive they must bear if the government policy is adopted. The benefit is any satisfaction, monetary or otherwise, that people believe they will receive if the policy is implemented.

People's perceptions of costs and benefits change over time, yet most people generally want the most benefit for the least cost. Rarely are policies implemented that impose high costs for low- or short-term benefits.

Majoritarian Politics

Policies that promise benefits to large segments of the population at a cost that most people will have to bear are called the policies of majoritarian politics. Such policies involve making appeals to large segments of the voters and their representatives. Examples are Social Security and defense spending. Everyone pays through taxes, everyone benefits from the program. Majoritarian politics usually reflects ideological differences or are often reached when there is wide consensus in the face of a crisis.

REAL-LIFE FACTS

Only after the widespread failure of banks during the Great Depression of the 1930s did the federal government enact legislation to regulate and insure financial institutions. In 2008, the government spent more than $1 trillion to stabilize the banking system in response to the credit crisis.

Interest Group Politics

In interest group politics, a proposed policy will benefit a small or concentrated group, with the cost incurred by them or another small group. These issues are generally fought out by highly organized interest groups.

An example of this is a law Congress passed that requires businesses to give 30 days' notice before large-scale layoffs. Union interest groups strongly favored the law as their members would directly benefit. Business leaders opposed the law as they would be the only ones to incur the salary cost for the 30 days.

Client Politics

Client politics refers to the benefit going to one small group, with a large portion or all of society bearing the cost. The group that receives the benefit is very motivated to get organized and galvanize support for the issue. Because the cost is spread out to so many, most people are unaware of the cost and it is marginally insignificant.

An example of client politics is farm price support. Farmers and large agricultural corporations benefit substantially; however, the public is unaware of how much it is costing them in taxes or in higher food costs. Pork-barrel projects are another example of client politics. Projects that favor individual districts are placed as riders on legislation. Congress members vote to approve the legislation knowing that they will each get something for their district. This process is called *logrolling.*

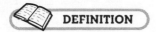 **DEFINITION**

Logrolling refers to mutual aid among politicians. It is the equivalent of saying, "You scratch my back, and I'll scratch yours."

Entrepreneurial Politics

Entrepreneurial politics refers to society as a whole receiving the benefit while the cost is absorbed by a small group. An example of this is the requirement that automobiles have certain safety mechanisms, such as airbags.

Society benefits because of the added safety measure, and the auto manufacturers must pay for installing the device. However, manufacturers then pass on the cost to consumers by way of increasing prices for cars.

How Does Policy Get Made?

Policy-making is about placing an item on the government's agenda and deciding what to do about it. The outcome of political struggles as they relate to policy matters will depend not only on who gains and who loses, but also on the perceptions, beliefs, and values of the key political players.

The policy-making process has five distinct stages:

Problem identification   What is the problem? How and by whom is the problem defined? Does the government need to act? As we have seen in this chapter, there are a variety of factors and people involved in problem identification.

Policy formulation   What should be done? Who should be involved in planning the policy?

Policy adoption   Who needs to act? Which branches of government are involved? Is the policy constitutional and legal?

Policy implementation   Once a policy is adopted there are some important questions to address: How should the policy be carried out? How much money should be allocated for the policy? How can the policy be administered effectively?

Policy evaluation   Is the policy working? How is the effectiveness of the policy measured? Who will evaluate the policy? Evaluation is very political because most program supporters and administrators will exaggerate their success and attempt to hide any cost overruns or waste.

Poverty and Welfare

The traditional solution to poverty in the United States has been through income transfers. This is commonly referred to as welfare, where income from the well-to-do is transferred via taxes to relatively poor groups through various programs. These programs have helped to reduce the number of people living in poverty in the United States. The most common programs include food stamps, housing vouchers, and medical assistance. Since the 1960s, hundreds of billions of dollars have been transferred to the poor through these programs.

Until 1996, the basic welfare program in the United States was known as Aid to Families with Dependent Children (AFDC). This program provided aid for children who did not receive adequate financial support from their fathers. Conservatives for many years criticized this program as perpetuating poverty by creating a culture of dependency on federal assistance. In 1996, the Republican-controlled Congress passed, and Democratic President William Jefferson Clinton signed, the Welfare Reform Act. At the signing ceremony for the act in August 1996, President William Jefferson Clinton said, "Today, we are ending welfare as we know it. But I hope this day will be remembered not for what it ended, but for what it began."

This legislation replaced AFDC with the Temporary Assistance to Needy Families (TANF) program. Under the TANF program, the federal government transferred the responsibility of welfare assistance to the states and funded this with block grants. The states now have to meet the cost of the welfare services they provide with the money allocated to them by the federal government. If states wish to provide more services than the block grant covers, the states must raise the additional revenues on their own.

The main objective of the Welfare Reform Act was to limit government spending on welfare at all government levels. One way it sought to achieve this was by limiting most welfare recipients to only two years of welfare assistance. After the two-year period was up, welfare payments would be discontinued unless the recipient was working. Secondly, the new law limited lifetime welfare assistance to five years. However, if the states wish to pay the full cost the benefits provide, they are not limited to the five-year rule. Practically speaking, however, most benefits terminate after the lifetime cap, since states cannot afford to absorb the full cost of benefits without federal assistance.

In 1974, Congress passed the Supplemental Security Income (SSI) program to provide minimum income for elderly Americans and persons with disabilities who do not qualify for standard Social Security benefits. Today, SSI is one of the fastest growing programs that assist Americans with need. In 1974, the cost of the program was $7 billion. Today, the cost is more than $40 billion. The government also provides assistance to low-income families and individuals through the food stamp program. In 1964, when the program first started, nearly 367,000 Americans were receiving assistance at an annual cost of $860,000. Today, more than 30 million Americans qualify for assistance at an annual cost in excess of $30 billion annually. In 1975, Congress passed the Earned-Income Tax Credit (EITC) program. This program gives back part or all of the Social Security taxes paid by low-income workers. Today, nearly 20 percent of all taxpayers claim an EITC at an estimated cost of more than $25 billion annually.

 MISINFORMATION

> Studies show that the public dramatically overestimates the number of African Americans in poverty. Although 75 percent of news and magazine pictures feature African Americans as the face of welfare, African Americans make up only 35 percent of welfare recipients. This depiction of welfare recipients is accompanied by the feminization of poverty, where from the 1970s onward, women became the predominant face of poverty.

Environmental Policy

Americans have been dealing with environmental issues ever since the colony of Massachusetts passed laws regulating water pollution. Since the 1880s, states have passed legislation controlling water pollution, sewage, and dumping in order to ensure a clean and safe water supply for its citizens. In 1948, Congress passed the Federal Water Pollution Control Act, which provided research and assistance to the states for pollution control efforts. In 1952, Oregon was the first state to pass laws regulating air pollution. The first federal laws dealing with air pollution were passed in 1955 with the Air Pollution Control Act.

Citizens and environmental interest groups generally support efforts by the government to ensure a clean air and water supply. Many industrial business groups oppose these efforts as an unfair burden placed on them by the government and as an impediment to their competitiveness in the open market, where they must compete with foreign businesses who are not burdened by costly government requirements and regulations.

Some of the most significant environmental legislation passed includes the following:

Clean Air Act (1963)   Assisted local and state governments in establishing control programs and coordinating research.

Water Quality Act (1965)   Authorized setting standards for discharges into waters.

Air Quality Act (1967)   Established air-quality regions. Required local and state governments to implement approved control programs or be subject to federal controls.

Clean Water Act (1974)   Established federal standards for water suppliers serving more than 25 people, having more than 15 service connections, or operating more than 60 days a year.

Oil Pollution Act (1990) Established liability for the cleanup of navigable waters after oil-spill disasters.

Clean Air Act (1990) Established national levels for air pollution and comprehensive air quality laws.

Environmental policies divide Americans largely along political and geographical differences. Presidents have issued Executive Orders that reflect their views and have created policies without Congressional action. President Obama, for example, has cancelled leases that would have allowed drilling for oil in the Arctic. Additionally, in 2015 President Obama issued Executive Order 13693 that cuts greenhouse gas emissions by 40 percent.

Taxes and Subsidies

As you read earlier in this chapter, taxes and subsidies are voted on by members of Congress. This world of taxes and subsidies creates a cycle of action and reaction by the government and some part of the public. This is commonly referred to as the *action-reaction syndrome.*

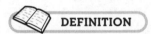 DEFINITION

> For every action on the part of the government, there is a reaction on the part of the affected public. This, in turn, results in government action in response to the public reaction, which then results with another reaction, and the cycle begins all over again. This is known as the **action-reaction syndrome.**

Individuals and businesses do not pay a lump-sum tax each year. Rather they are taxed based on progressive tax rates. Individuals at the highest tax rate seek to reduce their taxable income to the lowest possible amount in order to reduce their tax liability. In order to do so, Congress must pass loopholes—legal methods by which individuals and businesses are allowed to reduce the tax liabilities owed to the government.

In the 1940s, the highest tax rate stood at 94 percent. Today, that rate is 35 percent. This means that in the 1940s, the highest earners in America paid 94¢ on every dollar in taxes. In the 1980s, President Reagan persuaded Congress to reduce the highest rate to 28 percent. Today, the federal income tax has 7 brackets: 10 percent, 15 percent, 25 percent, 28 percent, 33 percent, 35 percent, and 39.6 percent. The amount you owe depends on your filing status and income level. The tax rate in the United States in graduated. That means that higher amounts of income are taxed at higher rates than on lower amounts. For example, the top rate only applies to income you earn above $415,000.

MISINFORMATION

Most people believe their income is taxed based on the total gross income earned. The marginal tax system in the United States means you are taxed at different rates based on the income bracket for that portion of your income. The first $9,225 is taxed at 10 percent for everyone and increases to 15 percent for the next bracket of $9,226 to $37,450 for single filers.

Closely related to the subject of taxes is the sustainability of the Social Security system. Social Security is funded by taxes and came into existence in 1935 as part of the New Deal legislation to alleviate the financial burden of many Americans during the Great Depression. Social Security guarantees a minimum level of pension benefits to all persons. Currently, Social Security tax collections exceed benefits, so the trust fund in which the excess monies are placed continues to grow. This trust fund is invested in government bonds. However, with the arrival of the baby boomer retirees, the monies collected will not be enough to pay the benefits. The government will be forced to sell the bonds in the reserve fund to pay out social security benefits to the nearly 75 million expected recipients. Some economists estimate that by 2030 the trust fund will be depleted and any future benefits will have to be paid from the taxes collected.

The government can act to address this looming crisis in several ways:

- Raise the Social Security tax rate

- Reduce the benefits paid

- Raise the age of eligibility to collect benefits

- Place a means test on all or some of the benefits

Some have called for the total or partial privatization of Social Security. Many conservatives in America favor this proposal as a way of reducing and ultimately eliminating government's role and all taxpayers' responsibility for a guaranteed pension benefit for all Americans. Liberals fear that privatization could jeopardize the long-term security of retirees who would now have to rely on the mercy of a volatile stock market. Given the recent economic meltdown in the U.S. economy and stock markets, any attempt to privatize Social Security will likely be met with passionate resistance.

Fiscal and Monetary Policy

Fiscal policy is defined as the "tax-and-spend" policy of the government to bring about changes in economic variables such as the inflation rate, the unemployment rate, and the rate of economic growth. Monetary policy is defined as the use of changes in the money supply to alter interest rates, which in turn affects the unemployment rate, interest rates, and the rate of inflation. Fiscal policy is the domain of Congress and the president. Monetary policy is executed by the Federal Reserve Bank, an independent agency not controlled directly by either the president or Congress.

The theory behind fiscal policy is fairly clear. When the economy is in a period of recession or contraction, the government should stimulate economic activity by decreasing taxes, increasing government expenditures, or both. Conversely, when the economy is expanding too rapidly and inflationary pressures are mounting, the government should reduce its expenditures, raise taxes, or both. This particular view of fiscal policy is an outgrowth of the theories of John Maynard Keynes. Practically speaking, however, once government has instituted new spending programs to stimulate the economy, it becomes difficult to abolish the program or spending line. When the economy improves, individuals and groups that benefit from the program lobby for continued funding.

The theory behind monetary policy is also straightforward. In periods of economic contractions, the economy should be stimulated by increasing the supply of money. This in turn lowers interest rates and encourages consumer and business borrowing and spending. In times of inflationary pressures, the money supply should be reduced to have a reverse effect. However, reducing the money supply can result in higher unemployment, which results in an economic slowdown. This is particularly destabilizing not only for the economy, but for society at large. Still, conservatives generally believe that monetary policy is the best way to manage the economy, as opposed to involving the government directly through stimulus programs.

Budget Deficits and the Public Debt

Every time the government runs a budget deficit—when it spends more than it receives in taxes—it must issue debt instruments to make up the gap. These debt instruments are U.S. Treasury Bonds, essentially IOUs that are sold to foreign governments, corporations, and individual investors that become part of the public debt. The public debt is defined as the total amount of money owed by the U.S. government. As the government budget continues to produce deficits, the net public debt increases.

In 2001, in response to the terrorist attacks in September of that year, with the economy already in recession, the government increased expenditures greatly. This resulted in even greater deficits than had been anticipated. The government has continued to increase its "security" spending. This, coupled with the wars in Afghanistan and Iraq, has raised the national debt to vertiginous levels.

The Great Recession of 2007–2009 caused deficits and debt to increase substantially. Revenue decreased and spending increased to levels not seen since World War II. Federal spending reached 25 percent of the GDP.

REAL-LIFE FACTS

During the presidency of George W. Bush, the net public debt of the United States has tripled from $3.4 trillion in 2000 to $10.6 trillion in 2008—only to further skyrocket following the financial crisis and Great Recession. Under President Obama, although annual budget deficits have been brought below Bush-era levels since 2014, the national debt will exceed $19 trillion by the end of 2016. This represents $58,000 in debt for every individual American.

The Least You Need to Know

- The most important aspect of the policy-making process is to get the issue on the government's agenda. Issues arrive on the agenda through some principal political players: interest groups, courts, the bureaucracy, political elites, and the media.

- Most public policies can be placed in a cost-benefit analysis framework. The nature of the issue will determine which groups emerge to support and oppose the measure.

- There are four categories of politics in the public policy arena: majoritarian politics, interest group politics, client politics, and entrepreneurial politics.

- The policy-making process has five distinct stages: problem identification, policy formulation, policy adoption, policy implementation, and policy evaluation.

Economic Policy, Foreign Policy, and National Defense

Economic policy can be divided into three different areas: fiscal policy, monetary policy, and trade policy. The goals of economic policy are to control inflation, unemployment, and economic growth. Economic policy also affects military spending and foreign aid.

Foreign policy and economic policy are very closely related. The economic status of the United States offers protection and opportunities for trade with other countries and economic growth. The United States' relationships with other countries are described in terms of alliances, treaties, and trade agreements. Nations work together to create a world of political stability and to expand trade opportunities.

In This Chapter

- The U.S. economic policies
- Major economic theories in the United States
- The Federal Reserve
- The U.S. military departments
- International alliances and trade pacts
- The United Nations

Economic Theories

The U.S. economy is based on the principles of capitalism. This theory is described in Adam Smith's *The Wealth of Nations,* published in 1776. Smith envisioned an ideal, self-regulating market economy as the "invisible hand" leading individuals in pursuit of their own interests and consequently the pursuit of society's interests as a whole. He found that labor, land, and capital are the three most important factors of production and the major determinants of a country's wealth.

Although capitalism is the main theory that drives the U.S. economy, other more modern theories have also contributed to economic policies over the years. Monetarism is an economic theory that focuses on the supply of money in the economy as the most important factor in determining the rate of inflation. Monetarists believe that inflation occurs when the government prints too much money. They suggest that in order to avoid the cycles of growth and recession, the government must print money at a steady rate that is proportional to the country's economic growth.

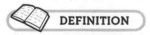 **ON THE RECORD**

"Money was all appropriated for the top in hopes that it would trickle down to the needy."

—Will Rogers

Keynesianism is based on the theory of twentieth-century British economist John Maynard Keynes. The state can spur economic growth and improve the stability of the private sector by creating the right level of demand and creating a circular flow of money. Following the Great Depression, Keynes argued that the government should increase spending by increasing the money supply or by buying up some of the market. This contrasts with the idea of capitalism because it implies government intervention in times of economic *recession.*

 DEFINITION

A **recession** is the reduction of a country's gross domestic product (GDP) for at least two quarters. It is a period of reduced economic activity in the business cycle.

Supply-side economists see economic growth in terms of creating incentives for people to produce goods and services (supply), such as adjusting income tax and capital gains tax rates. It is often combined with trickle-down economics, which is a theory that came about during Ronald Reagan's presidency. It was originally coined by humorist Will Rogers after the Great Depression to refer to the policy of providing tax cuts to businesses and rich individuals. The major features of Reagan's policies were similar to this in that he called for the reduction of taxes on capital gains, corporate income, and higher individual incomes.

Implementing Economic Policy

After World War II, the United States saw that foreign aid would not be enough to bring about the economic recovery of its allies. Europeans needed to sell their goods in foreign markets, so other nations lowered their *tariffs* and amended their strict trading rules. In 1947, the United States assisted in creating the General Agreement on Tariffs and Trade (GATT), an international trade agreement that more than 90 different countries have chosen to participate in.

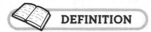 **DEFINITION**

Tariffs are taxes on imported goods or products.

The United States has progressively used more treaties like GATT to promote free trade and peace around the world. Members of GATT formed the World Trade Organization (WTO), an association created to encourage global trade and manage international trade disagreements. The United States has a special trade pact with the countries that border it. The North American Free Trade Agreement (NAFTA) began in 1994 and removed most trade restrictions between the United States, Canada, and Mexico, thereby increasing trade across the borders.

NAFTA has both positively and negatively affected the member nations. Those who support NAFTA point to the net rise in income and the decline in poverty in Mexico. Other economists have shown that NAFTA has been lucrative for business owners in all three countries, but has had a negative impact on farmers in Mexico and on U.S. workers in manufacturing and assembly industries who have lost their jobs. Critics of NAFTA believe that it has contributed to the growing levels of inequality in the United States and Mexico.

While the United States uses economic policy for the benefit of free trade, it also uses it as a political statement in the form of embargoes and sanctions. When the U.S. government feels that certain countries participate in deplorable acts such as torture, terrorism, diamond trading, narcotics distribution, and nuclear proliferation, it chooses to limit and sometimes even ban trade with that country. Currently, the United States has sanctions against North Korea, Sudan, and a few other countries; others have recently been lifted on Iran and Cuba. The United States also does not participate in arms-related trade with China. These policies are intended to isolate the country and put its government in a tough position, as not being able to trade with other countries can make its economy suffer greatly.

Fiscal Policy

U.S. fiscal policy is concerned with government spending and taxes. It can be classified as neutral, expansionary, and contractionary. A neutral fiscal policy indicates a balanced budget where government spending is equal to the money it raises in taxes. This has rarely been the case in American history. When the United States spends more money than it takes in, it's usually practicing an expansionary fiscal policy, either because it has no choice, such as in a time of war or a financial crisis, or because it's seeking to stimulate the economy by increasing spending, lowering taxes, or both. This usually results in a budget deficit.

In times of peace and economic prosperity, a contractionary fiscal policy reduces net government spending either through higher taxes, reduced government spending, or a combination of both. This usually results in a budget surplus so that, ideally, the government will have the resources to revert to an expansionary policy to counter the next economic downturn.

Government programs are mainly funded by taxes but they can also be paid for in other ways. Seignorage is the net money made from printing currency. It is known as the "inflation tax" because an increase in the amount of money in circulation causes inflation. The government can also borrow money from the population through the sale of bonds. Before bonds were invented, the government used to borrow money from private investors and other countries. The sale of bonds also helps to control inflation because the government does not need to print more money. To pay for programs, the government can also sell some of its assets (like land) or use money that it saved in times of a fiscal surplus.

REAL-LIFE FACTS

Foreign governments hold a large percentage of our national debt. Japan holds $644 billion, China $350 billion, the United Kingdom $239 billion, and the oil-exporting countries $100 billion.

The Federal Reserve

The Federal Reserve, or the Fed, is the central bank of the United States. It was created in 1913 to address banking panics and ensure the stability of the financial system. It is composed of a Board of Governors appointed by the president, the Federal Open Market Committee, 12 regional Federal Reserve Banks located in major cities around the United States, several private banks with a certain amount of stock in the Fed, and many advisory councils.

REAL-LIFE FACTS

There are 12 Federal Reserve District Banks, but only one state has two banks. Missouri is home to the fed banks in St. Louis and in Kansas City.

Bank panics occur because banks do not have enough cash in reserve to support simultaneous withdrawals from their customers. One way the Fed attempts to control this situation is by having an elastic currency, which means that the Fed can increase or decrease the money supply as needed. The Fed also clears checks from banks that other banks will not in times of economic uncertainty. The Fed also acts as a lender of last resort; it extends credit to banks in emergency situations when it would have a severe negative impact on the economy if it did not. The Fed charges these banks a discounted rate. This role of the Fed helps alleviate pressure and prevent finance companies from bankruptcy.

As the United States' central bank, the Federal Reserve is the bank of the federal government. It processes all of its financial transactions, often in billions and trillions of dollars. Deposits into the federal government's checking account with the Fed include tax deposits made by taxpayers. Withdrawals are made for government spending programs, among other things. The Fed also sells and redeems U.S. savings bonds and Treasury bills, notes, and bonds. It is the issuer of the national currency. The U.S. Treasury Bureau of the Mint and Bureau of Engraving and Printing actually produce the money and the Fed is responsible for passing it on to the banks.

The Board of Governors is responsible for supervising the private banks. It does not allow member banks to give out too many loans to people who cannot pay them back. It also punishes banks for overvaluing assets such as land, property, or security in order to control "asset bubbles," which inflate the market and can cause severe economic repercussions.

In the late 1990s and early 2000s, private banks and mortgage lenders increasingly took advantage of very lax oversight. As a result, there was excessive lenience and pressure on financial institutions to grant subprime mortgages that were then bundled into mortgage-backed securities and other high-risk lending instruments. Starting in late 2007, a real-estate downturn became a landslide as the asset value of homes declined and many borrowers found themselves with outstanding loans greater than the current market value of their home. The resulting wave in mortgage defaults and property foreclosures, and subsequent collapse of the worldwide financial market in those mortgage-based derivatives, triggered a financial panic and a global recession.

In order to address concerns it may have about the U.S. economy, the Federal Reserve has the power to act on its own without the approval of Congress or the president. The members of the Board of Governors are appointed by the president but serve staggered 14-year terms. This limits the influence any single president can have over appointments to the Fed, thereby limiting the influence of national politics. The chairman of the Fed is required to report to both the House and Senate semiannually on the state of the U.S. economy. Markets around the world try to decipher the testimony for clues to future Fed policy. Additionally, the Fed is required to make an annual report of its operations to the Speaker of the House.

Monetary Policy

Monetary policy pertains to the actions of the central bank, the Federal Reserve, to control the money supply and short-term interest rates. Interest rates and the money supply are inversely related because interest rates are the prices at which money can be borrowed. Therefore, if interest rates are low, there is an increase in the money supply, and vice versa.

The printing of money is regulated by the Federal Reserve. The goals of monetary policy include maximum employment, stable prices (inflation control), moderate long-term interest rates, and the promotion of secure economic growth.

Like fiscal policy, it can be classified as expansionary or contractionary. Expansionary monetary policy increases the total supply of money and is used in times of recession to decrease unemployment by lowering interest rates. If the Federal Reserve wishes to lower interest rates, it purchases government debt, usually treasury bonds held by the banks, thereby increasing the amount of cash in circulation. It can also lower the interest rate for other banks to borrow from them, thereby expanding the credit available to the American people.

The Fed can also reduce the reserve requirements, the assets that banks must have as cash available for the central bank. Banks typically only maintain a small portion of their assets in cash available for withdrawal; the rest is usually invested in mortgages and loans. By lowering the reserve requirement for cash availability, the Federal Reserve frees up more funds available for banks to provide loans, but it does increase risk if they're not invested in stable assets, as we saw after the financial crisis.

Contractionary fiscal policy is just the opposite. It involves raising interest rates in order to manage inflation in times of economic prosperity.

Foreign Policy

Foreign policy is the combination of strategies, actions, and positions that a nation takes in its interactions with other countries. This includes alliances, treaties, trade agreements, foreign aid, and the defense budget.

Up until World War I, the United States did not meddle very much in international affairs. It was a new and relatively weak nation with many problems of its own, the Civil War being one of the most significant. Geographically, the United States is also isolated from Europe and Asia by two very large oceans, with no airplanes or modern ships to cross them. Therefore, a policy of isolationism predominated, meaning that the United States avoided military alliances but did create many trade agreements. In 1823, President James Monroe established the Monroe Doctrine, which reinforced the United States' isolationist policy and warned Europe and Russia to stay out of the affairs of both North and South America. This doctrine was tested in 1861 when the French invaded Mexico. The United States helped the Mexicans in forcing the French to withdraw in 1867.

The United States revealed itself to be a strong military power when it defeated the Spanish in the Spanish-American War in 1898. By 1900, the United States had holdings around the world from Latin America all the way to the Philippines. President Theodore Roosevelt added the Roosevelt Corollary to the Monroe Doctrine, and the United States began to police Latin America, putting an end to revolutions in countries like Nicaragua, Haiti, and Cuba. In the 1930s, this policy was replaced by Franklin Roosevelt's Good Neighbor Policy, which sought to improve relations with Latin American countries by endorsing their sovereignty.

The twentieth century was marked by United States involvement in wars all over the world. World War II initiated the shift in foreign policy from isolationism to internationalism. The United States emerged as a military and economic superpower since European countries had all suffered through many years of war. The Allies desired collective security and formed the United Nations. The Soviet Union, a communist country, was the main threat to national security after World War II. This period became known as the Cold War because, while direct military action did not occur, relations were hostile between the United States and the Soviet Union. The Truman Doctrine of 1947 aimed to contain the spread of communism by protecting Greece and Turkey from falling under Soviet control.

China was also a communist nation and considered a Cold War foe, but U.S. foreign policy with China has always been very complex. Wars in Korea and Vietnam were fought to limit the influence of communist countries in Asia. In 1972, President Nixon paved the way for formal diplomatic ties between the United States and the People's Republic of China. The Soviet Union dissolved in 1991, ending the Cold War.

The challenges of the twenty-first century include the United States' diligent efforts to combat terrorism and the proliferation of nuclear weapons. The attacks of September 11, 2001, have altered the way the United States conducts foreign policy. No longer is the enemy one particular country and its armed forces; rather, the enemy is a network of terrorist organizations located across the world. The United States has used military action in Iraq and Afghanistan in the hopes of preventing further assault on the territories of the United States and its allies.

The United States must also worry about the proliferation of nuclear weapons in potentially unstable nations such as Pakistan, as well as North Korea and Iran, whose leaders have implied their willingness to use them in South Korea, Japan, Russia, China, and Israel. In 2015, the United States, China, Russia, France, the United Kingdom, and the European Union signed an agreement with Iran that would reduce and limit Iran's nuclear capabilities in return for the lifting of certain sanctions and unfreezing assets held in U.S. and European banks.

The Foreign Policy Establishment

The main symbol of foreign policy in the United States is the president. He is the one who decides on many global issues and represents the United States in the international arena. The president cannot do all of this by himself. He relies on a large staff for assistance in all matters of foreign affairs. The State Department is headed by the Secretary of State, the president's chief adviser on foreign relations. This officer helps to make and enforce policies, and manage the department, both at home and abroad. The State Department includes ambassadors, members of the foreign service, and diplomats. It also grants passports to American citizens.

ON THE RECORD

"In the wars of the European powers, in matters relating to themselves, we have never taken part, nor does it comport with our policy to do so. It is only when our rights are invaded, or seriously menaced that we resent injuries, or make preparations for our defense."

—President James Monroe

Ambassadors are the highest-ranking diplomats in their country. They are usually assigned to a foreign government or international organization to serve as the official representative of their country. The Foreign Service Act (1980) defined the members of the foreign service. They include the chiefs of mission, the ambassadors at large, members of the Senior Foreign Service, Foreign Service Officers and Specialists, and foreign national employees and consular agents. Members of the Senior Foreign Service are the corps of leaders and experts in the management of the Service and the performance of its functions. Careers in this department require passing intense oral and written examinations and an impressive résumé, as the positions are growing in popularity.

The Defense Department unifies the branches of the military. It was designed for civilian oversight of the nation's defense. The National Security Act of 1947 provides that the Secretary of Defense cannot have served on active duty for at least 10 years before being hired for that job. The Secretary of Defense heads the Defense Department and works in the Pentagon. Other members of the Defense Department include the chairman and vice chairman of the Joint Chiefs of Staff, the Army Chief of Staff, the Chief of Naval Operations, the Commandant of the Marine Corps, and the Air Force Chief of Staff.

REAL-LIFE FACTS

Ambassadors are not subject to the laws of the country in which they work. This is called diplomatic immunity.

The three military departments are the Army, Navy, and Air Force. Each is headed by a civilian secretary that reports to the Secretary of Defense. The Army is the oldest and largest of the armed services. It consists of the regular Army, the National Guard, and the Army Reserve. The Department of the Navy also oversees the Marine Corps, whose members are the combat-ready land force for the Navy. The Air Force is the United States' first line of defense. Its main tasks in times of war are to attack enemy air, ground, and sea forces and provide transport for other branches of the armed services.

Since it was created in 1775, the military has played a decisive role in our history. Currently, the military is composed of three million personnel, half of whom work on reserve. Conscription, or the draft, was introduced in the Union Army during the Civil War. It was not employed again until 1917. It was a very controversial topic in the twentieth century, but finally came to an end in 1971, when the draft renewal bill was approved for another two years. With the end of active U.S. ground fighting in Vietnam, December 1972 saw the last men drafted to the war.

The United States currently operates with an all-volunteer military. In addition to our Army, the State Department also employs several companies to provide support in dangerous areas that would be difficult for conventional U.S. forces. This area of the government is growing at a fast pace. Some people view this expansion as a way of privatizing the critical parts of the military. Critics of this trend see trouble in hiring private companies that are not ultimately accountable to a legislative body.

The U.S. Intelligence Community is made up of 16 separate agencies that work both separately and together to conduct intelligence activities to protect our national security and conduct foreign relations. The Central Intelligence Agency (CIA) is an independent agency of the U.S. government. Its primary function is gathering and analyzing information about foreign governments, corporations, and people in order to advise people in the government on policy. The other 15 agencies are offices or bureaus of the executive branch. The Federal Bureau of Investigation (FBI) is not a part of this group of agencies; rather, it is the primary unit of the Department of Justice. It serves as a federal criminal investigative body and a domestic intelligence agency.

The Department of Homeland Security was created in 2002 as a result of the terrorist attacks of September 11. It is responsible for tracking down terrorists, patrolling the nation's borders and ports, protecting the nation's infrastructure, preparing for and providing relief after emergencies and natural disasters, and defending the nation against chemical, nuclear, biological, and radiological warfare. The government believed that it would be more advantageous to have a centralized office to perform all of these functions. The ramification of this has been centralized accountability. This office has proven to be very effective since there have been no attacks on U.S. soil from foreign enemies. However, domestic terrorism, such as the bombing at the Boston Marathon and the San Bernardino massacre, is an increasing threat Homeland Security faces.

Foreign Aid

Foreign aid is money and resources that the United States allots for other countries. It has been a basic feature of U.S. foreign policy for more than 60 years. After World War II, the United States offered $12.5 billion to European countries through the Marshall Plan. Foreign aid does not come just in the form of money. The United States also helps countries by supplying them with troops and military resources. Foreign aid strengthens the economies and security of nations important to the United States, such as Israel and Iraq. Most of the money in foreign aid is used to buy American products, which in turn helps the American economy as well. Today, the United States spends nearly $38 billion a year on foreign aid, about one percent of the federal budget.

 MISINFORMATION

A World Opinion Poll found that Americans believed 25 percent of the federal budget goes to foreign aid. When asked how much they thought would be an "appropriate" percentage, the median response was 10 percent. In fact, just 1 percent of the federal budget goes to foreign aid.

Alliances

Alliances are associations of countries that are formed for mutual benefit. The United States is involved in certain alliances that have agreed to take collective military action to meet the defensive needs in a particular part of the world if it is deemed necessary.

The most important American alliance is NATO, the North Atlantic Treaty Organization. Formed in 1947 in order to protect Europe from the Soviet Union, it has 26 members that have all agreed to defend each other in case of an attack on one or more of the members. NATO has been involved in military efforts in Bosnia and Kosovo to end the civil war there and in Afghanistan to combat the Taliban.

The Rio Pact is another American alliance that unites the United States, Canada, and many Latin and South American countries. The ANZUS Pact of 1951 aligns the United States with Australia and New Zealand. The United States has similar pacts with Japan, the Philippines, and South Korea.

In the Middle East, the United States' primary ally is Israel. The United Nations recognized the nation of Israel in 1948, and there have been many conflicts over its territorial borders and overall existence. The United States has tried to be a mediator for peace in the Middle East. President Carter initiated a peace treaty between Israel and Egypt in 1979 known as the Camp David Accord. In the Oslo Accords of 1993, the Palestinian Liberation Organization (PLO) finally recognized Israel's right to exist. In turn, Israel also recognized the PLO as the representative of the Palestinian people.

Although the Oslo Accords seemed to be a turning point in Israeli-Palestinian peace agreements, recurring episodes of violence and retaliation continue to afflict that area of the world. The United States and the United Nations have tried to be the negotiators in this conflict and will continue to urge both sides to reach a compromise.

The United Nations

The United States saw the need to participate in international politics after World War II, as it emerged as one of the world's greatest military and financial powers. In 1945, the 50 victorious allies drafted the United Nations Charter. It was put into effect a year later "to save succeeding generations from the scourge of war." The main goals of the United Nations are international peace and security, the development of amicable relations between all countries, and the promotion of justice and joint action in response to international crimes and crises. Today, the United Nations has 192 members, which includes nearly every recognized independent country in the world. Its headquarters are on international territory in New York City.

MISINFORMATION

The United Nations does not have its own army. When the United Nations resolves to use military action, as it has done in Korea (in 1950) and Iraq and Kuwait (in 1991), it gathers a coalition of forces from participating nations.

The United Nations is divided into six administrative bodies: the General Assembly, the Security Council, the Economic and Social Council, the Trusteeship Council, the International Court of Justice, and the Secretariat.

The UN General Assembly includes all of the members. Sessions are held once a year to discuss any matter in the charter and to make recommendations for new members to the Security Council and other UN subgroups. The General Assembly alone can make amendments to the charter. The assembly also elects the 10 nonpermanent members of the Security Council, the 54 members of the Economic and Social Council, and the elective members of the Trusteeship Council. The assembly selects the secretary-general and the judges of the International Court of Justice along with the Security Council. Just like the Security Council, the assembly can admit, suspend, and expel members.

The Security Council is made up of 15 members. The United States, France, Britain, Russia, and China are the five permanent members. The 10 temporary members are chosen for two-year terms that are not immediately eligible for reelection. On important matters, nine affirmative votes are needed to pass a resolution. However, if one permanent member does not agree, then the resolution will not pass.

Because of this veto power, the Security Council's permanent members must always be working toward compromise and cooperation. Interestingly, abstaining from voting is not regarded as a veto.

The Least You Need to Know

- The United States' foreign and economic policies are closely connected and provide opportunities for economic growth and alliances with other countries.

- Economic policy in the United States incorporates trade, fiscal, and monetary policies. Trade policy deals with tariffs and trade agreements. Fiscal policies manage the federal budget, taxes, and government spending. Monetary policies control inflation, interest rates, and the money supply.

- The Federal Reserve is the central bank of the United States and plays a large role in regulating the interest rates and money supply. It also regulates private banks and helps in times of financial crisis.

- Foreign policy in the early United States was primarily isolationist. After WWII, the United States emerged as a world leader and began to form economic and military alliances with many countries. The most important agreements the United States participates in are NAFTA, NATO, and the United Nations.

- The United Nations is an organization of almost all the countries in the world whose purpose is to promote international law and security, economic development, human rights, and social progress.

Social and Environmental Policies

Social policies in the United States are shaped by many factors. Backed by political interest groups, it comes down to who will benefit from these programs initiated by either the federal government or the state, and how it is going to be financed.

This argument is the basis of the major social welfare programs of the United States. The constant push and pull between the federal government and state governments contributes to the funding and eligibility of social programs such as Medicare and Medicaid, each an example of no means and means-tested programs. This financing battle between federal and state is also at the root of the nation's energy policies and projects, and the discussion of the obvious harm that the environment will endure if an effort to change policy is not on the agenda.

In This Chapter

- Social programs in the United States
- Social issues
- Education policy
- Environmental policies of the United States
- Natural resources and alternative energy

The National Social Safety Network

Social welfare can be characterized into two different categories. The first caters to everyone without restrictions, also known as no means test. The other is known as means-tested, which applies to a *demographic* of people that fall below a certain income level.

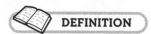 **DEFINITION**

A **demographic** is a portion of a population, typically involving age ranges, social class, race, income, education, employment status, location, and gender. Demographic data refers to selected population characteristics used in government, marketing, and/or opinion research.

Social Security in the United States is a form of social insurance that is funded through payroll taxes. Under President Franklin D. Roosevelt, Congress passed the Social Security Act of 1935, which provided benefits to the elderly and the unemployed, as well as a lump-sum payment at death. At the time, President Roosevelt felt it was important to safeguard the elderly population.

Between 1936 and 1996, the Aid to Families with Dependent Children (AFDC) program provided money to families in need. This was funded by both the federal and state governments. The cost of this program increased dramatically over the years. In 1993, during his first State of the Union address, President Clinton declared, "Later this year, we will offer a plan to end welfare as we know it … after two years they must get back to work, too, in private business if possible, in public service if necessary. We have to end welfare as a way of life and make it a path to independence and dignity."

In 1996, Congress passed the Personal Responsibility and Work Opportunity Reconciliation Act. This replaced AFDC with a more temporary program and made the states more financially responsible than the federal government. This new program limits recipients to a total of five years of support throughout their life and requires that recipients work or volunteer in the community.

Social Security

Old-Age, Survivors, and Disability Insurance (OASDI) is the basic social security program. It was established by the Social Security Act of 1935. It is supported by taxes on employers and workers. In 2007, the tax was 6.2 percent on the first $97,500 of a worker's income, which employers must match. People who are self-employed are taxed 12.4 percent of their income.

Medicare

Medicare is a federally sponsored health-care plan for all people over the age of 65 regardless of their medical history or income. It was added to the Social Security program in 1965. It is supported by taxes placed on employers and workers. Employees pay a 1.45 percent tax on their total annual income and employers must match it. The self-employed pay 2.9 percent of their total annual incomes.

Medicare's structure is organized into four parts. Part A pays for the care received in a hospital, nursing facility, home health care, or at a hospice. Part B pays for the care received from a physician, outpatient, and home health-care visits and preventive services. Part C is also known as the Medicare Advantage Program, which means that beneficiaries can join a managed care plan, such as a HMO, PPO, or private fee-for-service plan. Part D is the newest addition to Medicare, and it outlines the new outpatient prescription drug benefit, which is delivered through private plans that are in contract with Medicare.

 MISINFORMATION

Even though about 44 million people are enrolled in Medicare, they also have an additional form of supplemental coverage, as Medicare does not cover 100 percent of health-care costs. About 2.6 million Medicare beneficiaries are active employees who receive coverage from their employers and more than 7 million qualify as low income and are dual eligible for Medicare and Medicaid.

Medicare Reform

The debate over health care has divided the political parties on many occasions and the major reforms have been passed as interest groups seek their own agendas. The most noted transformation was made by President George W. Bush when he passed the Medicare Modernization Act (MMA) in 2003, which is the reason behind the newest addition to Medicare, Medicare Part D.

The role of prescription drugs has become more and more dominant as new and more expensive drugs are created. Patients see this as an additional financial burden as most of Medicare's population has modest incomes and resources. About 47 percent have incomes below 200 percent of the poverty level, meaning they have incomes well below the minimum level of income deemed necessary to achieve a decent standard of living. The MMA was meant to take on this problem by providing basic prescription drug coverage. This coverage was voluntary and is available only through insurance companies and HMOs. The benefit includes that the enrollee pay a monthly *premium*, an annual deductible, and 25 percent of the drugs' costs, adding up to $2,250. If the full costs of drugs lie between $2,250 and $5,100, the enrollee is responsible for those costs and Medicare Part D covers nothing. The coverage will pick up again at costs greater than $5,100, where Medicare Part D will cover 95 percent of the bill.

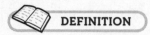 **DEFINITION**

> A **premium** is the amount paid or to be paid by the policyholder for coverage under the contract, usually in periodic installments.

This large gap is referred to as the "doughnut hole" and has stirred much controversy. Other specifications made were mandating a trial for a partly privatized Medicare system in six cities, donation of an extra $25 billion to hospitals in rural areas, higher fees for wealthier seniors, a pretax health savings account for working people, and support for electronic prescribing.

The MMA made two significant changes to Medicare. It proposed to establish income-related premiums and changed the standards for ways to pay back its debts. Since the birth of Medicare, it has operated on the trust funds that are financed by payroll taxes. The projected outlook on Medicare spending predicts that the reserves will be depleted by 2018. These fiscal challenges initiate a great deal of uncertainty about the future of Medicare.

The Patient Protection and Affordable Care Act

In 2010, Congress passed and President Obama signed the most significant reforms of the health-care system of the United States. This politically controversial legislation transformed how hospitals and doctors deliver medical services and aims to increase the quality and affordability of health insurance. States were able to set up health insurance exchanges to offer citizens lower rates. The federal government set up a federal exchange for citizens who reside in states with no exchanges. Insurance companies can no longer deny a person coverage due to a preexisting condition and cannot charge different rates regardless of sex. In two separate cases, the Supreme Court has upheld the constitutionality of the Affordable Care Act. Still, the debate concerning the role of the federal government in the health-care and health insurance sectors is sure to be a significant factor in the 2016 presidential election.

Medicaid

Medicaid finances the majority of medical services for low-income and disabled adults and children. This is a program that is run jointly by the federal and state governments and is a needs-based social welfare program, in comparison to Medicare, which is an entitlement program. The amount of federal government contribution ranges from 50 to 76 percent, depending on the state per capita income.

To qualify for Medicaid, individuals must first meet the financial criteria and also belong to one of the following groups: children, parents of dependent children, pregnant women, people with disabilities, or the elderly. The federal law states eligibility for these individuals who fall into these groups and who fall below specified income levels is guaranteed.

States have the power to increase Medicaid income eligibility beyond what the federal government allows; however, states cannot receive the funds to insure childless adults unless they have a federal waiver. Many states have expanded their Medicaid eligibility, but this depends widely by state.

Unemployment

The unemployment compensation program supports people who are currently unemployed but actively looking for employment. It was also established by the Social Security Act of 1935. This program is financed by federal and state taxes.

Unemployment compensation is given to an unemployed worker and is considered a type of social welfare benefit. This is financed through federal and state employer payroll taxes, and generally employers pay both the state and federal unemployment taxes if they pay their employees $1,500 or greater in any quarter of the calendar year and if they had at least one employee working during any day of the week for 20 weeks in a calendar year.

In 1939, Congress passed the Federal Unemployment Tax Act, which allowed the Internal Revenue Service to collect a yearly federal employer tax used to fund state agencies. This act also covered the cost of overseeing the Unemployment Insurance and Job Service program in all states. The government also pays for half the cost of expanded unemployment benefits and sets up a fund from which states can borrow to pay for the benefits. The federal government sets up broad outlines for coverage, but the states vary in the way they see who should receive these benefits.

Abortion and Reproductive Rights

Abortion, the termination of a pregnancy by the removal of an embryo or fetus from the uterus, has created much controversy as the political, legal, and cultural issues that surround it differ depending on the particular audience. Pro-choice believers affirm that abortion is a human right and the decision is up to the woman who has complete control on whether or not she chooses to terminate her pregnancy. On the other hand, pro-life advocates are opposed to abortion and believe that the embryo and fetuses are indeed alive and therefore human beings and in turn, abortion would be considered murder.

In 1973, the Supreme Court made a momentous ruling on abortion that will alter state and federal laws. In the case of *Roe* v. *Wade*, the decision proclaimed that a mother may abort her pregnancy for any reason, up until the "point at which the fetus becomes viable." The term *viable* was defined as being "potentially able to live outside the mother's womb, albeit with artificial aid. Viability is usually placed at about seven months but may occur earlier, even at 24 weeks." This ruling ultimately changed the course of history and even today, the legality of abortion is being questioned.

In the United States, it is legal for a woman to seek an abortion for whatever reason, may it be to preserve the physical and mental health of the mother, in cases of rape, or for social and economic reasons. Depending on the state, there are a number of laws on the regulation and limitations of abortion. Thirty-eight states require an abortion to be performed by a licensed physician, 19 states require an abortion to be performed in a hospital after a specified point in the pregnancy, and 18 states require the involvement of a second physician after a specified point. Yet 36 states prohibit abortions except when necessary to protect the woman's life or health, after a specified point in the pregnancy, most often fetal viability. Forty-six states allow individual health providers to refuse to participate in an abortion and 43 states allow institutions to refuse to perform abortions.

The Supreme Court has ruled on many cases that have involved the legality of various state laws regulating abortions. In 1992, in the *Planned Parenthood of Southeastern Pennsylvania* v. *Casey,* the Court refused to overturn *Roe* in a 5–4 decision. However, the Court upheld the state's right to impose restrictions on women seeking abortions. These restrictions include a mandatory 24-hour waiting period, the requirement that teenagers obtain the permission of at least one parent, and a requirement that women seeking an abortion procedure be given written materials that explain what the alternatives are. The Court ruled that the state cannot place an "undue burden" on women seeking abortions. In March 2016, the Supreme Court heard arguments in *Whole Woman's Health* v. *Hellerstedt.* The Court heard arguments in a case that requires abortion clinics in Texas to have doctors with admitting rights to hospitals. Opponents of the law believe the law is intended to reduce the number of clinics and, therefore, creates an "undue burden" on women seeking abortions.

  REAL-LIFE FACTS

One million American teenagers become pregnant each year and 78 percent of these pregnancies are unintended. Consequently, 35 states require some type of parental involvement in a minor's decision to have an abortion, 22 states require one or both parents to consent to the procedure, while 11 require that one or both parents be notified.

Gun Control

On June 26, 2008, the Supreme Court upheld the right of individuals to bear arms for hunting and for self-defense. Before this ruling, the debate revolved around whether the federal government should have a stronger presence in handgun and firearm regulation. The most vocal group against the federal regulations is the National Rifle Association (NRA), who argued that the Constitution states in the Second Amendment that individuals have the right to own and carry guns. Those in favor of more strict federal regulations include Handgun Control, the Brady Center, and the Center to Prevent Handgun Violence. They disagree with the NRA's interpretation of the Second Amendment, citing statistical evidence that people with guns cause injury and death to themselves and others. In 2010, the Supreme Court applied this Second Amendment right to the states. However, even though the government may not ban guns, prior court cases appear to support the government's right to regulate the purchase and use of guns.

 ON THE RECORD

"As long as there are guns, the individual that wants a gun for a crime is going to have one and going to get it."

—President Ronald Reagan

Gay Marriage

In 1996, Congress passed and President Clinton signed, the Defense of Marriage Act (DOMA). DOMA defined marriage as a legal union between one man and one woman for purposes of all federal laws, and provides that states need not recognize a marriage from another state if it is between persons of the same sex.

In 2003, the Massachusetts high court ruled that the state constitution allowed gay marriage. This ruling pivoted the issue of gay marriage to one of federalism and states' rights. Same-sex couples were now eligible to marry and were issued marriage licenses. In subsequent years, some states passed laws banning same-sex marriage, while some others began allowing same-sex civil unions. In 2008, Proposition 8 was a ballot proposition in California that sought to change the state constitution regarding marriage. Passage of this proposition by voters amended the California State Constitution by including "only marriage between a man and a woman is valid or recognized in California."

Starting in 2013, the position of the Supreme Court on the issue of gay marriage began to emerge. In a challenge to DOMA in *United States* v. *Windsor,* the Court overturned the law, which barred government from recognizing same-sex marriages. This meant that the federal government must recognize same-sex marriages established by marriage licenses issued by the states. In

2015, in the landmark case *Obergefell* v. *Hodges,* the Court ruled in a 5–4 decision that the fundamental right to marry is guaranteed by the Fourteenth Amendment of the U.S. Constitution.

Education

The states are in charge of their own education departments. It is the most expensive component of every state budget, representing more than one third of state spending. Primary and secondary education is mainly supervised by local governments, and their local taxes usually fund the school districts. States provide some aid to the schools and also set statewide standards and guidelines for the curriculum. State laws establish teacher-certification qualifications and the length of the school year.

At the college and university levels, the states play a more significant role. Every state has a public university program. California's is the largest in the country. Tuition is typically less at public colleges than at private schools. States understand that it is important to produce highly trained college graduates so that the state can prosper.

The Department of Education was created as a Cabinet level department in 1980. Prior to that, the department responsible for education policy in the country was marginal and insignificant, often a subordinate arm of a more powerful cabinet level department. The principal duty of the Department of Education is to provide federal assistance to the state and local agencies primarily responsible for education in the United States.

 ON THE RECORD

"The aim of education is to enable individuals to continue their education ... (and) the object and reward of learning is continued capacity for growth. Now this idea cannot be applied to all members of a society except where intercourse of man with man is mutual, and except where there is adequate provision for the reconstruction of social habits and institutions by manes of wide stimulation arising from equitably distributed interests."

–John Dewey

No Child Left Behind

President George W. Bush signed the No Child Left Behind Act in 2001, which was designed to improve America's public schools. Greeted with overwhelming bipartisan support, this created solid standards for what every child should know and learn in the subjects of math and reading in grades three through eight in each state. This also provided flexibility for all states in their use of federal education funds that allow them to use these dollars on programs that were proven to help most children learn. Additionally, it gave the opportunity for parents to obtain other education services and/or the option to transfer their children from failing schools, making them active participants in their child's education.

This act seeks to reduce the gap in educational achievements between high income and lower income students and also between minority and nonminority students. It made states accountable by implementing grant programs and federal funding to properly dispense these resources in areas of teacher quality, language proficiency, and after school enrichment. It also requires that progress and achievement of each child be made available in yearly report cards so parents can see how school performance and statewide progress measure against the quality of the education that their child is receiving and their progress in those subjects.

The No Child Left Behind Act has raised achievement for many children in all kinds of schools. Through NCLB, the Nation's Report Card showed improvement in fourth through eighth grade math and reading achievement. To further education reform, President Bush released "Building on Results: A Blueprint for Strengthening the No Child Left Behind Act." When Congress failed to reauthorize NCLB, President Bush and the Secretary of Education Margaret Spellings took steps to ensure its continued progress. The secretary gave states flexibility to help turn around schools in need of improvement and reinforced regulations that address the dropout rates, accountability, and student access to tutoring.

In 2015, Congress passed and President Obama signed, the Every Student Succeeds Act (ESSA). This new law replaces No Child Left Behind and was passed with support of both Republicans and Democrats. This new law drastically reduces the role of the federal government in education policy and hands over most of the decision-making powers to the states and local school boards. The new law keeps some key provisions of NCLB in place, including a federal testing schedule and requirements that schools annually report on achievement scores.

Vouchers

The case of education vouchers has faced much resistance from the academic arena. Milton Friedman, an economist, recommended the idea in 1955 when he argued that the shortcomings of public schools were due to the lack of free-market involvement and no accountability to parents, students, or even corporate interests. Therefore, this does not use resources or tax dollars efficiently and a poor education does not help anyone.

School vouchers are government-imposed credentials where students from underperforming schools are given money to attend the school of their choice. Teachers and parents alike are opposed to this approach as it takes away attention from improving public schools and creates conflicting standards for students. This would only promote the divide among racial, economic, ethnic, and religious distributions. As mentioned in Chapter 16, the charter school movement has expanded considerably in the United States in the last two decades.

Environmental Policies

More recently, concern has turned the focus onto the utilization of alternative energy sources. Environmental policies are a way to supervise and manage activities that can have a harmful effect on nature, in turn, reducing the results of problems from human impact. As globalization and technology advance, environmental health will affect everyone regardless of social, economic, or political affiliations, and will not discriminate against race, sex, or ethnicity. The objective of environmental health policies is to identify and respond to adverse environmental exposures and to manage those consequences.

The Environmental Protection Agency (EPA) was created by President Richard Nixon and it is designed to oversee the safety of human needs and in addition to preserving the qualities of air, land, and water. Since it was formed, the EPA has passed major laws that help to restore the quality of the environment and create standards for organizations and regular households to reduce their "carbon footprint."

Names of the Different EPA Offices

Office of Administration and Resources

Office of Air and Radiation

Office of Enforcement and Compliance Assurance

Office of Environmental Information

Office of Environmental Justice

Office of the Chief Financial Officer

Office of General Counsel

Office of Inspector General

Office of International Affairs

Office of Prevention, Pesticides, and Toxic Substances

Office of Research and Development

Office of Solid Waste and Emergency Response

Office of Water

Global Warming

Global warming is the average measure of the increased temperature of the Earth's atmosphere near the surface. This can be caused by natural or human causes; however, it usually refers to the result of the greenhouse gases released from human activities. Greenhouse gases are necessary because they keep the planet's surface warmer than it would be; nevertheless, when the concentration of these gases in the atmosphere increases at an exponential rate, the Earth's temperature begins to rise to where it can ultimately change the planet's climate patterns. Model projections show that the temperature will continue to rise and we will see increasing sea levels, extreme weather occurrences, and changes in the pattern of types of precipitation.

In 2002, the U.S. government proposed a plan that will reduce the greenhouse gas concentration by 18 percent over a 10-year period from 2002 until 2012. This concentration level is a measure of the gas emissions per unit of economic activity. This strategy can help to reduce the release of more than 100 million metric tons of gas emissions annually.

In 2010, President Obama started the America's Great Outdoors Initiative. This program is designed to preserve and protect key natural resources and natural features. In 2015, President Obama unveiled the Clean Power Plan, which aims to reduce the greenhouse gas emissions from coal-burning power plants.

Pollution from Automobiles

The Clean Air Act was ratified to tackle smog and air pollution and to improve public health. The United States passed several clean air laws that started with the Air Pollution Control Act of 1955 and then the Clean Air Act of 1963, which was the first federal legislation dealing with air pollution control. A few years later, the ratification of the Clean Air Act of 1970 resulted in a shift in the role of the federal government. It allowed the progress of complete federal and state regulations to limit release of toxins from stationary and mobile sources.

As a result, four regulatory programs were instated: the National Ambient Air Quality Standards, State Implementation Plans, New Source Performance Standards, and National Emission Standards for Hazardous Air Pollutants. These strategic programs helped to create and form the EPA. Many additional amendments were added, most recently, the Clean Air Act Amendments of 1990 added further provisions that attend to acid rain, ozone depletion, and toxic air pollution.

REAL-LIFE FACTS

Carbon monoxide forms when carbon in fuel doesn't burn completely. The main source of carbon monoxide in our air is released from motor vehicles.

Acid Rain

Acid rain indicates the mixture of wet- and dry-deposited material from the atmosphere that contains greater than normal amounts of nitric and sulfuric acids. The forbearer of acid rain comes from both natural (volcanoes) and man-made sources (fossil fuel combustion), which release sulfur dioxide and nitrogen oxides. Acid rain takes place when the gases in the atmosphere react with water, oxygen, and other chemicals to produce acidic compounds. These acidic compounds are released back into the environment through means of wet deposition such as acid rain, fog, and snow, or dry deposition like dust and smoke. The effects of acid rain are detrimental to our lakes and streams and damage the soil.

To attempt to reduce the harmful effects of acid rain, Congress has created the Acid Rain Program as part of the Clean Air Act Amendments of 1990. This program is to primarily accomplish environmental and public health benefits through the significant reduction in sulfur dioxide and nitrogen oxides gas emissions. The program engages in new and innovative ways to control air pollution while keeping it low cost to the public. It aims to limit sulfur dioxide emission from power plants to about 9 million tons per year starting in 2010.

Agricultural Pesticides

Rachel Carson was a writer, ecologist, and scientist most noted for her efforts to warn the public about the long-term effects of abusing the use of pesticides. In *Silent Spring* (Fawcett Premier, 1962), she challenged the methods of the government and the damage caused by a common pesticide called DDT. Carson was pinpointed as an alarmist and was attacked by the chemical industry and the government, but she continued to be outspoken about the deterioration of the environment through the use of pesticides.

At present, the EPA is in charge of the activities that contribute to food security in the United States, which include pesticide application. Ensuring the safety of the public with potential risks that occur when consuming foods that could have been treated with pesticides, it is responsible for the registration and tracking of pesticides before they are marketed and the renewal of older pesticides that certify current qualifications.

To better promote pest management and the quality of the environment, Integrated Pest Management (IPM) aims to utilize techniques to get the best results by disrupting the environment in the slightest way. Examples include using insects like ladybugs to control crop-destroying bugs and harvesting pest-resistant plant varieties. Modern biotechnology also makes possible the new breeds of plant varieties that are insusceptible to pesticides and/or threatening insects.

Consumers have taken a great interest in foods that have the minimal amount of chemical treatment. These organic foods claim to have no artificial food additives and are often processed with very few artificial methods. Several surveys have revealed that organic farms do not consume or release artificial pesticides into the environment and are beneficial in sustaining diverse ecosystems.

Recently, attention has turned to foods produced by genetically modified organisms, or GMOs. GMOs are used in agriculture as well as in biomedical research, and farmers around the globe have adopted GMOs to increase their food production. There is some controversy about the safety of these products, and medical experts say it is too soon to know what the long-term effects of GMOs will be on human health. The U.S. Food and Drug Administration currently does not require foods to be labeled as GMO.

 MISINFORMATION

Most organic food products do cost from 10 to 40 percent more than traditionally made products, but it is the fastest growing sector in the American food market. Whole Foods Market, a store devoted to selling high-quality natural and organic foods and products, had more than $6 billion in revenue in the year 2007 and has locations all over the United States as well as Canada and the United Kingdom.

Management of Natural Resources

There is no consensus on issues of the environment among certain interest groups. In the management of our natural resources, the National Resources Defense Council acts to pursue the vigorous protection of the Earth, including its people, animals, plants, and the natural ecosystems.

The thirst of our machines for oil has exploited nature and, as fuel costs soar and citizens are faced with uncontrollable bills, oil companies have continued to earn record-breaking profits. Offshore drilling can have a destructive effect on the environment as it threatens coastal lands, beaches, and wetlands. It also uses vast quantities of toxic and radioactive contaminants that can kill marine life as well as release pollutants into the air that contribute to the greenhouse gas effect. Lastly, oil spills can empty hundreds of thousands of gallons into the oceans, and cleanup methods will only eliminate a small fraction of that number.

Clean and renewable ways of alternative energy can guarantee lower energy use while preserving a healthy environment and more efficient uses of energy.

REAL-LIFE FACTS

Every American uses 300 to 700 plastic shopping bags per year. By eliminating this use, each person could save 3 to 7 gallons of crude oil. A city with about 100,000 people could save up to 14,000 barrels of oil per year.

Energy Innovations

Climate change and high gas prices coupled with government involvement and public outcry have pushed the legislature toward alternative and renewable energy. For example, wind power is the capability to take wind and transform it into a useful form like electricity. Large-scale farms have electrical grids where turbines provide electricity to isolated locations. Windmills are also used to pump water or grind grain.

Another example is solar power, which can generate electricity through heat from the sun. This is used in applications like architecture, urban planning, agriculture, heating, cooling, and ventilation. Finally, a particular kind of alternative energy is ethanol. Found primarily in corn, ethanol is clean-burning energy that fuels most approved automobiles and power machinery. Ethanol is biodegradable and reduces the amount of greenhouse gas emissions by 12 to 19 percent.

In 2010, U.S. Energy Secretary Chu announced a $120 million investment to launch the Energy Innovation Hub. The Hub is charged with advancing U.S. leadership in energy manufacturing through research. This research will help U.S. manufacturers and entrepreneurs compete in the global energy economy.

ON THE RECORD

"We sometimes emphasize the danger in a crisis without focusing on the opportunities that are there. We should feel a great sense of urgency because it is the most dangerous crisis we have ever faced, by far. But it also provides us with opportunities to do a lot of things we ought to be doing for other reasons anyway. And to solve this crisis we can develop a shared sense of moral purpose."

–Vice President Al Gore

The Least You Need to Know

- There are two kinds of welfare programs in the United States: means tested versus no-means tested. One program determines eligibility if a person falls below a certain income level while the other program is available to everyone without cognizance to income, respectively.

- Social health insurance is funded through employer and employee contributions to the Social Security Trust Fund, where beneficiaries are entitled as a matter of right. Public assistance is not the same, as it is paid for out of general tax income to people found to be in need, regardless of how much they pay in taxes.

- Social issues deal with policies that regulate and govern aspects of human behavior. Conservatives favor a more traditionalist approach while liberals tend to favor guarantee of equal opportunity.

- In our federal system of government, education policy and funding is left mostly to the states to manage. The federal government has maintained a Department of Education since 1867; however, it did not receive cabinet status until 1953, and became an independent department in 1980.

- Experts on environmental issues either agree or try to disprove the theories of what wrongful uses of natural resources can do.

Glossary

affirmative action   Policy that requires public and private organizations to take steps to overcome past discrimination.

American Dream   The widespread belief that we live in a land of opportunity and that individual initiative can bring about economic success.

aristocracy   A form of government in which power is held by the nobility.

authority   The rightful use of power that compels obedience.

bankruptcy   The legal proceeding in which the bankrupt's assets are distributed among the individuals or businesses to which a debt is owed.

bicameralism   A legislature made up of two houses.

bill   A proposal to a legislative body that will become a law if approved.

blanket primary   A variation of the open primary in which voters receive a ballot with all the candidates and can vote for any party that they choose.

block grants   Government aid under less restriction than grants-in-aid.

blue slip   The piece of paper that the chairman of the committee sends to senators informing them that the president has made a judicial nomination to a position in their home state and inviting them to object or offer support.

brief   A document that states the facts of the case, summarizes the lower-court decision, gives the argument of the lawyer, and discusses prior cases that bear on the issue.

bully pulpit   A public office of sufficiently high rank that it provides the holder with an opportunity to speak out and be listened to on any matter.

bureaucrat   A member of a bureaucracy, commonly within an institution of the government.

Cabinet   The advisory body traditionally made up of the heads of the executive departments and other officers the president may choose.

candidate   A person who is nominated in an election.

capitalism   An economic system characterized by private property, competitive markets, and financial incentives with limited government involvement.

caucus   A meeting of the members of a political party to select candidates or decide policy.

census   A count of the U.S. population conducted every 10 years by the Census Bureau.

centralism   A belief that the Constitution is the supreme law of the land (over state laws) and that the state government cannot interfere with a national government representing all the people.

closed primary   When a party's nomination election is limited to declared members of that party.

closed rule   Prohibits amendments of a bill or permits only members of the committee reporting the bill to make changes. This usually occurs with tax and spending bills.

coalition   A union of many persons of diverse interests who have come together to get their candidate elected.

coattails   Refers to riding into office on the popularity of a better-known candidate for a higher office.

concurrent powers   Powers held jointly by the national and state governments.

confederate government   An alliance of sovereign and independent states.

conservatism   A belief system centered on free enterprise, the right to private property, keeping the government as small as possible, strong leadership, strict moral codes, and pro-business policies.

constitutionalism   A government in which the people are sovereign and hold the government legally and politically accountable for how it exercises its powers.

contractionary   A fiscal policy in which there is a net decrease in government spending or increase in taxation revenue. It will lead to a smaller budget deficit or a larger budget surplus.

cooperative federalism   A system of government in which the national government and the states cooperate strongly in solving problems.

creationism   A belief based on the Bible that God created all life, including the Earth, universe, and human beings, in their original form, and they have not undergone any change or evolution.

decentralism   The belief that the Constitution is an agreement among the states to create a central government with limited authority that has no justification to interfere with the activities or authority of the states that have been reserved to them in the Tenth Amendment.

deficit spending   Occurs when the government expenses are greater than revenues and it borrows to make up the difference.

democracy   A system of government by the whole population or the eligible members of a state, typically through elected representatives.

demographic   Of or relating to demography; a portion of a population, especially considered as consumers.

despotism   Government ruled by a single leader in which all of his or her subjects are considered slaves.

détente   A French term, meaning a relaxing or easing; the term has been used in international politics since the early 1970s.

devolution revolution   A term referring to a period when intergovernmental relations and power shifted substantially in the direction of the states in the 1990s.

dictatorship   A government controlled by a ruler, called a dictator, who has complete authority over the country and has typically taken over by force, or at least rules by it.

direct democracy   A democracy in which the citizens debate and vote directly on all the laws and policies of government.

diversity   The quality of being different or varied or changeable.

divided government   When different branches of government are controlled by opposing parties.

doctrine of nullification   A doctrine that suggests states had the right to void a federal law that, in that state's opinion, violated the Constitution.

dual federalism   A system of government in which the states and the national government each remain supreme within their own spheres of authority.

encroachment   The gradual loss of citizens' rights and possessions to the government.

Enlightenment   A European intellectual movement of the late seventeenth and early eighteenth centuries emphasizing reason and individualism rather than tradition.

environmentalist   A person who is extremely concerned with the protection of the environment.

evolution   The theory based on Charles Darwin's studies that involves the process of gradual change in life forms over generations. It claims that humans are a part of this process and that they evolved from lower life forms.

executive order   A directive, rule, or regulation that has the same effect as a law.

expansionary   A fiscal policy in which there is a net increase in government spending or a fall in taxation revenue. It will lead to a larger budget deficit or a smaller budget surplus.

external efficacy   The ability of one person to make the government respond to their needs.

federal mandate   A law that requires states to take action in a certain area of public life or policy.

federal system   A system in which sovereignty is shared so that on some matters the national government is supreme and on others the state, regional, or provincial governments retain ultimate authority.

franchise   The right to vote.

franking   The privilege of free mailings by members of Congress.

gerrymandering   The process of drawing congressional district boundaries in bizarre or unusual shapes in order to favor one party over the other in a general election.

government   A political institution that has the power to enforce rules and impose order and stability on a society.

grants-in-aid   Money that the federal government grants to the states for use as part of the state budget. They are under strict regulation.

horizontal federalism   The activities, problems, and policies that require state governments to interact with one another.

impeachment   Charging the holder of a public office with misconduct.

incumbent   The current office holder.

interest group   A private organization that tries to persuade public officials to respond to the shared views of the group. An interest group tries to influence public policy.

internal efficacy   The ability of one person to understand and take part in political affairs.

joint committee   A committee formed by the concurrent action of the House of Representatives and the Senate.

jurisdiction   The right and power to interpret and apply the law.

Keynesianism   A school of economic thought in which the state should stimulate economic growth and improve stability in the private sector, through interest rates, taxation, and public projects.

legitimacy   The right to act a certain way.

libel   A published false statement that is damaging to a person's reputation.

liberalism   A belief system that favors and respects individual rights and freedoms, justice and equal opportunity, and an active government that provides many social programs.

libertarianism   A belief system that cherishes individual liberty and freedom and insists on sharply reducing the size of government.

logrolling   Refers to mutual aid among politicians. It is the equivalent of saying, "You scratch my back and I'll scratch yours."

majoritarian politics   Occurs when elected officials closely follow the preferences of the majority of the citizens.

malapportionment   Drawing the boundaries of political districts so that districts are very unequal in population.

monarchy   Rule by an individual who has inherited the role and expects to bequeath it to his or her heir.

monetarism   A school of economic thought concerning the determination of national income and monetary economics. It focuses on the supply of money in an economy as the primary means by which the rate of inflation is determined.

monotheism   The belief that there is only one God.

natural rights   John Locke's notion that people possess the God-given right to life, liberty, and property.

naturalization   The process of granting citizenship.

nomination   The process of candidate selection in an electoral system.

oligarchy   Government by a small group of people who share similar interests or family relations.

open primary   Any qualified voter may participate in the nomination process for a party's candidate.

open rule   Permits amendments within the time allotted to the bill.

orthodox   Conforming to what has traditionally been established as right or true.

parliamentary government   A government in which the executive (prime minister) is selected by a majority of the legislative branch (parliament).

pigeonhole   A bill that is introduced only because some constituent or special interest group has asked for it and then it is left to die because it has little broad support.

platform   The official statement of party policy on a wide range of issues.

polarization   The process by which public opinion divides and goes to the extremes.

political elite   People who have a disproportionate amount of power and influence in politics.

political party   A group of ideologically aligned people who seek to control the government by winning elections, holding public office, and determining public policy.

politics   The process by which groups of people make decisions; the science of government and public policy.

populism   The political doctrine that supports the rights and powers of the common people in their struggle with the privileged elite. Populism is usually seen as liberal on economic issues and conservative on social ones.

position issue   A point in which the candidates for the nomination or for office have different or opposing views on matters that divide voters.

premium   The amount paid or to be paid by an insurance policyholder for coverage under the contract, usually in periodic installments.

presidential government   A government with at least an executive and a legislative branch.

primary   A preliminary election to appoint delegates to a party conference or to select the candidates for a principal election.

progressive   Favoring or promoting activism, change, or innovation.

public opinion   The distribution of individual preferences of a given issue, candidate, or institution in a population.

quota system   A hiring system that gives preference to protected group members.

realignment   Occurs in an election when expanded suffrage and change in the society change the alignment of voters within parties.

recession   A term that describes the reduction of a country's gross domestic product (GDP) for at least two quarters. It is a period of reduced economic activity in the business cycle.

referendum   A process by which a law is referred to voters for final approval or rejection.

representative democracy   Also known as a republic, in which citizens elect government officials, who in turn make the laws and policies of the government.

runoff primary　A primary held between the two top vote-getters in the first primary election in order to determine a nominee.

seigniorage　The net revenue derived from the issuing of a currency.

select committee　A congressional committee created for a specific legislative purpose and for a limited period of time.

seniority rule　The occupancy of top positions on powerful congressional committees by the officials with the most years of service.

slander　The crime of making a false spoken statement that is damaging to a person's reputation.

socialism　A belief system that calls for government ownership of most sectors of the economy while maintaining democratic political institutions.

solicitor general　The federal government's chief lawyer. The third-ranking officer in the Department of Justice, the solicitor general is part of the executive branch.

sound bite　A carefully orchestrated event that news organizations can use in one minute or less in their program.

sovereign government　A government that is fully independent and determines its own affairs.

spoils system　The practice of giving jobs and favors of government to political supporters and friends.

standing committee　A permanent committee in the Senate that considers bills within a certain area of jurisdiction.

stare decisis　Latin for to stand by that which is decided, the principle to abide or adhere to decided cases.

statute　A formal, written law of a country or state, written and enacted by its legislative authority and then ratified by the highest executive in the government, and finally published.

suffrage　The right to vote.

supply side　A school of macroeconomic thought that argues that economic growth can be most effectively stimulated by using incentives for people to supply goods and services. The classic examples include adjusting income taxes and capital gains taxes.

tariff　A tax on imported goods or products.

tolerance　The ability or willingness to accept the beliefs, opinions, and actions of others.

treaty　A formal agreement between two or more countries.

trickle-down   A policy of providing tax cuts or other benefits to businesses and rich individuals in the belief that this will indirectly benefit the broad population.

tyranny   Cruel and oppressive government or rule.

unitary government   A centralized government that possesses all political power.

valence issue   A point on which the public is not divided, but looks to see which candidate is more strongly aligned with the public view.

whip   A party leader who makes certain party members are present for a vote and vote the way the party wishes.

yellow journalism   Refers to the use of sensationalized and exaggerated reporting by newspapers or magazines to attract readers.

Index